New Morning

New Morning

Emerson in the Twenty-first Century

Edited by

Arthur S. Lothstein
and
Michael Brodrick

SUNY
PRESS

Published by
State University of New York Press, Albany

© 2008 State University of New York

For information, contact State University of New York Press, Albany, NY
www.sunypress.edu

Production by Eileen Meehan
Marketing by Susan Petrie

Library of Congress Cataloging-in-Publication Data

New morning : Emerson in the twenty-first century / edited by Arthur S. Lothstein and Michael Brodrick.
        p. cm.
    Includes bibliographical references and index.
    ISBN 978-0-7914-7527-0 (alk. paper) — ISBN 978-0-7914-7528-7 (pbk. : alk. paper)
    1. Emerson, Ralph Waldo, 1803–1882—Criticism and interpretation.
I. Lothstein, Arthur S., 1980– II. Brodrick, Michael.

PS1638.N49 2008
814'.3—dc22

                                                                    2007041835

10 9 8 7 6 5 4 3 2 1

*To all the students
with whom we have shared Emerson and
whose lives have been enriched by their
encounter with him*

Contents

Forever Young: A Preface   ix
Michael Brodrick

Acknowledgments   xv

Dancing with Emerson   1
Deborah Digges

1   Emerson: An Introduction   3
Mary Oliver

2   The Single Vision   9
Robert C. Pollock

Windfall   49
William Heyen

3   Spires of Influence   50
John J. McDermott

4   Teaching for Lustres: An Essay on the Emersonian Teacher   67
Arthur S. Lothstein

The Continental College of Beauty   99
Mark Strand

5   Emerson at *The Gates*   101
David LaRocca

6   Taking Emerson Personally   122
John Lysaker

    Local Knowledge   139
      Paul Hoover

7   Face to Face with Emerson   141
      David Marr

8   Emerson's Natures: Origins of and Possibilities for
    American Environmental Thought   151
      Douglas R. Anderson

    Shudder   161
      Dorene Evans

9   Emerson and the Reinvention of Democracy: A Lesson
    for the Twenty-first Century   162
      Len Gougeon

10 Individualism, Natural Law, Human Rights: Emerson
    on "The Scholar" vis-à-vis Emerson on Reform   179
      Lawrence Buell

    For the Children   195
      Gary Snyder

11 After Emerson: Of General Knowledge and the
    Common Good   196
      Ann Lauterbach

    Letter to Lucia   209
      Ralph Waldo Emerson

    Contributors   211

    Index   215

Forever Young: A Preface

This book announces a new morning for Emerson, and I am writing this preface from the morning of my life. This is significant not only because Emerson loved young people but also because my life has grown richer in the shade of Emerson's wisdom. I have learned from him what it means to be young, although I do not mean chronologically young. For Emerson, youth has little to do with what the philosopher Santayana calls "physical time," which is the time measured by clocks and calendars. It has to do instead with intellectual flexibility. Lao-tzu calls it "softness."

Youth welcomes each moment gladly: delighting in objects of attention when they are good in themselves, surveying them hopefully for signs of improvement when they are not, and yielding gracefully when nothing useful can be gleaned from them. To be at ease in prevailing conditions and ready at the same time to exchange them for others, to love our lives but without demanding more time to live—I take it these are some of Emerson's most important lessons for our future.

Emerson is fond of double entendres, but the title of this book, *New Morning*, is not one. This is not a new *mourning*, a collection lamenting and resisting the disappearance of Emerson from print, from the college classroom, or from American culture. The purpose of this book is rather to celebrate his indelible presence in the fabric of American life.

Emerson often writes as if history were a terrible burden and threat to original thinking; but Emerson himself was a passionate student of history with a keen grasp of intellectual movements. He prized innovation and loved to break new ground, but he never forgot the value of preserving the whole human story. A new thought or a new morning is not absolutely new and would not be intelligible if it were; other thoughts and mornings have gone before, lending significance to those present now. The present, if not for the past, might be experienced, and this experience might be enjoyable, but it would not be meaningful. The meaning of anything derives largely from what precedes it: a new morning is meaningful if it renews old hopes or seems to promise the completion of something important or the continuation of something comfortable and familiar.

Today the word *history* sounds old-fashioned, and the study of history is becoming obsolete. Facts are picked up and tossed away as dead fragments instead of being husbanded and viewed in the ampler perspective of a living intellectual tradition. Reliance on Internet technology is crowding out the natural ties that bind us to our common past and relate facts to the concerns of our lives. The network of lived events in which mere information becomes knowledge and memory is fading in the glare of detached facts hanging in a vacuum, waiting to be gaped at and forgotten instantly.

The neglect of history in America is pernicious because it threatens to deprive us of the stories and personalities that give meaning and direction to our lives. In the twentieth century, the rise of secular skepticism precipitated an identity crisis on a large scale; the decline of history could have the same bewildering result in the twenty-first century. Life with no history is not an attractive prospect, but the twenty-first century faces a second hazard: we are living in the shadow of spiritual confusion.

Jewish and Christian scriptures confuse spirituality with politics and morals and even occasionally with violence. The German philosopher Hegel famously misused the idea of spirituality to apologize for the bloodshed of human history by rewriting it in terms of inevitable moral progress. The benefit of long hindsight should be enough to help us understand the issue in a clear light, but in contemporary American culture spirituality is frequently identified with trivial matters of personal conduct and partisan politics. In the world at large it is often invoked as motive and justification of terrorism and torture.

Emerson stands at the headwaters of a grand intellectual tradition that in many ways is uniquely American; this tradition is already in our blood and needs only to be distilled out by a little curiosity and sustained attention. The vitality of mind is at stake in all profound philosophizing, and nothing could be more objectionable to a mature human being than intellectual senescence. I know an excellent philosopher who many years ago wrote an essay on Emerson in which he referred to him only in the present tense. The piece was about to appear in print when a copyeditor telephoned to complain. "You can't refer to Emerson in the present tense," she said, "because Emerson is dead"; to which my friend replied: "Not for me!" I am convinced that by learning about Emerson and the living tradition he helped to found we can face the challenges of a new century with confidence and hope, putting off intellectual infirmity and becoming, in a sense, forever young.

In my introductory courses, I try to bring suffering alive for students who have known only privilege. Many of them recognize nothing out of the ordinary in the name *Cambodia* or in the name *Rwanda*. You may say these atrocities are old; perhaps you are right. It is becoming tiresome to complain that young people are ignorant of history. But the outlook is equally disheartening about more recent humanitarian disasters. A few students open their eyes at the mention of Sudan or Fallujah, but many do not know the news or do not connect sympathetically to the stories. One student responded to a remark about thousands of afflicted children in Congo by saying that such things must happen for the best.

Emerson knew how easily experience can wash over us but without our feeling the wet or the warmth or the chill of it. Sometimes even calamity does not touch us: "The Indian who was laid under a curse that the wind should not blow him, nor water flow to him, nor fire burn him, is a type of us all. The dearest events are summer rain and we the Para coats that shed every drop." Apathy is a sign of affective paralysis and thus of intellectual dotage. When we stop feeling, we become spectators rather than participants, as if ensconced behind glass. Life loses its luster and the welfare of others fades from view.

Immanuel Kant reserves a special category for the evil of acting as if principles could never govern our conduct. He calls it "radical evil" because it poisons good conduct at its roots by denying the conditions that make it possible. To surrender the very conditions of principled behavior is to give up the possibility of good conduct, and from here cynicism is only a few steps away. Cynicism is perhaps the most baleful symptom of intellectual old age: a hardening of the arteries of the mind against possibility. In a world of finite creatures in which we suffer to no end, it sings like a siren. But a youthful spirit, too busy imagining a better world, will not be drawn by the song.

Cynicism must have appealed strongly to Emerson, who was only eight years old when his father died of cancer—too young to grasp the awful significance of the event. He noted on a piece of paper that the word *fun* is contained in the word *funeral*. In December 1828, Emerson became engaged to Ellen Tucker. In his journal he wrote: "Oh Ellen, I do dearly love you." They were married the following September, but she was ill with tuberculosis. When she died in February 1831, Emerson was in the room with her and wrote: "One of the last things she said after much rambling & inarticulate expression was 'I have not forgot the peace & joy.' And at nine o'clock she died." He would think and dream of her for the rest of his life; a lesser person would have been crushed.

Emerson's brothers Charles and Edward also became tubercular. Edward died in 1834, Charles in 1836, the year Emerson's first book was published. In 1842, his cherished son, Waldo, died of scarlet fever; perhaps the "little waving hand" in "Circles" is Waldo's. Emerson delivered the eulogy at this friend Thoreau's funeral in 1862, and his house caught fire and burned in the last decade of his life, destroying his father's sermons. Ellen Tucker's letters were spared along with many of his books and papers, but Emerson would never be the same. He would not lecture in public again, and he began to lose his mental faculties. Dementia afflicted him in his final years so that when he attended the poet Longfellow's funeral in March 1882 he could not remember the name of the deceased.

In spite of so much grief, Emerson remained optimistic, not cynical, to the end of his life. He believed in goodness, in love, in beauty, and in the restorative power of absorption in the present moment. House burning in front of his eyes, Emerson stood back and was heard to remark: "But isn't it a magnificent blaze!" Behind his optimism lay an unshakable conviction that each new day is a divine gift, that mistakes can be forgotten and redeemed, and that while we are mentally young we are prisoners neither of the past nor of the future but live free at a perpetual beginning. No doubt Emerson felt the pains of mortality as deeply as the excitement of living, but his intelligence was youthful and supple, and he could live amiably with both. At the centenary of Emerson's birth, William James said of him: "He could perceive the full squalor of the individual fact, but he could also see the transfiguration."

As we age, the lenses in our eyes rigidify; they lose their former plasticity, and we become nearsighted. Intellectual old age is marked by a similar degeneration. Our mental lenses become stiff and inflexible; we lose the ability to see alternatives and whatever *is* comes to seem necessary. Christian writers rightly remind us to consider the lilies of the field and the birds of the air, which do not cry over the past or long for remote fulfillments; these beings seem to be content with the world as it is. But their contentment is not evidence of stoic resignation or hardness of heart, nor indolence nor inactivity; on the contrary, it flows from the most perfect activity and flexibility. If they became conscious of themselves it would be as movements of what Taoists call the "endless knot of nature."

Human beings tend to resist the flow of events because we want to control our individual destinies. Relinquishing control can seem like defeat or death: when our bodies are healthy our hearts want growth and progress. Once, just before dawn, Walt Whitman looked up at a sky bright with stars and said to his soul: "*When we become the enfolders of those orbs, and the pleasure and knowledge of every thing in them, shall we be fill'd and satisfied then?*" And the reply came: "*No, we but level that lift to pass and continue beyond.*" The sentiment is familiar to all of us, and Whitman is echoing Emerson's words in "Circles" and elsewhere; but spiritual expansion requires youth and flexibility, not stubborn striving and the mania of individual control, which are sure signs of a superannuated intellect.

For Emerson, flexibility is the highest virtue, being seed and root of all intellectual growth and spiritual development. His philosophy is one of softness rather than rigidity, patience rather than haste, understanding rather than judgment: a fountain of youth from which our minds are invited to drink. Emerson writes: "We grizzle every day. I see no need of it. Whilst we converse with what is above us, we do not grow old, but grow young. Infancy, youth, receptive, aspiring, with religious eye looking upward, counts itself nothing and abandons itself to the instruction flowing from all sides." This almost rapturous movement onward and upward is quintessentially Emersonian; it is also quintessentially American.

Emerson's philosophy has found its way into the bloodstream of American culture because Americans are most at home on the frontiers, imperiled and sustained by their drives and their ideals. On the one hand, we want a philosophy that is friendly to moral progress and material success, and Emerson is, after all, the original author of the maxim Hitch your wagon to a star. But how can drives and ideals sustain us unless we also know how to be satisfied with present goods even when they are incomplete and unfinished? Emerson's philosophy delights as much in progress as in the simple enjoyment of the fruits of material and conscious life; it flourishes in America because it teaches us how to love the journey on which we have always been so heroically embarked.

Most traditions offer answers to the great mysteries of life, such as the doctrine of the soul's immortality, and some think Americans have no tradition because they have produced no final answers. Writing on the significance of the frontier in American life, Frederick Jackson Turner has this to say: "American social development has been continually beginning over again on the frontier. This perennial rebirth, this fluidity of American life, this expansion westward with its new opportunities, its continuous touch with the simplicity of primitive society, furnish the forces dominating American character." Can we not recognize ourselves in questions as much as in answers? America has always been a question, a beginning, a "perennial rebirth" on a new frontier. To be American is to be young in an Emersonian sense; it means loving questions as much as answers, journeying as much as arriving.

While our minds are young, the whole world is new. The most insignificant thing absorbs us, and we do not ask where it leads. The mystery of the growing grass does not ask to be found out. "The blowing rose is a new event; the garden full of flowers is Eden all over again to the small Adam; the rain, the ice, the frost, make epochs in his life." The mentally aged inquire only about the use and function of things; they quickly grow tired of the present and focus their minds on distant goods. They teach us to demand the future. But the future will come without our demands and will be sweeter if we do not try to force it. So much beauty remains to be enjoyed if we can live the way children do: "forever new to life." If we can, then seeking and finding will be one for us, and we will have mastered the art of living.

Of the seasons of the year Emerson loved spring the best. Joel Porte, who understood him well, could see that he lived in "perpetual expectation of the season of renewal" and that this was his "true faith." The last stanza of Emerson's poem "The World-Soul" reads:

> Spring still makes spring in the mind
>   When sixty years are told;
> Love wakes anew this throbbing heart,
>   And we are never old.

II

The editors want to present Emerson as our contemporary, as a voice still living and still speaking powerfully to the concerns of the living. We also want to make Emerson more accessible to students and the lay educated public and to make him more readily teachable. To celebrate Emerson's work as a poet and his profound influence on American poetry from Whitman to Dickinson to Mary Oliver, we have interleaved short poems between some of the chapters. These are either about Emerson or written in an Emersonian spirit; they represent the work of acclaimed living American writers.

The essays and poems included herein are mainly original, but where we could find a previously published work of superior value, such as Robert Pollock's "Single Vision" or Mark Strand's original version of "The Continental College of Beauty," we did not hesitate to include it. We are also excited to reproduce Emerson's letter to a little girl of thirteen, Lucia, who thought of him as a spiritual teacher. This letter has not appeared in print in more than a hundred years, and in it Emerson speaks not only to Lucia, but to all his spiritual children.

We have also been concerned to highlight the interdisciplinary character of Emerson's work. His interests were as various and far ranging as his moods, and we want to present an Emerson who continues to speak relevantly across disciplinary lines. Emerson was an idealist and a naturalist, an ancient and a modern, a philosopher and a divine. He was an artist and a lover of art with his own aesthetic. He was a champion of democracy and civil rights, including the rights of women and native Americans: he said he did not want to live in a country in which slavery existed. Emerson was a forerunner of contemporary environmental philosophizing and activism; he is also the grandfather of much American philosophy and literature.

The essays we have anthologized speak to the wide spread of Emerson's concerns, all of which are alive and pressing today. We have assembled them here not to ensure that Emerson will continue to be read. He will be read inevitably. Our desire is to restore him to his beloved "strong present tense."

Michael Brodrick

Acknowledgments

Above all, I want to thank John J. McDermott, who introduced me to Emerson more than forty years ago and whose continuing friendship and inspiration has been one of the great blessings of my life. My friend and former colleague Paul Sherwin connected me to the poet Paul Hoover and reconnected me to the poet Ann Lauterbach. My conversations with him about Emerson and other philosophical and literary matters have been a major source of insight for both my writing and teaching. I also want to thank my former colleague Norbert Krapf for introducing me to the poet Bill Heyen and for his generosity and friendship over the years. My wife, Dorene, has encouraged the project from the beginning, and her brilliant editorial skills have been invaluable in the shaping of my own work. Finally, I want to thank the countless number of students with whom I have shared Emerson for more than thirty-five years at C.W. Post, NYU, the New School, and in other academic and nonacademic settings.

—Arthur S. Lothstein

I am grateful for my family's encouragement and for the constant support of John Lachs.

—Michael Brodrick

God had infinite time to give to us; but how did He give it? In one immense tract of a lazy millennium? No, but He cut it up into neat succession of new mornings, and, with each, therefore, a new idea, new inventions, and new applications.

—R. W. E.

Dancing with Emerson

Deborah Digges

The wide pavilions of the old Post Road
from western Massachusetts toward Concord
one night past three, as I drove slowly in,
just freshly plowed, were empty.
The fields flapped out on either side,
climbing the blue hills like eternity.
There at the prison rotary
I could go only round
at last to dance with Mr. Emerson.
Oh waltz with me to guardhouse radios
playing night music for the stalled,
the jailors and the jailed locked in their crimes
like songs you live by.
Mr. Emerson, hello.
Do me the honor here outside the wall
strung with barbed wire where once was meadow.
My hand in his and his about my waist
outside the gates we whirled the circle.
And so I told him, shy, with due respect,
you were my first love, Mr. Emerson.
And this was early March,
Northeast the worst of months,
the snow piled high, like a rotunda.
I blizzard-fated, blind and scared,
and for the first time in my life
my dance card was empty.
Without a word, he such a gentleman
held my hand, and I so lightly his
as searchlights scanned the prison yards,
and dance we did, my Mr. Emerson.
I drive that road so many seasons, drive hours
toward home or coming into Boston.
It was enough that only once we danced,
less time it takes to slip the wire,
or dip the quill, or kiss a man.

Chapter 1

Emerson

An Introduction

Mary Oliver

*T*he distinction and particular value of anything, or any person, inevitably must alter according to the time and place from which we take our view. In any new discussion of Emerson, these two weights are upon us. By time, of course, I mean our entrance into the twenty-first century; it is more than two hundred years since Emerson's birth in Boston. By place, I mean his delivery from the town of Concord, and his corporeal existence anywhere. Now he is only within the wider, immeasurable world of our thoughts. He lives nowhere but on the page, and in the attentive mind that leans above that page.

This has some advantage for us, for he is now the Emerson of our choice: he is the man of his own time—his own history—or he is one of the mentors of ours. Each of these possibilities has its attractions, for the man alive was unbelievably sweet and, for all his devotion to reason, wondrously spontaneous. Yet as time's passage has broken him free of all mortal events, we begin to know him more clearly for the labors of his life: the life of his mind. Surely he was looking for something that would abide beyond the Tuesday or the Saturday, beyond even his first powerful or cautionary or lovely effect. "The office of the scholar," he wrote in "The American Scholar," "is to cheer, to raise, and to guide men by showing them facts amidst appearances." The lofty fun of it is that his "appearances" were all merely material and temporal—brick walls, garden walls, ripening pears—while his facts were all of a shifty vapor and an unauthored goodwill: the luminosity of the pears, the musics of birds and the wind, the affirmative staring-out light of the night stars. And his belief that a man's inclination, once awakened to it, would be to turn all the heavy sails of his life to a moral purpose.

3

The story of his life, as we can best follow it from its appearances, is as follows. Ralph Waldo Emerson was born in 1803; his father, William Emerson, died in 1811. The family—his mother, two sisters, and five brothers— were poor, devout, and intellectually ambitious. Death's fast or slow lightning was a too-frequent presence. Both girls and one boy died in childhood; Emerson's brothers William, Edward, and Charles survived only into early manhood. The only remaining brother was Robert, who was a man of childish mind. As the poet Walt Whitman for most of his life took responsibility for his child-minded brother, Eddie, so did Emerson keep watch over this truculent survivor.

Emerson graduated from Harvard College, then divinity school, and in 1829 he began preaching at the Second Church (Unitarian) in Boston. In that year he married the beautiful but frail Ellen Tucker. Her health never improved, and in 1832 she died. Emerson was then twenty-nine years old.

I think it is fair to say that from this point on, the greater energies of his life found their sustenance in the richness and steadfastness of his inner life. Soon after his wife's death he left the pulpit. He had come to believe that the taking of the sacrament was no more, nor was meant to be more, than an act of spiritual remembrance. This disclosure he made to his congregation, who perhaps were grateful for his forthrightness but in all honesty did not wish to keep such a preacher. Soon after, Emerson booked passage to Europe. He traveled slowly across the Continent and, finally, to England. He was deeply touched by the magnificence of the past, so apparent in the cities, in their art and architecture. He also made it his business to explore the present. The list of those he met and talked with is amazing: Coleridge, Wordsworth, Walter Savage Landor, John Stuart Mill among them. His meeting with Thomas Carlyle began a life-long friendship, their letters going back and forth across the Atlantic until Emerson's death.

Emerson returned from Europe and established a manner of living that he would scarcely alter for the rest of his life. He married again, a young woman named Lydia Jackson. In his journals, which he had begun in college and never abandoned, he tore down wall after wall in his search for a style and for ideas that would reach forth and touch both poles: his certainty and his fluidity. He bought a house in the town of Concord, an easy distance from Boston yet a place with its own extraordinary style and whose citizens were farmers, tradesmen, teachers, and the liveliest of utopians. Here, as husband and father, as writer and lecturer, Emerson would live for years his seemingly quiet, seemingly peaceful life.

The best use of literature bends not toward the narrow and the absolute but to the extravagant and the possible. Answers are no part of it; rather it is the opinions, the rhapsodic persuasions, the ingrafted logics, the clues that are to the mind of the reader the possible keys to his own self-quarrels, his own predicament. This is the crux of Emerson, who does not advance straight ahead but wanders to all sides of an issue; who delivers suggestions with a kindly gesture; who opens doors and tells us to look at things for ourselves. The one thing he is adamant about is that we *should* look—we *must* look—for that is the liquor of life, that brooding upon issues, that attention to thought even as we weed the garden or milk the cow.

This policy, if such it might be called, he established at the start. The first book he published was called *Nature;* in it he refers, with equal serenity, to "Nature" and to "nature." We understand clearly that by the first he means "this web of God"—everything that is not the mind uttering such words—yet he sets our lives down among the small-lettered noun as well, as though to burden us equally with the sublime and the common. It is as if the combination, and the understanding of the combination—the necessary honoring of both—were the issue of utmost importance. *Nature* is a text that is entirely about divinity, and first purposes, a book of manners, almost, but for the inner man. It does not demean by diction or implication the life that we are most apt to call "real," but it presupposes the heart's spiritual awakening as the true work of our lives. That this might take place in as many ways as there are persons alive did not at all disturb Emerson, and that its occurrence was the beginning of paradise here among the temporal fields was one of his few unassailable certainties.

In 1836, at the issue of this initial volume, and in the first years following, he was a man scarcely known to the world. Descended from seven generations of preachers, in conventional terms a failed churchman himself, he held no more important post than his membership in the Concord volunteer Fire Association. If he tried to be at home among the stars, so too he strove to be comfortable in his own living room. Mentor to Thoreau and neighbor to Hawthorne, the idiosyncratic Bronson Alcott, the passionate Margaret Fuller, the talkative Ellery Channing, and the excitable Jones Very, he adorned his society with friendliness and participation. His house was often full of friends, and talk. Julian Hawthorne, then a young boy, remembers him sitting in the parlor, "legs crossed and—such was their flexibility—with one foot hitched behind the other ankle. Leaning forward, elbow on one knee, he faced his guests and held converse." There was an evening when his daughter Ellen called him away to talk to the butcher about mutton. It is reported that he rose mildly to do as he was bid. And there is another story, as he reports it himself in his journal, on a June day: "Now for near five years I have been indulged by the gracious Heaven in my long holiday in this goodly house of mine, entertaining and entertained by so many worthy and gifted friends, and all this time poor Nancy Barron, the mad-woman, has been screaming herself hoarse at the Poorhouse across the brook and I still hear her whenever I open my window."

Emerson was the leading member of the group we know as the New England transcendentalists. It is hardly a proper philosophy; certainly it is not a school of thought in which all members were in agreement. Impossible such a finding would have been with the various sensibilities of Concord! For each member, therefore, it must be reported somewhat differently. For Emerson, it devolved from Coleridge and German philosophy, from Swedenborg, no doubt from half a hundred other voices as from his religious beliefs and his own appreciation of the world's more-than-utilitarian beauty. For Emerson, the value and distinction of transcendentalism was very much akin to this swerving and rolling away from acute definition. All the world is taken in through the eye, to reach the soul, where it becomes *more*, representative of a realm deeper than appearances: a realm ideal and sublime, the deep stillness *that is*, whose whole proclamation is the silence and the lack of material instance in which, patiently and radiantly, the universe exists. Emerson would not turn from the world, which was domestic, and social, and collective, and required action. Neither would he swerve from that unperturbable inner radiance, mystical, forming no rational word but drenched with passionate and untranslatable song. A man should want to be domestic, steady, moral, politic, reasonable. He should want also to be subsumed, whirled, to know himself as dust in the fingers of the wind. This was his supple, unbreakable faith.

His certainty that a man must live also in this world, enjoined with the similar faith of the other transcendentalists, was no small force in the New England of the 1830s and 1840s, especially in speech and action in behalf of abolition. Slow as he often was to express outrage, Emerson burst forth in his journal thus: "This filthy enactment [of the Fugitive Slave Law] was made in the 19th century, by people who could read and write. I will not obey it, by God." And he did not.

Writing that loses its elegance loses its significance. Moreover, it is no simple matter to be both inspirational and moderate. Emerson's trick—I use the word in no belittling sense—was to fill his essays with "things" at the same time that his subject was conceptual, invisible, no more than a glimmer, but a glimmer of immeasurable sharpness inside the eye. So he attached the common word to the startling idea. "Hitch your wagon to a star," he advised. "The drop is a small ocean." "A foolish consistency is the hobgoblin of little minds." "We live amid surfaces, and the true art of life is to skate well on them." "Sleep lingers all our lifetime about the eyes, as night hovers all day in the boughs of the fir tree." "The soul makes the body." "Prayer is the contemplation of the facts of life from the highest point of view," he says, and suddenly that elite mystical practice seems clearer than ever before and possible to each of us.

Of course his writing is made up of the nineteenth-century sentence, so nimble with commas. The sparks of his expression move forward softly and reasonably, in their shapely phrases—then they leap. He rests upon the gnomic as a poet will rest upon meter and comes not to a conclusion but to a pause in which the reader's own impetus, given such a bright shove, takes over. And yet it is not ornamental eloquence, but natural, fecund, ripe, full of seed and possibility. Even, or especially (it is his specialty, after all), when talking about the utterly unprovable, he sends out good news, as good reports come all day from the mockingbird, or the soft tongues of the Merrimack. The writing is a pleasure to the ear, and thus a tonic to the heart, at the same time that it strikes the mind.

Thus he wrote and lectured, often in Boston and New York but also as far west as Missouri and beyond. He did not especially like travel, or being away from home, but he needed the money and trusted the lecturing process as a way for him to develop and polish his essays for eventual publication.

In 1847 Emerson, by then an established writer and widely honored on both sides of the Atlantic, returned to England. The audiences for his lectures were large and curious. Crabb Robinson, in his diary of those years, relates first his own response and then the reaction of the writer Harriet Martineau:

> Tuesday, I heard Emerson's first lecture, "On the Laws of Thought;" one of those rhapsodical exercises of mind, like Coleridge's in his "Table Talk," and Carlyle's in his Lectures, which leave a dreamy sense of pleasure, not easy to analyze, or render an account of. . . . I can do no better than tell you what Harriet Martineau says about him, which, I think, admirably describes the character of his mind. "He is a man so *sui generis*, that I do not wonder at his not being apprehended till he is seen. His influence is of a curious sort. There is a vague nobleness and thorough sweetness about him, which move people to their very depths, without their being able to explain why. The logicians have an incessant triumph over him, but their triumph is of no avail. He conquers minds, as well as hearts, wherever he goes; and without convincing anybody's reason of any one thing, exalts their reason, and makes their minds worth more than they ever were before." 9th June, 1848.

That we are spirits that have descended into our bodies, of this Emerson was sure. That each man was utterly important and limitless, an "infinitude," of this he was also sure. And it was a faith that leads, as he shows us again and again, not to stasis but to activity, to the creation of the moral person from the indecisive person. Attachment to the Ideal, without participation in the world of men and women, was the business of foxes and flowers, not of men, not of women. This was, for Emerson himself, difficult. Outwardly he was calm, reasonable, patient. All his wildness was in his head—such a good place for it! Yet his certainty that thought, though it might grow most robust in the mind's repose, was sent and meant for participation in the world, never altered, never ebbed. There are, for myself, a hundred reasons why I would find my life—not only my literary, thoughtful life but my emotional, responsive life—impoverished by Emerson's absence, but none is greater than this uncloseting of thought into the world's brilliant, perilous present. I think of him whenever I set to work on something worthy. And there he is also, avuncular and sweet, but firm and corrective, when I am below the mark. What we bring forth, he has taught me as deeply as any writer could, is predictable.

But let him have the last word. In his journal he wrote: "I have confidence in the laws of morals as of botany. I have planted maize in my field every June for seventeen years and I never knew it come up strychnine. My parsley, beet, turnip, carrot, buck-thorn, chestnut, acorn, are as sure. I believe that justice produces justice, and injustice injustice."

Chapter 2

The Single Vision

Robert C. Pollock

*A*n interpretation of Emerson which would claim to do him Justice is by no means a light undertaking. For, contrary to what seems to be a widely held opinion, he was a very complex person who thought deeply and subtly about serious matters. Indeed, the closer we come to the man himself the better we can estimate the difficulty of making a just appraisal of his essential genius.

Today, thanks to the painstaking efforts of scholars, it is possible to gain a rounded appreciation of Emerson's achievements. At the very least, we can now see that Emerson resists easy classification, and that, moreover, there is little excuse for certain misconceptions regarding him which owe their currency to the habit of pouncing upon certain words of his taken in isolation and with little regard for his basic motivations, spiritual, intellectual, and esthetic.

A contemporary scholar sums up extremely well what any serious reading of Emerson should teach us, when he says: "We are wrong to think of him as an Olympian seer, playing in solitude with Platonic abstractions. The power of his writing rests not simply on his craftsman's skill, though that was great, but on the compulsions and conflicts, the revelations and the doubts, the glories and the fears which struck fire in his imagination and compelled him to bring them to definition. Genius is the daughter of such necessity. Because he has this kind of power he will continue to be read." While we might find fault with any statement which would seem to identify Platonism with abstractions in the pejorative sense, we must still agree with the main idea expressed by this author, especially when he goes on to say of Emerson that "his life of thought was not, as it has generally been represented, an eventless and static thing, to be defined and assessed, like merchandise, by a process of random sampling," and when he says, further, "In following it we are watching a process that is always absorbing wherever it is encountered—the action of a superior imagination taking possession of its world."[1]

However, if we are to make this general assessment of the living quality of Emerson's work complete, we should stress not only the dynamism of
his life and thought and the great power of his imagination, but also his capacity for highly disciplined thinking. And here again a contemporary author sums up the matter for us when she says (in reference to Emerson's
ideas of literature and art) that "at no point was he soaring into a vague
empyrean of irresponsible speculation, but was always sustained by the support of other thinkers, however disparate these thinkers may be from each
other," and when, in addition, she tells us that his esthetic theory "is a better rationalized esthetic than his critics have generally suspected."[2]

But while Emerson was primarily a literary figure, he found himself in the
situation where he had to function constructively on a theoretical level, and
not merely with respect to poetry and literature, but in relation to reality as a
whole. And the burdens imposed by such a diversity of interests were bound
to have unhappy results. As a literary figure he had to concern himself with esthetic theory, inasmuch as he wanted to show that esthetic sensibility has an
indispensable function within the whole structure of knowledge. His avowed
aim was to demonstrate the objective status of esthetic experience, while justifying a symbolistic method in literature. Moreover, the need for a reap-
praisal of human existence in its entirety was keenly felt by him, especially
since he could see that the problems confronting him as a writer and poet
waited for their solution on the answer to questions of a philosophical nature.

From first to last an artist, Emerson paid the price of his diverse efforts, even laying himself open to the charge that his "failing was a lack of
literary purposefulness."[3] Still, we may well question whether "a lack of literary purposefulness" exactly states the case, for it remains true that he
played no small part in fortifying and expanding esthetic sensibility, as the
author just quoted has himself shown.

Although Emerson spent much time brooding over philosophical matters, he never for a moment fancied himself a philosopher in any purely
formal or technical sense of the term. Far from it, for he made no bones
about his deficiency in the sort of thinking that produced the works of a
Hume or a Butler. Yet, if we read his *Journals* along with his *Essays*, we
surely cannot avoid seeing that he was capable of a high and sustained
philosophical seriousness which puts the stamp of significance on much of
what he says. Indeed, as it has been rightly said, "the height and depth of
his thought" is one of his "distinguishing excellencies."

Emerson was first and last "an artist in the medium of theory."[4] And, as
an artist he brought something of value to his philosophical reflections,
namely, an esthetic sensibility which held him fast to a concrete and experiential method. This method in no way implied a derogatory view of philosophical speculation, although it did fasten his attention on the strange and
complex process by which experience is converted into thought. Others

might disparage knowing and the contemplative life, but, as one who had imbibed copiously of Plato's wisdom, he grasped the importance and even the sublimity of soaring speculative thought. However, the sustaining purpose of his philosophical efforts was simply to extend consciousness through direct insight and to enlarge man's vision of the world.

Emerson was quite content to translate his philosophical ideas into the broadest human terms, without trying to work them into a strictly philosophical form. Systematic thinking of a sort there would be, of course, but he would mainly content himself with the kind of system which consists in "dotting a fragmentary curve, recording only what facts he has observed, without attempting to arrange them within one outline."[5] Thus, all things considered, Emerson's approach was characterized by good sense and modesty, and if his thought may at times seem to defy abstract logic, it possesses, notwithstanding, a logic of its own, a logic of life, which is validated in the depth of personal experience.

At every step of the way, Emerson worked on two levels at once, that of principles and that of experience, for he saw with far more than ordinary clarity that men were suffering from an impoverishment of both principles and experience. But it was especially with the level of experience that he concerned himself, since he knew that while principles were absolutely essential, they would hardly manifest their truth to men who had already imposed artificial limits on experience. How could they possibly pay heed to his religious, ethical, and esthetic teachings, if they regarded the religious, ethical, and esthetic components of experience itself as strictly out of bounds? He accordingly applied himself to the business of restoring to human life a whole range of experience from which it had arbitrarily detached itself. Having himself in mind, as well as others, he noted the extraordinary facility with which we insulate ourselves from our own experiences, even from those that we might ordinarily regard as overpowering. In fact, it would seem that, more often than not, nothing really touches us, and "the dearest events are summer-rain, and we the Para coats that shed every drop." Clearly, then, "the Indian who was laid under a curse that the wind should not blow on him nor water flow to him, nor fire burn him is a type of us all."

But Emerson knew that if men shunned what was most valuable in their experience, it was because they had accepted the fiction of a split universe, that is, a universe in which the life of the spirit is insulated from man's life in nature. What had once been regarded as inseparable had been cleft asunder, with the unhappy result that a devoutly religious attitude to life, the contemplative spirit, and poetry itself were thought to be quite foreign to man's growing preoccupation with his earthly habitation. And mechanistic philosophy had provided this separatism with an aura of intellectual respectability which lay like a black cloud over human consciousness. Hence, it would be necessary to overcome this deadly separatism by liberating man from the mechanistic nightmare, while showing that we cannot even begin to relate ourselves properly to our natural environment unless we bring to it the inner world of the spirit.

In other words, Emerson was determined to cast out the devils of the mechanistic outlook which had alienated men from their own deeper experiences. He had no intention of stifling interest in the world of nature. On the contrary it was his purpose to bind men more closely to that world by effecting a thoroughgoing transformation in their perception of it. He would make them see that they had been living at second hand and had become so dulled to a cosmos teeming with surprising relationships, that they had failed to note the most revealing relationship of all, that between the world of visible things and the world of spirit accessible to man. They would thus discover that every contact with the material environment involved them in a mysterious contact with a higher world. And once this was seen, the split universe would be banished as a pernicious delusion, for men would know that their true habitat is the one all-inclusive environment which embraces spirit as well as the world of nature. No longer would these planes of reality be regarded as merely juxtaposed to each other, nor would material nature be looked upon as man's sole environment. Men would, therefore, set about the business of re-fashioning their lives within the all-inclusive universe of an older tradition; and within this universe they would recover an experiential wholeness.

When Emerson asserts that "we are so much strangers in nature as we are aliens from God," he is not merely upholding the primacy of the spiritual world, but he is also implying that, together, the spiritual world and the world of nature form one single reality, one universe in which man lives his life. And he is implying, further, that man cannot even naturalize himself, cannot really plant his being within the natural world until he has gained some sense of the higher world of spirit which is half-revealed and half-hidden by material nature. Even the naturalist, in the Emersonian view, cannot strictly be called one "until he satisfies all the demands of the spirit," for "the best read naturalist who lends an entire and devout attention to truth will see that there remains much to learn of his relation to the world, and that it is not to be learned by any addition or subtraction or other comparison of known quantities, but is arrived at by untaught sallies of the spirit, by a continual self-recovery, and by entire humility." Man is but a dwarf until he accepts his own elemental power to view nature in such wise that even the landscape, "every glimpse of which hath a grandeur," is perceived as a face of divinity. Let man grasp the exalted truth that "the noblest ministry of nature is to stand as an apparition of God" and science itself will be kindled "with the fire of the holiest affections" and "God will go forth anew into the creation."

Emerson's every line takes on new meaning once we see what he is driving at. Unwearyingly he strove to free men from the delusion of a split universe, which, as he knew, had reduced human life to a fragmented state. On one side, religion was losing a certain cosmic and natural quality, and, on the other, man's life in nature was being stripped of its spiritual dimension. Religious life was fast becoming a lopsided and even freakish affair, and man's contact with nature had lost a certain spiritual rapport essential to it. Faith in God had become detached from a lived awareness of nature as that which "brings tidings from spiritual realms," while faith in science and machinery subsisted apart from any faith in divine causes. Having lost their bearings in the universe whose source and foundation is the eternal One, men had become strangers to their own experience. Man, therefore, had to recall what in truth he is, a being who holds together within himself the "poles of the Universe," and who is the very meeting place of spirit and nature. He must thus widen to infinity his conception of himself, since he embraces "on one side elemental order, sand-stone and granite, rock-ledge, peat-bog, forest, sea and shore; and on the other part, thought."[7]

Alfred Noyes touches on this fundamental Emersonian standpoint in declaring that "Emerson was the first writer in American literature to begin that great work of the future—the finding and maintaining of that central position which has been temporarily lost in an age of specialists, that central position from which we shall again see 'all things in one,' as Thomas a Kempis could see them." And there can be no doubt that Noyes has correctly singled out that in Emerson which more than anything else should enable us to enter more sympathetically into his thoughts and attitudes.

As we have said, Emerson had no intention of loosening man's vital connection with the material environment. He fully appreciated the positive aspects of the naturalism that had made its appearance in modern times. For example, he saw it as a real triumph of the human spirit that man had put away his small measure in viewing nature, in gaining a sense of her "large style." Thus what others regarded as but a moment in the development of a scientific attitude, he saw as a significant stage in man's spiritual ascent. The spiritual significance of the new naturalism did not escape him, and for that reason he could rejoice because man had expanded to infinity his conception of nature while acquiring an ineradicable conviction that he and nature proceed from one identical root.

To Emerson the whole modern sense of nature was illumined by his own outlook rather than by that of mechanistic philosophy. Especially when we consider the cluster of feelings which well up so spontaneously within us at the mere sight of natural objects, as, for example, when we "anticipate a supersensual utility in the sun and stars, earth and water."[8] True, the impressions of nature may fall so feebly on us that we fail to sense this "supersensual utility." But, in that case, it is the function of the poet to remedy this defect, in helping us traverse the whole scale of experience. Yet if the poet is indispensable, so too are the philosopher and the seer, for these latter can supply the vision which will make men more sensitive to nature's promptings regarding the realm of the "supersensual." And through this vision men will easily understand why their contact with nature is able to arouse in them a spirit of reverence. Moreover, they will become more responsive to the necessary lessons in which nature exercises the mind of man, the "lessons of difference, of likeness, of order, of being and seeming, of progressive arrangement; of ascent from particular to general; of combination to one end of manifold forces." Finally, they will be the grateful recipients of one of nature's fairest gifts, namely, an "integrity of impression made by manifold objects," and through which, for example, the stick of timber is distinguished from the tree of the poet.

Working on two levels at once, that of principles and that of experience, Emerson set out to remove the blinkers from men's eyes, so that they might perceive the indescribable wonders of a world which so loudly proclaims the hollowness of the mechanistic hypothesis. Above all, he wanted men to evaluate properly the mysterious congruity which subsists between them and the natural world. For he felt certain that when the full implications of this congruity are grasped, inward spiritual life and life in nature would be joined together, and the ancient precept "know thyself" and the modern precept "study nature" would at last be fused into one maxim. To spiritually minded men who had discovered their ties with nature, nothing, surely, could be more liberating than the knowledge that soul-searching and a searching of earth and sky are not alien to each other, and that if the eyes of the soul "wander incessantly to the unfathomable abyss,"[9] the eyes of the body should be endlessly engaged in a closer scrutiny of nature.

People were awed by this rather strange man who could marvel before the spectacle of his own inward life and yet feel the marrow of the world in his bones. They heard him proclaim that "when a man lives with God his voice shall be as sweet as the murmer of the brook and the rustle of the corn," and that "as a plant upon the earth, so a man rests upon the bosom of God." But they also heard him say of man that "so much of nature as he is ignorant of, so much of his own mind does he not yet possess."

As they listened they felt he was really before them and standing solidly behind his words, and that he was speaking "*from within*, or from experience," and not "*from without*, as spectators merely." But apart from the authentic note in his message, he himself had declared that "if a man do not speak from within the veil, where the word is one with that it tells of, let him lowly confess it." Still at times, they must have been somewhat puzzled to hear one and the same person speak so earnestly of spiritual matters and yet so vividly of the ordinary things of life. There before them stood a man whose spiritual gravity and power of inward absorption brought forcibly to mind an image of the Puritan mystic, and from whose lips yet poured forth a profusion of magical phrases affirming his belief that nature, as "the city of God," was no vain show. And when he offered them his own version of what it means to accept nature as "the city of God," they were more certain than ever that he was speaking "from within the veil."

II
An Authentic Naturalism

It might be said by way of objection that Emerson's concern to join together religious life and life in nature is, in the final analysis, meaningless, inasmuch as he seems to equate religion with pantheism. And here an objector might cite a contemporary scholar who asserts that although at times Emerson "sounds very much as if he believed in God," the "higher will" he acknowledges "can be described only in pantheistic terms." But a closer study of Emerson will most certainly lay bare the inadequacy of such a view. Indeed it would seem that the more balanced interpretation is offered by another writer who denies that Emerson's position can be classified under the term pantheism, or, for that matter, under such terms as emanationism, or evolutionism. For, as he says, none of these terms "precisely and exhaustively characterizes his solution of the problem of contingency." In this writer's view, we may perhaps summarize it best in "saying that the entire force of the first and absolute cause is directed to the actuality of the individual, to every individual, and that every individual exists by the full influx of the first cause." "This conception," he tells us further, "does not in any way raise the question of the identity of the individual with the absolute cause, for the reply is apparent before the question takes form: the individual, by its individuality, cannot be equated with the Absolute; the Absolute by its infinity, cannot be exhausted, either by a single individual or by an infinity of individuals."

Emerson's thought on the Absolute and the finite is characterized by his desire to take account of both unity and duality. If the Absolute is indeed the cause and ground of all things, it nevertheless does not reduce them to nullity through its all-enveloping reality. As a matter of fact, Emerson was congenitally unable to view any question one-sidedly and statically, for his mind was, one might say, spontaneously dialectical, and it was just this natural disposition which made Plato's dialectical procedure so congenial to him. Emerson's characteristic way of approaching questions is also seen in his treatment of the problem of experience itself, for he views it sometimes monistically and sometimes dualistically. But his attitude was, as he said, "somewhat better than whim at last," for, as has been well said, for Emerson "each extreme was tacitly conditioned by a third view in which both became partial."[10] Clearly, then, his attitude to the fundamental question of the relation between the world of nature and the Absolute was anything but capricious. He did not deliberately seek out inconsistency. But neither did he shy away from it when he found it staring him in the face from the very center of his own thinking and his own experience. Quite the contrary, for inconsistency prodded him into an inescapable awareness of a wider standpoint in which opposites would find their reconciliation.

Emerson wished to bring to focus a certain truth, namely, that nature, as "the city of God," is the indispensable medium of intellectual and spiritual discernment. As the product, not of manifold power, "but of one will, of one mind," of the Supreme Being, or "the eternal ONE," whose attribute is self-existence, nature is an ever novel effect descending from above and in an unbroken obedience.[11] Thus, as the descending manifestation of spirit, nature is no stranger to man. In truth, it is bound to the human spirit by ties whose occult and mysterious character account for the intimations and suggestions which permeate man's experiences of the natural world.

Parenthetically, let us note here that in holding to this doctrine of nature as a manifestation of a supramaterial realm, Emerson attributed so much independence to the human spirit in its power to apprehend nature's deeper meanings, that at times he sounds like a subjective idealist. But his real intent is merely to stress the profound interiority of the human spirit. The spirit of man in its inwardness is, as it were, the terminus of a spiritual utterance whose source, while beyond time and space, yet reaches man through the instrumentality of nature. Idealism appealed to him only as a means of upsetting the complacency of the materialist, and throwing into relief the reality of mind, not only "as a part of the nature of things," but as a part which yet occupies a highly unique position in its relation to spiritual reality. He saw idealism as "a hypothesis to account for nature by other principles than those of carpentry and chemistry." But in denying the existence of matter, idealism fails to satisfy the demands of spirit, and "leaves me in the splendid labyrinth of my perceptions, to wander without end." How he felt regarding this denial of the reality of matter can also be seen in a later essay, when, in speaking of our contact with things in nature, he says, "These enchantments are medicinal, they sober and heal us. These are plain pleasures, kindly and native to us. We come to our own, and make friends with matter, which the ambitious chatter of the schools would persuade us to despise."[12]

Emerson particularly wanted to show that there is something transpersonal in human personality which explains the connection between human knowledge and the abyss of being, as well as man's ability to perceive the spiritual dimension in things. This transpersonal something is, of course, the divine presence itself. As he says, "Into every intelligence there is a door which is never closed, through which the creator passes." Hence, if deep calls unto deep, if the spirit of man can be so profoundly perceptive of the whole scale of being, it is because "the Maker of all things and all persons stands behind and casts his dread omniscience through us over things." All thinking is, at bottom, a "pious reception," for, "when we discern justice, when we discern truth, we do nothing of ourselves, but allow a passage to its beams." Therefore it can be rightly said that "the intellect, seeker of absolute truth, or the heart, lover of absolute good, intervenes for our succor."

Emerson attempted to "pluck the strings of tension" in men by contrasting their habitual state of consciousness with a truly human state. In place of that original relation to the universe to which every man is called, there was a blind and ignorant following of custom, and a "squalid contentment with conventions," and "satire at the names of philosophy and religion."[13] Men were living at second hand and had accepted penny-wisdom substitutes for what was authentic. Even when men yearned to drink deeply of life, they were enslaved by the grotesque notion that living one's life had to be postponed from day to day.

No mere generalizer or a propounder of formulas, Emerson merely wished to resuscitate a primal state of consciousness in which man feels his continuity with the great world around him, experiencing a sense of participation and of barriers swept away, and in addition, a sense of contact with a spiritual source of things. Subtle links of continuity on the one hand and, on the other, a vivifying relation to the realm of spirit in the depth of the soul—together these constitute the basis of a rounded human experience. But how was he to make others aware of his? Would he not have to penetrate to "the aboriginal Self" in man, in order that the primordial experiences might stand revealed? Would he not also have to contend with the blight of sophistication—an "impudent knowingness"—and a spurious "second thought" which kills primal conviction?

In the light of Emerson's desire to create a new fusion of religious life and life in nature, we can see why he would envision morality itself in cosmic terms. Mere moralism would have been repugnant to him, for he found it necessary to view everything, morality included, within the setting of a real universe (i.e., Nature in the large sense, which includes spirit). "But speak the truth," he says, "and all nature and all spirits help you with unexpected furtherance. Speak the truth, and all things alive or brute are vouchers, and the very roots of the grass underground there do seem to stir and move to bear you witness." Only when men feel that as men they are strong "by the whole strength of nature" will they have the power to withstand "the maxims of a low prudence" which declares the "first duty is to get land and money, place and name."[14]

For Emerson it was never a question of a spiritual versus a naturalistic outlook, since, as we have seen, he steadfastly refused to recognize any split between the higher and lower worlds. We would say that for him the real opposition lay between a genuinely spiritual outlook and a spiritual outlook which was denatured. It seemed to him that everything was conspiring to make religion something artificial in the universal scheme, something apart from man's life in the world of nature. While rationalism and mechanistic philosophy had done their part in promoting this death-dealing separatism, religion itself, at least the religion of his own forbears, had prepared the ground in its lack of a cosmic root. When he complained that the miracle was no longer "one with the blowing clover and the falling rain," he was merely reminding men of the delusion of the split universe. Indeed, so completely had this separatism dulled their senses, that they no longer regarded the marvelous interlacing of processes in nature as "the endless circulations of the divine charity [which] nourish man."

As the enemy of a denatured outlook, Emerson strove to make men more sensitive to their natural environment. Man's sense of wonder and his instinct for the mystery in things were enfeebled, and it was necessary to restore them to full vigor. The curtain had to be raised from the most ordinary facts, to discover their secret and enthralling wonders. Man had to be taught to marvel again at the miracle of being, so that "the light of rising and of setting suns, . . . the flying cloud, the singing bird, and the breath of flowers" will not seem alien to the deeper promptings of the spirit. Man had to be free from a prison of his own making, if he was to repossess a primal wisdom which includes a vision of nature, and even more fundamentally, spiritual understanding, or knowledge of God, which Emerson identified with "*matutina cognitio*," the morning knowledge of the Schoolmen, as against "*vespertina cognitio*," or evening knowledge, which is the knowledge of man.[15]

Man is imprisoned in man. Therefore, he, Emerson, would dedicate himself to the business of freeing him. Men were by no means content with their condition. They naturally wanted to live their own lives, they were thirsting for real existence and loved "to be caught up into the vision of principles." They would therefore know how to respond to one who understands that "The imaginative faculty of the soul must be fed with objects immense and eternal.[16] Men yearned to do something worthwhile, something truly in keeping with human nature and which would make its absolute demands upon them and which they could do with all their heart. Yet the essential appeal capable of stirring men to their roots was lacking, the appeal which would base itself on a true understanding of man's desire for an all-embracing unity of life. Scholars, thinkers, and writers were making no vital communication to society, and the public disregarded them. Accordingly, in speaking the words which would reanimate man with a consciousness of his true dignity and the unity proper to human life, Emerson felt he was doing something that was in its own way as necessary as the labors of the Abolitionists. Apparently conscience-stricken for a spell by what he deemed his remissness in not aiding the antislavery fight, he regains perspective in reflecting that he had quite other slaves to free, the "imprisoned spirit" and "imprisoned thought."[17]

III
An Ancient Tradition

In ancient classical philosophy Emerson found that very fusion of spirituality and a cosmic sense which he knew to be coeval with the human spirit. And in his quick response to this ancient outlook, which was as manna to his soul, he was experiencing what Catholic thinkers down the years had experienced before him. No matter how deficient the ancient thinkers were in terms of the more comprehensive vision of things vouchsafed to the believing mind of the Christian, they had, nonetheless, a magically evocative power which could be found nowhere else and which had a transforming effect on all who came in contact with them. But what was especially entrancing to Catholics was just that vision to which Emerson was groping, and whose essential feature was a great structured universe in which man has his place as a true cosmos within a cosmos.

Given such a vision, so congenial to the Catholic spirit, how else could Catholic culture develop save by remaining true to it? That is why we find medieval Catholic culture so completely dominated by the notion of an all-inclusive universe in which the whole spiritual order has its place. It was natural, therefore, for the medieval man to regard the world of the spirit as an actual part of his environment and as capable of acting on him and influencing him as things in time and space. When we consider that in modern times the very notion of "universe" has been stripped by physical science of its larger connotation, and that the essential vision has paled even for many religious people, we can more readily appreciate Emerson's efforts to recapture it.

Let us dwell for a moment on this great scheme envisioned by the ancients and to which several schools of thought contributed. For our purpose it will be enough to consider the contribution of Platonists and Stoics. On one hand, the Platonists had taught a doctrine of a transcendent spiritual reality, while yet offering to men's minds the spectacle of a structured scheme in which the world of man had its fixed place. The Stoics, on the other hand, believed in the dynamic immanence of a rational principle which permeates the universe to its innermost core, leaving nothing untouched. Despite the shortcomings of the Platonist view, it has remained a tower of strength to Christians; and as for Stoicism, it, too, while even more glaringly defective, has yet given new shape to human consciousness. Both aspects of that ancient vision found new scope in Catholic Christianity—Platonic transcendence and that outlook which found magnificent expression in *The Hymn of Cleanthes* or in Marcus Aurelius' "O dear city of Zeus."

There is significance in the fact that Emerson himself exhibited in some degree these two strains, the Platonic and the Stoic. His Platonism is evident in his doctrine of a spiritual reality beyond the world of the senses, a spiritual reality which is directly accessible to us. It is also revealed in his cherished view that every fact can be given its widest horizon by being raised from one level to another. To him Plato "represents the privilege of the intellect, the power, namely, of carrying up every fact to successive platforms and so disclosing in every fact a germ of expansion."[18] This expansion from one level to another of every fact is organic and has, moreover, an objective import, since "the mind does not create what it perceives, any more than the eye creates the rose."[19] The objects in our physical environment thus represent more than themselves, since they constitute the germ of an infinite meaningfulness.

As for Emerson's Stoicism, one can say that no ancient Stoic was more overcome than he before the great spectacle of a universe whose humblest forms bespoke divinity. Nor did any Stoic feel more deeply than he the divine immanence which manifested itself to him in the opulence of natural forms and the power and magnificence of nature's processes.

We know, of course, that Emerson was also influenced by Asiatic writings. Hence we can sum up the various influences by saying with Santayana that "he felt his affinity to the Hindoos and the Persians, to the Platonists and the Stoics." But these Asiatic traces by no means separate him from the great tradition of thought stemming from classicism and Christianity, since this tradition is also heavily indebted to the East. We might, indeed, characterize this tradition as essentially an effort to reconcile the notion of limit and measure, in which the Greeks excelled, with the sense of the measureless and boundless, which was more congenial to the Eastern mind. Emerson himself turned toward the East because its mode of thinking appealed to his own sense of an all-pervasive Infinite. Yet he loved Western ways of thinking, for in them he found what he also regarded as indispensable, namely, the classical respect for form and measure. Thus, in full approval of both Eastern and Western orientations, he can say, "if the East loved infinity the West delighted in boundaries."[20]

In his attempt to recapture the single vision of the older tradition, Emerson was severely handicapped by a lack of knowledge of the way in which that vision took shape down through the centuries. Still, it must be acknowledged that, despite grave defects, and considering his practical aim, something great emerges in his conception.

If we bear in mind his desire to view moral and spiritual life within the framework of a great cosmic order, we can deal more justly with his failure to confront the problem and mystery of evil more adequately than he did. Undoubtedly he was hard pressed by the fact of evil. If his placid outward demeanor often conveyed an easy optimism, we should not be deceived, since this was in some measure the result of a severe inner discipline. Besides, his own personal tragedies, which had been shattering experiences, were quite enough to shock him out of a self-complacent optimism.

Yet, if Emerson felt the reality of evil, how was he to accept it without jeopardizing his notion of a great ordered scheme which was ruled by intelligence and not by brute force? If evil was real, so was the order of the universe and its rational principle. How, therefore, deal with evil while yet showing that the universal order always holds sway, and with it the goodness which is bound up with the unity of things? As we know, he apparently solved the problem to his own satisfaction by having recourse to the view that "against all appearance, the nature of things works for truth and right forever,"[21] thereby making evil fade away as a result of the beneficent action of Goodness itself. Thus a "Beautiful Necessity" reigns over things, always assuring the triumph of the good. If this is indeed Emerson's view, then it would appear that evil has been banished as illusory, so eager is he to safeguard the cosmic order in which truth and justice are seen as operating with a certain impersonal force. And nature itself, which, in other contexts, is presented by him as a living presence manifesting divinity, is turned into a convenient abstraction.

If Emerson had made a serious study of Catholic thought, he would have been struck by the masterful way in which the problem of evil is handled, in full awareness of the ultimate mystery and yet with no essential violation of the cosmic outlook of the ancients. If anything, that cosmic outlook is deepened and broadened. For to these Christian thinkers, no matter how grave the disorder introduced into the world, the power of an omnipotent and creative God always stands above it, making evil serve the Divine Plan for the whole universe. Evil itself is, therefore, never a total disorder, for it, too, is ordered. What we have, then, in the Catholic conception is a magnificent optimism which, nevertheless, does not diminish by one iota the factuality of evil or its gravity. In the framework of Catholic doctrine, evil does not fade away under the magic wand of a beneficent necessity or through a more or less automatic process of universal compensation, nor can it be disregarded through an easy confidence in Goodness itself. On the contrary, evil becomes all the more terrible as the violation on the part of free rational beings of an order which has been freely and lovingly instituted by God Himself.

Clearly, Emerson's optimism lacked a proper metaphysical foundation. However, when we set out to criticize it we should at least keep in mind its basic motivations. We can, if we wish, link it in part with Emerson's desire to fortify human initiative. But we should also remember his effort to restore to religious life a profound sense of cosmos, so that spirituality would illumine and transfigure man's life as a cosmic being. Nor should we overlook his stubborn belief that at the heart of things there is that which makes untenable the tragic view of life, such as we find it in classical civilization with its conception of an overruling Fate. Obviously, his optimism has its roots, not in the ancient pagan world, but in a world which is under the sign of

Christianity; and if, in upholding it, he was forced into evasions in handling the problem of evil, the answer, strangely enough, is to be found in his yearning for a reconciliation of inward spirituality with the cosmic sense— a reconciliation which is certainly one of the glories of the Catholic tradition.

Emerson's approach to the problem of evil is particularly regrettable in view of the fact that he had dedicated himself to the task of reattaching men to their own experience. His ruling passion was fidelity to the data of experience, yet he was driven to violate the data in dealing only obliquely with that which bites so deeply into our lives, namely, evil itself. Today, we are painfully aware of what has been called "the gods and devils of the human soul." Emerson, it would seem, resolutely averted his gaze from the devils. Yet he felt impelled to do so in order to restore to life a certain massive and cosmic grandeur which had formerly been associated with religion, and which in modern times had been diverted from it. Perhaps he also felt an overwhelming need to shut out the devils with whom the religion of his own forebears had made him all too familiar, in order to win back his own dignity and freedom as a human being and to regain a proper view of the universe and man's spiritual ties with it. Undoubtedly, too, he was reacting against a religious conception which had become all too personal in excluding ideas like "universal justice" and "universal truth," which had once aroused deep religious emotion. To one like himself who was profoundly affected by Plato's doctrine of archetypal Ideas, universal justice and universal truth were living realities and never mere abstractions. Considering, then, all aspects of Emerson's optimism, we can appreciate the fact that despite its shortcomings, it represents in some degree a real effort to restore an older conception of things.

It has in fact been said that Emerson "was trying to describe an ancient way of seeing by means of a modern vocabulary which had been designed to repress it."[22] Specifically, what the author, here quoted, has in mind is Emerson's concern with an organic apprehension of things in contrast to "intellectual perception," which, according to Emerson, "severs once for all the man from the things with which he converses."[23] As he shows, Emerson set himself against the modern reduction of the thinking ego to a destructive abstraction, in seeing clearly that "an interest in the *how* more than the *what* of knowing would eventually be 'punished by loss of faculty.'"[24] But Emerson's fidelity to the "*what* of knowing" was tied in with his effort to rehabilitate human experience and with it man's relations to a spiritual and cosmic order. Thus he was indeed trying to restore an ancient way of seeing and to an extent which should command our respect. Most certainly, he was offering men a glimpse of the true dimensions of human existence, despite the resistance offered him by the very vocabulary at his disposal and by ingrained habits of thought which could only be dissolved by a kind of violence on his part which also had the effect of throwing him off center.

We have emphasized the empirical character of Emerson's approach. Granting that he violated this empiricism in his handling of the problem of evil, although for reasons which were by no means petty, it is still true that he believed with all his heart in an experiential method. The strength of his belief can be measured by the fact that his search for the single vision in no way caused him to turn his back on the world of multiplicity. "A faithful reporter of multiplicity,"[25] he was unfailingly sensitive to the boundless diversity of things. And like the great thinkers of the Greek world, he had no intention of obliterating boundaries and limit, for, as he says, "the very definition of the intellect is Aristotle's: 'that by which we know terms or boundaries.'"[26] How he felt in the matter is also evident from his educational advice: "Give a boy accurate perceptions. Teach him the difference between the similar and the same. Make him call things by their right names."

Emerson knew only too well that reality resists every attempt to reduce it to an undifferentiated whole, such as is to be found in a materialistic or a spiritualistic monism. "Recognize the inextinguishable dualism," he writes in his *Journal*, "[b]ut also show that to seek the Unity is a necessity of the mind." But apparently this conviction of Unity is not only rational but also a matter of belief, for he writes, "A believer in Unity, a seer of Unity, I yet behold two."[27] More likely then, this search for unity arose not only out of "a necessity of the mind," but out of what he elsewhere describes as "*the universal impulse to believe, that is the material circumstances and is the principle fact in the history of the globe.*"

As to nature itself, what he beheld was a wondrously diversified world, exhibiting everywhere amazing contrasts and a polarity of opposites. "Nature is upheld by antagonism," he says, and when he looks upon God as the very resolution of all such antagonism, he is merely pointing up his acceptance of its cosmic and fruitful character. But Emerson's keen awareness of diversity and antagonism was not without its painful side, as we may gather from his words, "Cannot I conceive the Universe without a contradiction?"[28]

True enough, as it has been noted, his attempt to view the endless variety of things in relation to "the absolute End" often led him to a too rapid ascent from diversity to unity. But it would be wrong to interpret such an ascent as mere flight from the complexity of the world. On the contrary, Emerson sought multiplicity out, experiencing real exultation in perceiving nature's inexhaustible opulence. But, nonetheless, he believed with every fiber of his being in the essential relatedness of all things; and the unity he envisaged was fully concrete—"the inexplicable continuity of this web of God," in which "contrary and remote things cohere." Things are strictly related, and no matter how small or large the range of our perception, we find, not merely "surprises and contrasts," but a "guiding identity" running through them.

There can be no doubt that Emerson had a lived awareness of this wholeness, and that it was activized by contact with the simplest objects in nature. But if he was capable of total absorption in ordinary things, his heart fairly danced with joy before the variety of nature's forms and "the majestic beauties which daily wrap us in their bosom." And even the single glimpse became a moving experience when it was caught up in the panoramic view and when in his imagination he projected it against the background of the world and the universe, and when finally he saw it in relation to the all-fair, "the ever-blessed ONE," whose infinity encircles the humblest of objects.

Nothing so plainly demonstrates Emerson's sensitivity to the complexities of the real world as his grasp, not merely of a universal relatedness, but of its dynamic character. The astonishing interplay of the most divergent things and the ceaseless tension of opposites fascinated him. Spellbound before so enthralling a spectacle, he wished that others might perceive it as vividly as he did, for he knew how effectually it could arouse the intellect from a state of torpor and lethargy.

But Emerson saw much more than a world teeming with opposition and tension, for he was too keenly perceptive of life and motion to miss the universal rhythm which nothing escapes. Thus he writes: "That great principle of Undulation in nature, that shows itself in the inspiring and expiring of the breath; in desire and satiety; in the ebb and flow of the sea; in day and night; in heat and cold; and, as yet more deeply ingrained in every atom and every fluid, is known to us under the name of Polarity,—these 'fits of easy transmission and reflection,' as Newton called them, are the law of nature because they are the law of spirit." And with the "solar eye" of his spirit he beheld how rhythm pervades man's life as an individual and his life in relation to all that lies around and beyond him. In one sovereign moment he is face to face with his own baffling uniqueness; but, in the inescapable flow of life, this experience gives way to one in which the individual is drawn out of himself and into the embrace of the universe. Always there is this rhythmic movement, this universal Undulation, an ebb and flow, an oscillation of states.

The intellect itself is not immune, for its daily history is characterized by a ceaseless alternation between expansion and contraction. Thus, no matter where he looks, Emerson finds unfailing manifestations of a universal rhythm, which governs spiritual as well as cosmic processes: "[T]he chemical and ethereal agents are undulatory and alternate; and the mind goes antagonizing on." And this rhythm also shows itself in the relation between the spiritual and material sides of human life, and between thought and action, perception and expression, struggle and repose, breadth of life and intensity of life, society and solitude, culture and originality, history and character. To flout this universal rhythm is to do violence to the simplest facts of experience, while exposing oneself to the crudest errors through a static conception of things. But when we grasp the true proportions of rhythm, we gain a new insight into the wonderfully dynamic unity of the universe and its awesome necessities.

Clearly, then, no interpretation of Emerson has any claim to adequacy which does not do full justice to that which inspired his every thought and word—his synoptic vision. Such a vision forbids any discrediting of the world of nature which lies expanded before us. It also rules out every fragmenting conception in making manifest what has so often been overlooked by good philosophers, namely, the extreme importance of the category of relation. Hence, Emerson's unfailing concern with unity was justified, for he knew that nothing can be viewed in isolation in a universe which is truly a universe, and whose unity, moreover, is dynamic. "Nature is intricate, overlapped, interweaved and endless," and the single vision does not permit the weaving of "a spotted life of shreds and patches." The togetherness of all things was thus for Emerson the primal truth, and in his fidelity to it he was the worthy heir of a great tradition in which we find some of the greatest of the Christian mystics. And like these mystics he knew that one cannot seek God with the whole of one's being without attempting at the same time to view Him and all things in one great vision.

IV
An Authentic Individualism

Emerson's habit of seeing things in the widest context, that is, in relation to the Universe and finally to the eternal ONE, governs his conception of human individuality. Accordingly, we should think twice before applying to his view the term *individualism* in its derogatory sense. The implacable foe of fragmentation, he could never rest satisfied with any conception of individuality which would make of it a spiritually self-sufficient entity, and one devoid of all ties to the universe. Everywhere in his works we find statements of the essential Emersonian doctrine. Nothing can escape from the "magic circle of relations,"[29] for "relation and connection are not somewhere and sometimes, but everywhere and always."[30] And it is this insistence on the fact of a universal interrelation and interpenetration of things which is behind his statement that "to the young mind every thing is individual, stands by itself." He is not denying individuality; he is merely pointing to the fact that, with the growth of understanding and knowledge, we discover how separate things are yet bound together by common roots which run underground.

The Emersonian viewpoint is also clearly stated in a variety of ways. Thus he tells us that "nothing is quite beautiful alone; nothing but is beautiful in the whole. A single object is only so far beautiful as it suggests this universal grace." Again he asserts that in order to be beautiful a thing must have "a certain cosmical quality, or a power to suggest relation to the whole world, and so lift the object out of a pitiful individuality."[31] "The fable of Proteus has a cordial truth," he writes. "A leaf, a drop, a crystal, a moment of time is related to the whole, and partakes of the perfection of the whole. Each particle is a microcosm, and faithfully renders the likeness of the world."

As for man himself, he, too, must be viewed in his relatedness, for he, above all, is "a bundle of relations," whose "power consists in the multitude of his affinities, in the fact that his life is intertwined with the whole chain of organic and inorganic being."[32] "Our life," he says, "is consentaneous and far-related. This knot of nature is so well tied that nobody was ever cunning enough to find the two ends."[33]

We may expect, then, that his view of human individuality is far more intricate and subtle than is ordinarily supposed. In general, it may be said that his conception took shape within a framework of ideas fashioned out of his determination to uphold both the diversity of things and that Blessed Unity which "compels every atom to serve an universal end." Thus, while he lays stress on the originality and uniqueness of each individual person, he can yet speak of the unity of all men in a way which sounds like a full-fledged monism. No one has insisted more than Emerson on the need for individual self-culture, and no one in his day so completely exemplified a certain aloofness from society, which was dubbed "scholastic asceticism." Still, it was Emerson who said that "man is explicable by nothing less than all his history," and that "our knowledge is the amassed thought and experience of innumerable minds."[34] It was he also who declared that "so massive is our debt to tradition that in a large sense, one would say that there is no pure originality."

However, although Emerson regards the unity of mankind as real, this unity seems to have but an ideal status, inasmuch as it operates largely in and through each individual consciousness, taken in isolation, rather than through the actual expansion of communal life. Apparently, in his view the single individual, as such, develops a social consciousness, thereby bringing unity down to earth as a recognized value. It would appear, therefore, that Emerson failed to see the way in which the growing unification of mankind finds its actual embodiment in and through the evolution of concrete society as a whole. He could, indeed, envisage a gradual improvement of society, but the relation between the development of society and its structures on the one hand and expanding social consciousness on the other seems to have escaped him. Hence he can rejoice because "the world is awakening to the idea of union,"[35] and still fall back into an isolationism which is content with a merely ideal rather than an actual concrete union.

Nevertheless, by way of compensation, Emerson's doctrine not only puts a much-needed stress on social consciousness as it expands within the depth of personal life, but it also gives to the unity of mankind a transcendent status which is no abstraction, having behind it all the splendor and reality of the Platonic Idea, which, in the Emersonian framework, seems to have a creative energy. As we see, then, Emerson's conception upholds the unity of mankind as an absolute value, and he really apprehended this value in its objectivity. Emerson's sense of value was very great, and it manifests itself here as clearly as in so many other things with which he concerned himself. Nevertheless, although he upholds the unity of mankind as a value, while throwing into focus the role of the individual person in bringing that value down to earth, he still failed to grasp that side of the process of unification which has to do with social and institutional development. However, he was certainly not alone in an age which was just beginning to discover the reality of society *qua* society. Besides, the circumstances of his day were such as to make imperative his stress on the inward and personal consciousness of mankind's unity, in grounding that consciousness, not in a purely evolutionary process, regarded materialistically, but in each individual's vital relation to a spiritual and transcendent sphere.

Unity was so intensely real to Emerson that for him the real opposition lay, not between individuality and sociality, but rather between a genuine form of individuality, which maintains its anchorage in the eternal and absolute value of unity, and the spurious form, which has sundered itself from that value. Emerson's quarrel with the society of his day was, therefore, not the expression of a rank individualism. It was simply the outgrowth of his conviction that this society promoted not the true form of individuality, but mere particularism, or the spurious form. To him it seemed that society had reduced what should have been a unity, consciously experienced, to a hodgepodge of individuals, who having in the depth of their spirit suffered amputation from the trunk, "strut about so many walking monsters." Men fear to express what they are, as though they "are ashamed of that divine idea which each of us represents," and in forgetting their eternal moorings, are so reduced to a fragmentary status that they are hardly to be reckoned as individual characters. In this degenerate state, they are unable to resist the process of aggregation which rides roughshod over them, and, instead of having truly personal fates, are "reckoned in the gross" and are called the "mass" and the "herd."

In thus appearing to make the actualization of mankind's unity in time purely a matter of individual consciousness and self-culture, Emerson was not able to view history in a way which would bring it to life. For history, after all, is essentially the process of man's unfolding within the developing forms of associated life. Nevertheless, Emerson's conception was not without value, even in regard to history, since it enabled him to show that, as the fruit of a living relation of the human soul to a world beyond space and time, the very aspiration toward unity must ultimately be explained from above rather than from below.

At a time when evolutionism was in the air, and when men were beginning to regard things *sub specie temporis,* Emerson's insistence in viewing history *sub specie aeternitatis,* that is, in terms of a reality transcending the temporal order, is not to be scoffed at. In his own way, Emerson was offering resistance to an absolute immanence, especially of the materialistic type. For not only could he proclaim the sacredness of history, but he could also affirm the absolute originality of the individual person, as well as the openness of the human soul to a spiritual world beyond the world of matter. He was therefore helping substantially to form an atmosphere in which a historically minded man like Orestes Brownson could arrive at a more realistic view of society and history, without ceasing to stress the transcendent dimension and the individual's vital relation to it.

Emerson's affirmation of the vertical or spiritual as against the horizontal or temporal axis in history served a practical purpose, for it lent a certain metaphysical support to his appeal to men to rid themselves of a deadly fixation on the past which made them its slavish imitators. If history is in some real sense sacred, if its relation to the Eternal One runs right through it as a primary fact, then that relation is just as real in the living present as it was in the past. Men had to be brought to a realization that a divine force is operative here and now, and in a town meeting as well as in the great centers of culture. He would make them see that the world is "plastic and fluid in the hands of God," and that each moment breathes its own immortal breath. The world has felt God's impulse in the past and would feel it again, and men must have the courage to respond to it. Men must recognize a "transcendent destiny," in viewing themselves as "redeemers and benefactors, obeying the Almighty effort and advancing on Chaos and the Dark." Clearly, then, "it is the office of a true teacher to show that God is, not was; that He speaketh, not spake." If man fears to implant himself firmly in the present, and "with reverted eye laments the past, or heedless of the riches that surround him, stands on tiptoe to foresee the future," it is a sign he lacks faith not only in the God of history, but in the human soul itself through which God makes Himself heard.

Manifestly, Emerson was not acclaiming the value of individuality in a merely emotional or irresponsible way. For he knew that men would remain impervious to any doctrine of salvation which was directed only to the soul in general, rather than to the individual soul. In an age as socially and politically ebullient as the nineteenth century, a sense of individual human dignity and freedom was not wanting. But the modern dichotomy between religious life and life in the world showed itself once again, and the new feeling for the dignity of each individual was being severed from its spiritual roots. Emerson, of course, saw this and expounded a doctrine which aimed at a deepening of consciousness in order that the new élan toward the realization of individual dignity and freedom might be transformed into a passionately held religious conviction. His appeal, therefore, was strictly to the individual soul and not to the mass of men, and he sought to make the individual soul aware of its true proportions in relation to the universe and divinity.

We have made the point that Emerson's true purpose was to differentiate between a genuine and a spurious individuality, and not to introduce antagonism between individual self-culture and community-mindedness. The dominant theme of unity, so profusely expressed in his works, forbade any doctrine of the individual which would controvert it. We can see this still better when we realize that he was trying to show that true individuality is to be measured by one's power to live, each in his own way, the universal life. Thomas Mann expresses exactly what we think was Emerson's true doctrine: "The world hath many centres, one for each created being, and about each one it lieth in its own circle." Individuality and universality are, therefore, not opposed, since the individual is no mere fragment of the universe, being rather a focal point, or point of concentration. Emerson's view of the individual thus seems to be a reflection of a doctrine which from its presentation by Leibniz has had a notable career in European thought. For in Emerson we have the constant refrain of an individually wrought wholeness of human life, which is intrinsically bound up with the larger scheme of things.

Emerson's cosmic conception certainly suggests this doctrine of the individual as representative of the whole, as, for example, in the following assertions: "The entire system of things gets represented in every particle",[36] "The world globes itself in a drop of dew"; "The value of the universe contrives to throw itself into every point." His essential teaching is also suggested by his statement that "The true doctrine of omnipresence is that God reappears with all his parts in every moss and cobweb."

As for man, Emerson observes that "every mind is different; and the more it is unfolded, the more pronounced is that difference." But he takes care to add that the elements entering in the individual "tend always to form, not a partisan, but a possessor of truth.[37] The unfolding of individuality is hence necessarily tied in with a growth in universality; and even when we aim at a petty end, "our act arranges itself by irresistible magnetism in a line with the poles of the world."[38] Willy-nilly, the individual is enclosed in a real universe and serves its purpose, consciously or unconsciously. And when "the particular man aims to be somebody; to set up for himself; to truck and higgle for a private good" he will learn that "pleasure is taken out of pleasant things, profit out of profitable things, power out of strong things, as soon as we seek to separate them from the whole."

In showing the true role of individuality as against mere particularity, Emerson cannot emphasize enough the truth that "A man is a method, a progressive arrangement; a selecting principle."[39] For it is through one's inborn capacity and traits, one's peculiar temperament and talents that a true position in the scheme of things is established. Each individual is thus called to live the life of the whole by following the line of his own essential bias and by holding to his own vantage point. Away from this vantage point, the world becomes merely external and alien, and history itself loses its meaning. That is why Emerson can say in regard to history, "[E]very mind must know the whole lesson for itself—must go over the whole ground," and also that "the hours should be instructed by the ages and the ages explained by the hours." History too has its centers, one for each individual, and it concentrates its force, not on human nature in the abstract, but on a living being who, as an individual, occupies one of these centers.

If we examine a volume published in 1826, Sampson Reed's *Observations on the Growth of the Mind*, a book which impressed Emerson at the time, we find statements which bring out the idea of true individuality as constituting the very gateway to a larger life. Reed is endeavoring to show that the mind must grow from an internal principle, and that even from infancy it is endowed with a principle of freedom which should be respected, and with propensities peculiar to itself which will govern its power of absorbing what is peculiarly adapted to it. But what is particularly worth noting is the following: "It becomes us then to seek and cherish this *peculium* of our own minds, as the patrimony which is left us by our Father in heaven—as *that by which the branch is united to the vine* (emphasis added)—as the forming power within us, which gives to our persons that by which they are distinguished from others."

Emerson likewise regards true individuality as that by which each is rooted in a common ground of being and life. In recognizing that "[e]ach mind has its own method," he was not adopting a crass individualism. He was merely accepting a fact and tracking down the implications in terms of his spiritual-cosmic doctrine. And the primary implication, that which blazoned across his consciousness, was the individual's absolute importance as an original way of expressing the whole, as one of an infinite number of variations on the same theme. Hence, when a new mind is sent into the world, we should wait and see what this new creation is, and "of what new organ the great Spirit had need." For indeed "The charm of life is this variety of genius, these contrasts and flavors by which Heaven has modulated the identity of truth, and there is a perpetual hankering to violate this individuality."[40]

The irreplaceable uniqueness of every human person is at the very forefront of Emerson's thought, and he regards the coming of a person as a veritable irruption into the world, and through which universality is given a new and diversified expression. As a singular spiritual subject each individual is called to occupy his own position in the scheme of things, and in doing so discovers his mysterious contact with the spiritual foundation of things as well as with nature itself. Later, William James would express the same sort of thing in saying, "Knowledge about life is one thing; effective occupation of a place in life, with its dynamic currents passing through your being, is another."

Emerson wished to emphasize the validity of experience, even of the most personal sort, when one lives his life truly, that is, as an authentic individual. As he says:

> The poet, in utter solitude remembering his spontaneous thoughts and recording them, is found to have recorded that which men in crowded cities find true for them also. The orator distrusts at first the fitness of his frank confessions, his want of knowledge of the persons he addresses, until he finds that he is the complement of his hearers;—that they drink his words because he fulfills for them their own nature; the deeper he dives into his own privatest, secretest presentiment, to his wonder he finds this is the most acceptable, most public, and universally true. The people delight in it; the better part of every man feels, This is my music; this is myself.

In the light of Emerson's doctrine we can sense the intensity of his feeling when he says: "Is it not the chief disgrace in the world not to be an unit; not to be reckoned one character—not to yield that peculiar fruit which each man was created to bear." Indeed it was this penetration into the deeper meaning of individuality which made him sensitive to that inner push in each individual by which he seeks actualization, and which so often produces an extravagance of movement, even eccentricity. Thus he says, "to every creature nature added a little violence of direction in its proper path, a shove to put it on its way; in every instance a slight generosity, a drop too much." And so it happens that nature makes men "a little wrong-headed in that direction in which they are rightest."[41]

There is one thing that remains to be said regarding Emerson's doctrine of the individual. For while this doctrine has a perdurable value, it has nonetheless a certain bourgeois tinge which recommended it to those who were concerned only with mere self-affirmation and self-esteem. Emerson, we cannot forget, was a child of bourgeois culture, a thriving bourgeois culture, and his thought is quite understandably colored by it. Incontestably, bourgeois culture advanced personal values, but it also contributed to their deformation. Considering that his doctrine was given a certain shaping by the age in which he lived, it is not surprising to find lines in his works which conjure up the bourgeois image rather than the deeper reality he was vitally concerned with. Besides, the wider significance attributed to the individual in his authentic doctrine had to be disentangled from his own natural egoism, of which he had his fair share. We would expect, therefore, inevitable confusions, which only a lifetime of personal growth could eliminate, at least in part.

V
Symbolic Vision

We have yet to consider that which lies at the heart of the Emersonian approach, namely, the desire to reconstitute and validate the symbolic consciousness, since it is in and through this consciousness that man experiences the power of material things to convey something beyond themselves. As a being who lies open to God, man is able to sense the supersensual value of things. For nature, as a descending manifestation of spirit, as the very apparition of God, is primarily a living symbol of that which lies above it.

As a symbol of spirit, the most prosaic fact or dull, heavy, despised thing can become, to the aroused intellect, a gift of precious gems, "an Epiphany of God."[42] Hence it can be said that "We learn nothing rightly until we learn the symbolical character of life." Knowing this, "the highest minds of the world have never ceased to explore the double meaning, or shall I say the quadruple or the centuple or much more manifold meaning, of every sensuous fact. . . . For we are not pans and barrows, nor even porters of the fire and torchbearers, but children of the fire."[43] As "children of the fire," it is natural, therefore, for men to revere nature, the symbol, even "with coarse but sincere rites," and for the poet to resign himself "to the divine *aura* which breathes through forms."

Since nature is a symbol, it can be used as a symbol. And it is here that language performs its highest and truest function. Words, of course, "cannot cover the dimensions of what is in truth," yet symbolic language can suggest in a forceful way what is finally inexpressible. And Emerson himself amply demonstrated in his discourses this power of the living word to convey the truth of what was ultimately beyond the grasp of the mind—an elusive yet shining realm of knowledge. For, as Santayana rightly says, in referring to those who venerated Emerson: "More than the truth his teachings might express, they valued the sense it gave them of a truth that was inexpressible."

If nature is indeed the symbol of spirit, "in the whole, and in every part," then the highest function of language is to convey the larger meaning of things. For through the living metaphor, natural objects, as the emblem of spirit, bring forth answering echoes in the psyche, hinting at realities which escape the grasp of mere concepts and generalizations taken by themselves. It is this fact which leads Emerson to declare as follows: "The use of symbols has a certain power of emancipation and exhilaration for all men. . . . We are like persons who come out of a cave or cellar into the open air. This is the effect on us of tropes, fables, oracles and all poetic forms." It follows, therefore, that a language which has gone stale, having lost its quality of living metaphor, its symbolic depth, is one which has become, in fact, a barrier to experience and to the normal ascent of the mind from the world of things to the realities of spirit. Having declined into abstractions which are no more than ostensive signs and practical instruments, such a language is no longer one with the living fact, and is thereby rendered incapable of performing its highest function. And when language loses its evocative power, its power to stir up energies and mysterious sympathies and to suggest truths far beyond what is given in the visible world, "wise men pierce this rotten diction and fasten words again to visible things."

In its growth, language exhibits the nonarbitrary character of all natural development. As Emerson says, "each word is like a work of Nature, determined a thousand years ago, and not alterable. We confer and dispute, and settle the meaning so or so, but it remains what it was in spite of us. The word beats all the speakers and definers of it, and stands to their children what it stood to their father."[44] "Language," he says again, "is a city to the building of which every human being brought a stone; yet he is no more to be credited with the grand result than the acaleph which adds a cell to the coral reef which is the basis of the continent."[45]

In line with his view of a certain inevitability in the growth of language, Emerson believed that the symbol, despite its poetic origin, is something found rather than made. Thus he asserts that "this expression or naming is not art, but a second nature, grown out of the first, as a leaf out of a tree."[46] But, nevertheless, he still insists on the transitory character of the symbol, "for all symbols are fluxional; all language is vehicular and transitory." While reaching depths of the psyche inaccessible to mere abstract statement, a true symbol is yet never more than a temporary vehicle, and having performed its function, it leaves the spirit independent of the visible object which originally awakened inner perception.

The contact with things of nature is indispensable, inasmuch as man's spirit is interwoven in the fabric of nature, and the roots of thinking reach farther into the natural world than is commonly supposed. But in leaping beyond the boundaries of time and space, the human spirit always manifests its privileged position with respect to the outer world. Hence symbolic experience is a flowing thing which stimulates the ascending life of intuitive thought, an experience which implies an organic union of spirit and nature, but of a type which permits thought to leave the things of material nature far behind.

We should overlook neither the Stoic aspect of Emerson's outlook nor the Platonic. It is the Stoic aspect which is in evidence when he plays up the organic relation which binds the human spirit to the universal scheme. But it is the Platonic aspect which shows itself in his view that man is the closest point of contact with a transcendent order which surrounds and envelopes nature. By virtue of his spiritual nature man is receptive to the influence of Absolute Spirit, or, if we wish, the Logos, which is also the archetypal principle behind nature. Man possesses, therefore, an intuitive power, which, while prompted by nature and the knowledge of nature gathered by the sciences, is endowed, nonetheless, with a certain intrinsic independence. Thought's function is not merely to provide us with transcripts of the outer world, for it occupies an original position in the universe by virtue of its power to rise infinitely beyond the world of visible things. Enjoying as it does a vital contact with the Infinite, thought has an implicit content which is inexhaustible; hence the widening scope of consciousness, as thought soars upwards in an ascending spiral, always seeking an exodus from every closed circle which would stifle the impulse to infinitude.

How well Emerson's very presentation of an idea conformed to his conception of thought as an expanding life is attested in the following characterization by Francis Thompson: "In some of these essays he is like a great eagle, sailing in noble and ample gyres, with deliberate beat of the strong wing, round the eyrie where his thought is nested." Emerson, he tells us further,

> has his own mode of progression. The gyres are widening gyres, each sweep of the unflagging wing is in an ampler circuit. Each return of the idea reveals it in a deeper and fuller aspect; with each mental cycle we look down upon the first conception in an expanded prospect. It is the progression of a circle in stricken water. . . . And thus the thought of this lofty and solitary mind is cyclic, not like a wheel, but like the thought of mankind at large; where ideas are always returning on themselves, yet their round is steadily "widened with the process of the suns."[47]

But, as we have said, Emerson regards symbolic sight as essential to the very process by which an organic expansion of meaning takes place. That is, in his view the intuitive operation of the mind is sustained and nurtured by poetic imagery, and through such imagery the implicit, latent, and mysterious content of thought becomes a luminous presence. Consequently, thinking at its very deepest is one with the symbolizing process. Nevertheless, for Emerson, the human psyche, in all its profound interiority, plays a highly autonomous role in relation to the outer world.

The poetic image is therefore all-important in that interiorizing process by which the whole of nature is taken into thought. Stimulated by such a viewpoint, Emerson spared no effort to find the appropriate image which would bring the inner world of the spirit to life. And how well he succeeded can be gathered from the following lines by the aforementioned poet:

> No prose-writer of his time had such resources of imagery essentially poetic in nature as Emerson—not even Ruskin. His prose is more fecund in imagery, and happier in imagery, than his poetry—one of the proofs (we think) that he was not primarily a poet, undeniable though some of his poetry is. With such figurative range, such easy and inexhaustible plasticity of expression, so nimble a perception, this iterative style was all but inevitable.

That opulent mouth could not pause at a single utterance. His understanding played about a thought like lightning about a vane. It suggested numberless analogies, an endless sequence of associated ideas, countless aspects, shifting facets of expression; and it were much as if he should not set down a poor three or four of them. We, hard-pushed for our one pauper phrase, may call it excess in him: to Emerson, doubtless, it was austerity.[48]

It is interesting to note that Emerson was enthralled, not only by Plato's power to achieve "transcendental distinctions," but also by his method of appealing to ordinary things in building up his thought, for "he fortified himself by drawing all his illustrations from sources disdained by orators and polite conversers; from mares and puppies; from pitchers and soup-ladles; from cooks and criers; the shops of potters, horse-doctors, butchers and fishmongers."[49]

Clearly, in Emerson's view the perceptual experience which underlies the élan of thought and its sense of vanishing limits has esthetic sensibility as an indispensable dimension. "The images," he writes, "the sweet immortal images, are within us—born there, our native right, and sometimes one kind of sounding word or syllable awakens the instrument of our souls and sometimes another."[50] And if the power is in the image, that is because the power is in nature itself, which, as symbol of spirit, is congenial to our faculties. "Our music, our poetry, our language itself are not satisfactions, but suggestions," which yet have the power to pierce the wall of insensibility which screens us from a whole realm of meaning which mere abstract generalization is powerless to reach. Referring to the kind of metaphor or analogy which relates "inner" experience to "outer" experience, he writes, "[T]here is nothing lucky or capricious in these analogies, but they are constant and pervade nature. These are not the dreams of a few poets, here and there, but man is an analogist, and studies relations in all objects. He is placed in the center of beings, and a ray of relation passes from every other being to him."

Obviously then, an organic language is indispensable to the normal functioning of spirit and mind, and is the necessary vehicle in that whole process by which man takes the universe into himself. Originally each word was a stroke of genius in providing the imaginative medium in and through which thought itself could expand toward infinity, like inspired eloquence which compels the listener to enter immediately into truth. It was the work of an intellect which took its direction from its celestial life, while abandoning itself to the nature of things and allowing itself to be caught up into the life of the Universe. Today as yesterday, the restoration of language to its organic character depends on men who understand that besides the privacy of the power of the individual man "there is a great public power on which he can draw, by unlocking, at all risks, his human doors, and suffering the ethereal tides to roll and circulate through him."[51]

Considering the role of Platonism in Emerson's attempt to rehabilitate symbolical consciousness, we can see why there is in him a tendency to make the relation of symbol to its visible object transitory and even somewhat tenuous. As it has been said, Emerson flees from "the material aspect of the symbol to the idea represented and from that idea to others,"[52] thereby achieving a type of symbolism which is "ideal rather than structural." However, as this author points out, there is compensation in the Emersonian attitude, for "the symbol represents the result of that creative process by which the poet participates in the flowing action of nature; if it is well wrought, it will produce the same immediate effect of spiritual elation which objects of nature inspire. It is thus the point of contact between men and the material world." Yet to do Emerson strict justice, it was not so much a matter of flight from matter as an attempt to give full scope to man's openness to a transcendent world of spirit, while rooting him at the same time in the world of nature. Emerson wished to show that inner perception or symbolic sight has an organic and nonarbitrary character which results not only from man's participation in "the flowing action of nature," but from his reception of an in-streaming light from a higher world. The whole creative process of the poet, who comes closer to things than others, is, therefore, one in which an intuitive element is fused with a sensuous element. That is why, in Emerson's view, it is "not metres, but a metre-making argument that makes a poem—a thought so passionate and alive that like the spirit of a planet or an animal it has an architecture of its own, and adorns nature with a new thing."

In a theory like Emerson's which tries to fuse into one single experience suprasensuous and sensuous elements, there is apt to be a certain undue weighting on the side of the "ideal," as against empirical fact. In history a balance between the inner world of the spirit and the outer world of the senses has been seldom achieved, and the historical moment with its need to accentuate one position as against another has resulted in a kind of zigzagging through which man has gradually perceived the possibilities of each. We might also add here that if men have felt impelled to envisage a balance, it is because they were steeped in Christianity, gaining from it the strength to cleave to the given facts and even to penetrate more deeply into them, while yet soaring upward to a realm of infinite truth.

Emerson combed the literature of East and West in his quest for symbols which had been fashioned by the genius of a people, and to which we must return if we would recapture an experience once vividly possessed. These symbols are indeed indispensable; but so, too, are the symbols which have sprung to life in our own age, and of which we must make full use. For, like every age, ours has made its contribution to human experience, and also to the imaginative process without which experience cannot be intellectually and spiritually assimilated. And what is true of our age in general is most certainly true of the New World itself. Therefore, it behooved Emerson to remind his generation that it still awaited its poet, and that it lacked the genius to recognize the values of its incomparable materials. As he says, "Our log-rolling, our stumps and their politics, our fisheries, our Negroes and Indians, our boasts and our repudiations, the wrath of rogues and the pusillanimity of honest men, the northern trade, the southern planting, the western clearing, Oregon and Texas, are yet unsung. Yet America is a poem in our eyes: its ample geography dazzles the imagination, and it will not wait long for metres."

VI
A Puritan, a Romantic, and an American

Once we gain the proper standpoint in interpreting Emerson, we can see why the sweeping generalizations that have been mustered against him are rather unsatisfactory. Most certainly the attempt to dispose of him by classifying him as a devotee of the so-called romantic religion of self-deification is futile. Even if we do find in him a strain of romanticism, this does not constitute by itself an indictment, for the interpretation of romanticism is very much an open question, and will surely be recognized as such when we gain a better perspective of history and its underlying exigencies. Like all great movements in history, romanticism represents a crucial moment in the very unfolding of human life, and it was inevitable that there would be a tension between the new and the old and a confusion of aims, resulting from the failure to grasp the true implications of what was being freshly perceived. Therefore, we must avoid the simplistic interpretation which would discern in romanticism nothing but a religion of self-deification.

Moreover, we should shun the temptation to conjure up easy generalizations concerning modern history, as, for example, the view that the leading motif from the Renaissance on is this deifying self-assertiveness, which, it has been argued, was also the great motivating force behind romanticism.

This oversimplified approach is untenable, for it confuses the issue by identifying the unfolding of personal life in history with a "titanic assertion" of human self-sufficiency. Surely it is somewhat inaccurate to lump together the very emergence of human personality in a historical process with the deviations and excesses to which it has invariably given rise.

In his many works Don Luigi Sturzo, the eminent sociologist and historian, has effectively demolished any view of things which takes no account of a real historical process, which, as he has abundantly shown, is bound up with the very unfolding of human personality. In his *Church and State* he writes, discussing Dante, "The personality of man and Christian as sung by Dante has continued its unceasing evolution up to our time, and will develop still further." Regarding romanticism itself, he asserts that despite the literary and artistic excesses of romanticism, "the underlying exigencies of the Romantic movement were sound: a return to historical, traditional, ethnical, religious and popular values. . . . Such a balance between past and present could be achieved only through a violent eruption, which in its impetus would overthrow established and crystallised positions."

Another author has come forward in defense of romantic and post-romantic literature. According to him, vitalities came to expression in this literature which, despite the fact that they "may not be couched in recognizable Christian forms, are not *ipso facto* to be defined as un-Christian or idolatrous."[53] Indeed he believes them to be defensible expressions of something inherent in Christian faith. And expressly mentioning both Emerson and Wordsworth, he insists that "a powerful latent Christian tradition is to be found in their work."

History is far too complex an affair to permit of our disposing of a man's lifework with a few pigeonhole generalities. Emerson is a case in point, for in him great historical forces came to expression, forces which, as we have intimated, have a core of rightness, even if he himself was not able to express them with an ideal perfection. And this essential core of rightness is all the more important because it has to do with a certain primordial pattern of human experience rather than with abstract theories as such.

There is no doubt that Emerson absorbed much from romanticism, for he found in it elements that were congenial to his own point of view, not the least of which was an expression of the newly emerging esthetic sensibility to whose further liberation he had dedicated himself. But if the romantic strain was strong in him, so was the Puritan, which, moreover, served as a powerful disciplining factor. Nor should we forget that he was also an American, wonderfully sensitive to the possibilities that lay concealed in the New World, and aware also of the fecundating effects of America upon the imagination itself.

Let us dwell briefly on Emerson's relation to his own Puritan lineage. The aforementioned writer who finds in Emerson "a latent Christian tradition" declares that Stuart Sherman "rightly identifies the Puritan lineage in Emerson, however obscured." And Sherman's "chief theme," he tells us, "is that Emerson transmits in new and revitalized form 'the vital forces of the great moral traditions, while at the same time he emancipates them from the dead hand of the past.'" But, curiously enough, in listing the elements in Emerson which reflect this lineage, this author makes no mention of that which surely lies at the heart of Puritanism, at least in its primary expression, namely, a transcendent and religious direction of life.

It is important to stress the fact that Emerson was protesting against any view of reality which ignores its spiritual dimension. In other words, any humanistic doctrine of the flat, horizontal type would be unpalatable to him. In fact it was just this religious orientation of his thought which accounts for his nostalgia when he looked back at his Puritan ancestors. "There was in the last century," he says, "a serious habitual reference to the spiritual world, running through diaries, letters and conversation . . . compared with which our liberation looks a little foppish and dapper."[54] And in his journal he writes, "I thought yesterday morning of the sweetness of that fragrant piety which is almost departed out of the world." Musing over this lost piety, his nostalgia must have become especially sharp when he recalled, "An old lady who remembered these pious people said of them that 'they had to hold on hard to the huckleberry bushes to hinder themselves from being translated.'"[55]

Emerson's preoccupation with the spiritual problem boiled down to the essential question, how "to replace for us the piety of that race [the Puritans]?" For, although Puritan piety had its attractive side, it yet sprang from a theological outlook against which he was revolting. Emerson's beloved and redoubtable Aunt Mary may have hit home in her jibe that he knew only a few bugbear words of Calvinism, but, for all that, he was too immersed in that tradition not to have grasped something of its essential character and spirit.

Even if there was a lingering trace of the "Puritan mystic" in him, he knew that Calvinism went counter to his own understanding of things, especially his conception of man and the world of nature and of the relation between them. As regards human nature, Calvinism narrowed its power and scope in a way that was entirely repugnant to him. For, in Emerson's view, human nature is the very bedrock of religious life in its intrinsic competence to reach a knowledge of moral and spiritual truths, and in its receptivity to a continuous influx of light. Thus his affirmation: "We lie open on one side to the deeps of spiritual nature, to the attributes of God. Justice we see and know, Love, Freedom, Power."

The alien character of Calvinism in relation to the Emersonian doctrine is easily seen when we consider that its great emphasis on the absolute and creative Will of God, made at the expense of the Divine Intelligence, was not likely to bring to the forefront the notion of nature as reflecting its Maker in its very meaningfulness as well as in its organic unity. Nor could the Calvinist view of the universe effectively resist the mechanistic philosophy which reduced poetry to the status of an ornament, with no claim to any validity in terms of an organic experience. Yet, as we know, the early Puritans made use of a vital symbolism, but they were still burdened by a certain opposition between their basic theological outlook and the human exigency to symbolize. Hence as Kenneth B. Murdock has said, the more a religious writer adhered to this Protestant tradition, "the farther he left behind him the Catholic theory that it was permissible to make frank use of sensuous material and to appeal to the senses in worship and religious art. Also the more difficult his task as an artist."

True enough, Calvinism had an appreciable effect on man's creative activity, but that activity was shorn of much of its human value. Man is plunged into a creative activity which, in making manifest a conformity to the Divine Will, likewise makes manifest the elect of God. But even when surrounded by a mystical aura, such activity was of an external conquering character, entirely alien to the kind of relationship envisioned in Emerson's conception. Thus, human nature, "girt in the poison robes of depravity," to recall a phrase familiar to transcendentalists, confronts a universe whose significance as a manifestation of divinity has been effectively nullified— a universe which would hardly answer to Emerson's claims on behalf of symbolic consciousness.

The Calvinist doctrine may have proved useful up to a point, in putting iron into the blood of men engaged in the grim work of subduing the wilderness. For a fatalistic spirit held them to their task. Indeed, Emerson perceived a certain grandeur in their granitelike attitude, especially when contrasted with the state of affairs in his own day. "Our America," he says, "has a bad name for superficialness. Great men, great nations, have not been boasters and buffoons, but perceivers of the terror of life, and have manned themselves to face it."[56] And if all great nations and great literatures had this sense of "something which cannot be talked or voted away," the Calvinists must be given their due, for, he avers, "Our Calvinists in the last generation had something of the same dignity. They felt that the weight of the Universe held them down to their place. What could *they* do?"

But whatever might be said in defense of Calvinist doctrine as it affected human activity, it is a fact, nonetheless, that it introduced grave distortions of elemental truths. And when in the natural course of events human experience once again expanded spontaneously to the full circle of normalcy, the Calvinist doctrine clearly betrayed its inadequacy. Certainly this inadequacy was made manifest in man's creative enterprise itself. For man cannot pursue his creative task without taking the universe into himself, as something meaningful and lovable. Everything in the outer world must be, so to speak, interiorized by him, even the very landscape, for as Emerson said, nothing should be left unrepresented, and "yonder mountain must migrate into his mind."[57] In a hundred ways, through the arts and by means of knowledge, what was merely external thus becomes a potent force in the very depth of man's being.

In America, the need to build up a meaningful relation to the environment assumed mammoth proportions, thereby accentuating the "divided consciousness" already so manifest among the Puritans. For in America a new tension developed between a spiritual orientation and life in time and space, since, along with their religious orientation, men were inevitably taken up with a world whose raw incompleteness was an irresistible challenge to human achievement. But instead of making this tension fruitful, Calvinism turned it into a bitter inner conflict, so that men alternated between a religious longing surcharged with mystical feeling and a materialistic urge to dominate and possess. The split between religion and life in the world seemed complete, and it was to overcome this very split that Emerson offered his conception, designed primarily to illumine human experience itself and its unitary pattern.

We must credit Emerson with exceptional acumen in perceiving that the essential solution lay in the direction of a thoroughgoing transformation of outlook, so that men might once again possess an ancient wisdom regarding the organic unity of things, while grasping the full scope of their relation to the universe. As we have said, Emerson was functioning on the experiential level, aiming at a restoration of experience in its organic unity, so that the inseparability of sensuous and suprasensuous elements might be made manifest. In fact, as we have suggested, he was trying to restore an older way of viewing things which we would broadly identify with a tradition at once classical and Catholic. While he fell short of an adequate comprehension of that tradition, still, he was aiming at something close to it, and this despite the fact that he permitted his rejection of Puritan Christianity to cloud his mind in regard to Catholic Christianity itself. But even here the entire story remains to be told, since there are indications in his *Journals* that he was by no means insensitive to the majesty and sublimity of Catholic Christianity.

If only he had had a better acquaintance with the classical-Christian tradition, he would have been entranced by its marvelous fusion of elements so dear to him: a sense of an all-embracing Universe which infinitely surpasses the physical universe of modern science (hence the medieval notion of *Natura* as an all-containing reality); a profound attachment to material nature regarded as, in some real sense, sacramental, and as manifesting, therefore, in its every atom, the divine presence; and, following from this, a high regard for the value of symbolic consciousness, which, despite the Catholic passion for logic, always held its own; an awareness of the structural unity of experience, embracing sensuous, intellectual, and mystical elements; an unshakable conviction of man's power to transcend in the very act of knowing a "vicious dualism" of subject and object; and an equally unshakable conviction of man's natural aptitude for transcendent truth; and last, a superb mastery of the classical sense of limit and measure along with an exalted awareness of Infinity and the immeasurable.

VII
Americans and an Ancient Tradition

The vital comprehensiveness of the Emersonian standpoint cannot be missed if we but study it seriously, and with historical understanding. And what will emerge from such a study, as of special importance, is the fact that Emerson belongs in a wider tradition than that of the American humanists. As it has been said:

> Emerson could not remain the exclusive property of the American humanists. He has done much to enrich their tradition, but the "leaping lightning" of his spirit sprang from their grasp when they sought to confine him within the sharply-defined boundaries of their critical world. The bad effect of neohumanist criticism upon readers of Emerson has been to close their eyes to the existence of that element of mysticism in Emersonian thought, which, embarrassing though it may be, is the highest rationale Emerson has offered of art's value in the world of man. In the event of a new upsurge of faith, this element in Emerson's aesthetic may again take on the fresh colors which it wore for nineteenth-century seekers.[58]

We have already pointed to the ancient tradition against which we must project Emerson's thought if we are to bring all its meaning and value to the surface. However, the importance of his thought is still further augmented by the fact that he was no isolated figure in American life, for he belongs in the company of those Americans who have sought for an integral conception of things which would be adequate to a full human experience. Without dwelling on Brownson (whose debt to Emerson and transcendentalism in general is far greater than is usually realized), there was, significantly, at the beginning of our philosophical development, Jonathan Edwards, and in recent times, Charles S. Peirce, the most brilliant figure in our own golden age of philosophy. Both thinkers stood for an all-inclusive viewpoint which would not only take account of a transcendent realm of spirit and idea, but would also give an absolute significance to man's life in time and space. Edwards, it is true, grounded himself in the theology of Calvin, but, nevertheless, he broke through its confines in his doctrine of a God, who, in joy, has created a world which is indescribably lovely and utterly lovable. And in his view of the visible world as a disclosure of that which lies above and beyond it, he was upholding the very doctrine which was to find such ample expression in Emerson. Here certainly was a thinker who was rediscovering for himself elements of an ancient tradition, and so effectively that he has been favorably compared with great medieval Catholic figures. And as for Peirce, considering his many-sided doctrine, nothing could seem more natural than that he should acknowledge, as he does, his close ties with medieval Catholic thought.

In the light of all that we have presented, there can be no doubt that Emerson is indeed representative of a very significant trend in American life, a trend which will be more thoroughly explored once it is perceived. No one has more consistently stressed human dignity and human possibilities within the framework of a real world than Emerson, and yet he was profoundly concerned with the need to emphasize the primacy of man's spiritual orientation. Like those others we have mentioned, he saw that a spiritual direction of life does not uproot man from his own temporal world but rather fastens him to it more integrally and more securely and in a way which furthers his innate dignity as a rational and spiritual being. This spiritual emphasis is brought out by Robert Caponigri who tells us that for Emerson "morality in human life looks not from man to man, but directly from the individual to the absolute spiritual forces whose theatre he is." And another contemporary scholar has this to say: "However much Emerson may have altered the idea of self-reliance to fit the drama of his life, the self and its experience of dependence on a higher source of spiritual power became the ground of his vision."[59] And he also states that Emerson's "daily problem was to maintain a living connection between the horizontal-worldly and the vertical-otherworldly, to live on as many of the platforms of experience that intervened as he could."[59]

Emerson, therefore, was no alien figure when he spoke out to the American people, for he was a living reminder of truths which American experience itself rendered inescapable. We can even say that his whole effort to achieve a meaningful relation between the world of matter and the world of spirit was profoundly American, for, certainly, Americans would never be brought to an effective awareness of things spiritual through mere disparagement of things material.

It is usually supposed that Emerson was appealing to a people whose souls had become subject to the dollar, and who were bartering away their human birthright for petty gain. This is an oversimplification, for Emerson was keenly aware of the positive forces that were stirring the souls of men, and it was to these that he appealed in helping men overcome that in them which was ignoble and degrading. He estimated correctly the power of acquisitiveness in a world of such boundless physical resources as America, but he also knew that men would never gain the strength to withstand the maelstrom of acquisitiveness unless their living contact with so promising an environment were radically transformed. Above all, he saw that materialism must be fought not simply by affirming the higher universe of the spirit but by helping men rid themselves of the "divided consciousness" and therefore of the "split universe" which was ravaging American life and rendering a great people spiritually impotent.

Emerson had a universal appeal in his day, because he had something valuable to offer. Communities everywhere, even the more simple communities of the West, were impressed by his message and felt the "high voltage" in his discourses. If he did not always succeed in fusing idea and symbol in his poetry, he demonstrated his power with the symbol in his spoken essays, and often with dazzling effect.

He was a born phrasemaker, and what he had to say hit home. This man whose visage had something of the American Indian about it, and who, like the Indian, was keenly alert to his surroundings, even when he seemed most Olympian in his air of detachment, spoke a language which stirred men deeply. And he spoke with a directness and simplicity which went straight to the heart of his listeners. In this respect we can hardly do better than cite these words of the French critic Charles Du Bos: "The natural elevation, the directness, the sanity of Emerson: in him always the terseness of the spoken word, of a word spoken by a man who has never had to achieve simplicity, in whom it is as inborn as the sound of his voice: those are the qualities that, when I was a youth of seventeen and knew nothing of America, led me to think of Emerson as the greatest American, and, leaving all question of genius aside, those are the qualities that today make America lovable to me."

Emerson, as we have said, never spoke to men in the mass, but always directly to each individual soul to whose primordial experience he could make his appeal, and with a simple dignity which excluded the slightest suggestion of condescension. Moreover, he never remained long on the heights, for he was soon back on familiar ground, conversing in terms of everyday experience, and demonstrating anew the sincerity of his words: "I embrace the common, I explore and sit at the feet of the familiar, the low."

He did not merely call on men to throw off the shackles of conformity, and resist circumstances. He did not merely hurl denunciations, although he knew how to make people wince when he bemoaned the fact that man had become "the treadle of a wheel," "a tassel at the apron-string of society," "a money-chest."[60] Nor was he content to declare that man "skulks and sneaks through the world," that he has "foreclosed his freedom, tied his hands, locked himself up and given the key to another to keep."[61] True to the transcendentalist creed of always affirming the positive, he sought to communicate the need for a total reorientation of the mind and spirit by opening men's eyes to the reality, not merely of ideas, but of their perceptual experience of truth. And in calling attention to such experience of the immediately given, he insisted that it was not a matter of mere choice, for such perception "is not whimsical, but fatal." Furthermore, he challenged the crude notion that spiritual truths can be evaluated by those who ignore the spiritual data themselves, as when he says, "the definition of *spiritual* should be, *that which is its own evidence.*"

He succeeded in bringing sublime truths into an immediate and even matter-of-fact relation to everyday concerns, and indeed so effectively that he broke the spell of one's routine, whether of the mechanic, the cooper, the miller, or the lawyer, relating one's being and even one's very craft and skill to the universal scheme, so that each one felt that his life was truly intertwined in it. To men keenly aware of new-found rights, he spoke of the basic right which must be cherished above all else, the right "to traverse the star-lit deserts of truth."[62] He made the dedication to truth something as elemental and attractive as the right to appropriate space in the wilderness, and as exciting. He asked his audiences why they should renounce their right to seek truth "for the premature comforts of an acre, house and barn." And in unforgettable phrases he dwelt on the primacy and necessity of speculative thought, while taking care never to violate the American instinct for action and practicality. Indeed he elevated action to a higher dignity by insisting that without it "thought can never ripen into truth," inasmuch as action in its higher meaning has to do with the way in which a man conducts his life. Action was thus all-important, because, as he also affirmed, man's very "health and erectness consist in the fidelity with which he transmits influences from the vast and universal to the point on which his genius can act."[63] "Of what use is genius," he asked, "if the organ is too convex or too concave and cannot find a focal distance within the actual horizon of human life?"

He touched off something in the souls of men, not by drawing a veil over the things they knew so well and loved, or by underrating perceptual experience, but rather by revealing the poignant beauty of the near at hand, which speaks of a still higher beauty apprehended only by the inner eye of the mind. And as he discoursed, the ordinary objects one met along the way became alive with mysterious meanings, and one suddenly realized that his hundred acres of plowed land were located not simply in America, or on the terrestrial globe, or even in the physical universe, but within the widest reaches of infinity itself. But when he spoke of religion as the very basis of an all-inclusive and organic consciousness, men found themselves restored to a primal experience in which religion is seen to have the same organic and functional position in the universal scheme as nature's processes, and, indeed, as all true art, whether of St. Peter's at Rome or of an American clipper ship.

Henry James, the younger, in his essay on Emerson is endeavoring to explain Emerson's power. He recalls that Matthew Arnold had contested Emerson's complete right to the title of man of letters. "Yet," says James, "letters surely were the very texture of his history." But James himself feels constrained to acknowledge a germ of truth in Arnold's view, for, as he says, Emerson "is a striking exception to the general rule that writings live in the last resort by their form; that they owe a large part of their fortune to the art with which they have been composed." In fact he declares that "it is hardly too much, or too little, to say of Emerson's writings in general that they were not composed at all." Indeed Emerson, in James's view, "differs from most men of letters of the same degree of credit in failing to strike us as having achieved a style."

But of Emerson's "importance and continuance," he seemingly has no doubt, believing that in this he "shall probably not be gainsaid by those who read him." As for those who do not, they "will hardly rub him out."[64] And he then comes to the nub of the matter, for, according to him, Emerson "did something better than any one else; he had a particular faculty, which has not been surpassed, for speaking to the soul in a voice of direction and authority. . . . It penetrates further, it seems to go back to the roots of our feelings, to where conduct and manhood begin; and moreover, to us to-day, there is something in it that says that it is connected somehow with the virtue of the world, has wrought and achieved, lived in thousands of minds, produced a mass of character and life."

In the light of all that has been said, these words of Henry James are surely loaded with meaning. And the more we ponder them the more we must acknowledge that whatever we may think of Emerson's style, we must yet concede that he had the literary power to communicate something of prime importance—what we have called the "single vision"—and by means of a symbolical consciousness which he possessed to a superlative degree. Valiantly and unremittingly he dwelt on the absolute importance of this vision, while showing how man's "continual self-recovery" is bound up with the deepening to infinity of his self-knowledge, since he is in truth a being who holds within himself the "poles of the Universe."

Notes

Robert Pollock wrote with a profusion of notes; the editors have removed such as did not seem vital for purposes of scholarship or understanding and edited others for consistency of style.

1. Stephen E. Whicher, *Freedom and Fate* (Philadelphia: University of Pennsylvania Press, 1953), 173.

2. Vivian C. Hopkins, *Spires of Form* (Cambridge, MA: Harvard University Press, 1951), 225.

3. Charles Feidelson, *Symbolism and American Literature* (Chicago: University of Chicago Press, 1953), 123.

4. Ibid., 158.

5. Ralph Waldo Emerson, "Natural History of Intellect," in *The Complete Works of Ralph Waldo Emerson*, ed. Edward Waldo Emerson, vol. 12 (Boston: Houghton Mifflin, 1903–04), 11.

6. Emerson, like so many authors of his day, tended to prefer the language of "man" and "men" to that of "woman" and "women." Robert Pollock seems to have developed the same preference. For both writers this was largely a matter of convention rather than of blindness or insensitivity, so that where they have written "man" or "men" we should understand "men and women," "human beings," or "humanity."

7. Ralph Waldo Emerson, "Fate," in *The Complete Works*, 6:22.

8. Ralph Waldo Emerson, "The Poet," in *The Complete Works*, 3:5.

9. Ralph Waldo Emerson, *The Journals of Ralph Waldo Emerson*, ed. Edward Waldo Emerson and Waldo Emerson Forbes, vol. 2 (Boston: Houghton Mifflin, 1909–14), 223.

10. Feidelson, *Symbolism*, 124.

11. Ralph Waldo Emerson, "The Method of Nature," in *The Complete Works*, 1:199.

12. Ralph Waldo Emerson, "Nature," in *The Complete Works*, 3:171.

13. Ralph Waldo Emerson, "Literature," in *The Complete Works*, 5:254.

14. Ralph Waldo Emerson, "Literary Ethics," in *The Complete Works*, 1:185.

15. Emerson, "Nature," 1:73.

16. Emerson, "The Method of Nature," 1:216.

17. Ralph L. Rusk, *The Life of Ralph Waldo Emerson* (New York: Scribner's Sons, 1949), 368.

18. Ralph Waldo Emerson, "Plato: New Readings," in *The Complete Works*, 4:81.

19. Ibid., 82.

20. Ralph Waldo Emerson, "Plato; Or, The Philosopher," in *The Complete Works*, 1:49.

21. Ralph Waldo Emerson, "Worship," in *The Complete Works*, 6:219.

22. Feidelson, *Symbolism*, 126.

23. Ibid., 127.

24. Ibid., 124.

25. Ibid., 123.

26. Ralph Waldo Emerson, "Education," in *The Complete Works*, 10:17.

27. Emerson, *Journals*, 4:248.

28. Ibid., 249.

29. Emerson, "Education," 10:128.

30. Emerson, "Fate," 6:31.

31. Ralph Waldo Emerson, "Beauty," in *The Complete Works*, 6:303.

32. Ralph Waldo Emerson, "History," in *The Complete Works*, 2:36.

33. Emerson, "Fate," 6:36.

34. Ralph Waldo Emerson, "Quotation and Originality," in *The Complete Works*, 8:200.

35. Ralph Waldo Emerson, "New England Reformers," in *The Complete Works*, 3:266–67.

36. Ralph Waldo Emerson, "Compensation," in *The Complete Works*, 2:97.

37. Emerson, "Quotation and Originality," 8:201.

38. Emerson, "Compensation," 2:110.

39. Ralph Waldo Emerson, "Spiritual Laws," in *The Complete Works*, 2:144.

40. Emerson, "Education," 10:137.

41. Emerson, "Nature," 3:185.

42. Emerson, "Education," 10:132.

43. Emerson, "The Poet," 3:4.

44. Emerson, *Journals*, 8:100.

45. Emerson, "Quotation and Originality," 8:199.

46. Emerson, "The Poet," 3:22.

47. Francis Thompson, *The Works of Francis Thompson*, vol. 3 (London: Burns and Oates, 1913), 235.

48. Ibid., 234.

49. Emerson, "Plato, Or, The Philosopher," 4:55.

50. Emerson, *Journals*, 1:334.

51. Emerson, "The Poet," 3:26.

52. Hopkins, *Spires of Form*, 133.

53. Amos N. Wilder, *Modern Poetry and the Christian Tradition* (New York: Scribner's Sons, 1952), 41.

54. Ralph Waldo Emerson, "The Sovereignty of Ethics," in *The Complete Works*, 10:203–04.

55. Ralph Waldo Emerson, "Boston," in *The Complete Works*, 12:193.

56. Emerson, "Fate," 6:5.

57. Emerson, "Education," 10:131.

58. Hopkins, *Spires of Form*, 228.

59. Sherman Paul, *Emerson's Angle of Vision* (Cambridge, MA: Harvard University Press, 1952), 9.

60. Emerson, *Journals*, 4:242.

61. Emerson, "Education," 3:53.

62. Emerson, "Literary Ethics," 1:186.

63. Emerson, "The Method of Nature," 1:208–09.

64. Henry James, "Emerson," in *The Art of Fiction* (New York: Oxford University Press, 1948), 238–39.

Windfall

William Heyen

Eating an apple, I think of Emerson
in another coach
traveling to a thousandth lecture. This time,
maybe it's summer, he's passing
apple orchards in Ohio where
he half dreams a bumblebee

sipping nectar—in its belly, a mite
glows with mite joy. In the mite's belly,
other living things the size of atoms

climb mountains . . . but he's tired
of revelation. It's certain the cosmos
is an orchard, or tree, or single bee

bearing the whole apple future, & Concord,
from one field to another,
& bearing him. He'll invite this audience

to find & live the secret of any windfall,
to try, for god's sake, to love
that which is obvious, & themselves.

Chapter 3

Spires of Influence

The Importance of Emerson for Classical
American Philosophy

John J. McDermott

And, striving to be man, the worm
Mounts through all the spires of form.
    —*Ralph Waldo Emerson, "Nature"*

*P*erhaps the title of this chapter should be "Why Emerson?" as that
would better reflect how I came to write this piece. It is not so much
that I have had to become convinced of the singular importance of the
thought of Emerson, for the writing and teaching of Joseph Blau[1] and
Robert C. Pollock[2] long ago made that clear to me. Rather the query about
"Why Emerson?" proceeds from my study of the classic American philosophers, especially William James, Josiah Royce, and John Dewey. Despite
their differences and disagreements, often extreme in both personal style
and doctrine, these powerful and prescient philosophers did have at least
one influence in common—the thought of Ralph Waldo Emerson.

Another major figure of the American classical period, George Santayana, seems to be a case apart. Santayana had an abiding interest in Emerson's thought and refers frequently to Emerson in his own writings. His
judgments on Emerson vary from admiration and affection to pointed and
even harsh criticism. I do not think that Emerson was a significant influence
on Santayana. Nonetheless, his published assessments of Emerson at the beginning of the twentieth century are contextually interesting, especially as
they contrast with those of James, Royce, and Dewey.

50

The remaining two major figures of the classical period, C. S. Peirce and G. H. Mead,[3] appear to be much less directly influenced by Emerson. Parenthetically, however, we do find a text in Peirce about Emerson which is intriguing and perhaps merits further inquiry in another context. In "The Law of Mind," published in 1892, Peirce wrote:

> I may mention, for the benefit of those who are curious in studying mental biographies, that I was born and reared in the neighborhood of Concord— I mean in Cambridge—at the time when Emerson, Hedge, and their friends were disseminating the ideas that they had caught from Schelling, and Schelling from Plotinus, from Boehm, or from God knows what minds stricken with the monstrous mysticism of the East. But the atmosphere of Cambridge held many an antiseptic against Concord transcendentalism; and I am not conscious of having contracted any of that virus. Nevertheless, it is probable that some cultured bacilli, some benignant form of the disease was implanted in my soul, unawares, and that now, after long incubation, it comes to the surface, modified by mathematical conceptions and by training in physical investigation.[4]

The wary and tough-minded response of Peirce is not atypical of a philosophical assessment of Emerson. Indeed, even those philosophers who acknowledge their debt to Emerson lace their remarks with dubiety about his fundamental assumptions and unease about much of the rhetoric of his formulation. Nonetheless, James, Royce, Dewey, and Santayana, each in his own way, find it necessary to evaluate the importance of Emerson in the light of their own developing positions. Before turning to these judgments, it should be helpful if I sketch the Emersonian project in cultural and philosophical terms.

The central theme of Emerson's life and work is that of *possibility*. In an anticipation of the attitude of Martin Buber, Emerson believes that "we are really able," that is, we and the world are continuous in an affective and nutritional way. It is human insight which is able to "animate the last fibre of organization, the outskirts of nature."[5] Emerson's persistent stress on human possibility is fed from two sources: his extraordinary confidence in the latent powers of the individual soul when related to the symbolic riches of nature and his belief that the comparatively unarticulated history of American experience could act as a vast resource for the energizing of novel and creative spiritual energy. The often oracular style of Emerson should not cloak the seriousness of his intention when he speaks of these possibilities. In this regard, the key text is found in his Introduction to the essay "Nature."

> Our age is retrospective. It builds the sepulchres of the fathers. It writes biographies, histories, and criticism. The foregoing generations beheld God

and nature face to face; we, through their eyes. Why should not we also enjoy an original relation to the universe? Why should not we have a poetry and philosophy of in-sight and not of tradition, and a religion by revelation to us, and not the history of theirs? Embosomed for a season in nature, whose floods of life stream around and through us, and invite us, by the powers they supply, to action proportioned to nature, why should we grope among the dry bones of the past, or put the living generation into masquerade out of its faded wardrobe? The sun shines to-day also. There is more wool and flax in the fields. There are new lands, new men, new thoughts. Let us demand our own works and laws and worship.[6]

We of the twentieth century may not grasp the radical character of Emerson's invocation, standing as we do on the rubble of broken promises brought to us by the great faiths of the past, be they scientific, social, or religious. But Emerson made no such promise and cannot be accused, retroactively, of bad faith. His message was clear. We are to transform the obviousness of our situation by a resolute penetration to the liberating symbolism present in our own experience. We are not to be dependent on faith hatched elsewhere out of others' experiences, nor, above all, are we to rest on an inherited ethic whose significance is due more to longevity and authority than to the press of our own experience. Surely, Emerson's nineteenth century, which was barely able to absorb the recondite theology responsible for the transition from Presbyterianism to Unitarianism, had to blanch at his bypassing the issue entirely, while calling for a homegrown "revelation." The radical character of Emerson's position at that time was given historical credence by the reception given to his Divinity School Address, delivered two years after "Nature" and one year after "The American Scholar." Using a tone more modest than either of those, Emerson in effect told the graduating class of Harvard Divinity School that the tradition they had inherited was hollow and the Church to which they belonged "seems to totter to its fall, all life extinct."[7] As in "Nature," he again called for a "new hope and new revelation."[8] The upshot of this address was that for nearly thirty years Emerson was unwelcome as a public figure in Cambridge.

Now, more to the point of the present discussion is Emerson's doctrine of experience and his emphasis on relations, both central concerns of the subsequent philosophical thought of James and Dewey. In his essay "The American Scholar," Emerson points to three major influences on the development of the reflective person: nature, history, and action or experience. In his discussion of the third influence, Emerson provides a microcosmic view of his fundamental philosophy. He makes it apparent that he does not accept the traditional superiority of the contemplative over the active life. Emerson tells us further, "Action is with the scholar subordinate, but it is essential. Without it he is not yet man. Without it thought can never ripen into truth."[9] It is noteworthy that accompanying Emerson's superb intellectual mastery of the great literature of the past and his commitment to the reflective life is his affirmation that "Character is higher than intellect."[10] Living is a total act, the functionary, whereas thinking is a partial act, the function. More than twenty years after the publication of "The American Scholar," Emerson reiterated his commitment to the "practical" and to the "experiential" as the touchstone of the thinking person. In his essay "Fate" he considers those thinkers for whom the central question is the "theory of the Age." In response, Emerson writes: "To me, however, the question of the times resolved itself into a practical question of the conduct of life. How shall I live? We are incompetent to solve the times."[11] The human task for Emerson is not so much to solve the times as to live them, in an ameliorative and perceptive way.

Emerson's generalized approach to inquiry is clearly a foreshadowing of that found subsequently in James, Dewey, and Royce. Too often, Emerson's anticipation of these thinkers is left at precisely that general bequest, whereby the undergoing of experience is its own mean and carries its own peculiar form of cognition.[12] What is less well known is that Emerson also anticipated the doctrine of "radical empiricism," which is central to the philosophy of James and Dewey. I do not contend that Emerson's version of relations had the same psychological or epistemological genesis[13] as that of either James or Dewey. Yet, *mutatis mutandis*, Emerson did affirm the primary importance of relations over things and he did hold to an aggressive doctrine of implication. Further, his metaphors were more allied to the language of continuity than to that of totality or finality. Finally, Emerson shared that modern assumption which began with Kant and is found repeated in James and Dewey—namely, that the known is, in some way, a function of the knower.

Emerson's attitude toward implicitness, relations, and the partially constitutive character of human inquiry helps us to understand him in other ways as well. Why, one might ask, would Emerson, a New England Brahmin, have a proletarian epistemology? That is, how could Emerson write as he did in "The American Scholar," a paean of praise to the obvious, to the ordinary? The text, as read to the audience at the Phi Beta Kappa celebration of 1837, was startling.

> I embrace the common, I explore and sit at the feet of the familiar, the low. Give me insight into to-day, and you may have the antique and future worlds. What would we really know the meaning of? The meal in the firkin; the milk in the pan; the ballad in the Street; the news of the boat; the glance of the eye; the form and gait of the body.[14]

Emerson immediately provides the response to the rhetorical question posed above. For the "ultimate reason" why the affairs of the ordinary yield insight traces to Emerson's belief that "the sublime presence of the highest spiritual cause lurks, as always it does lurk, in these suburbs and extremities of nature."[15] His version of the world is not characterized by hierarchies, nor by fixed essences, each to be known as an object in itself. Rather he stresses the flow of our experience and the multiple implications of every event and every thing for every other experience had or about to be had. Nature brings with it this rich symbolic resource, enabling all experiences, sanctioned and occasional, to retract potentially novel implications of our other experiences. The novelty is due both to the unpredictability of nature[16] and to the creative role of human imagination. Of the first Emerson writes:

> Nature hates calculators; her methods are saltatory and impulsive. Man lives by pulses; our organic movements are such; and the chemical and ethereal agents are undulatory and alternate; and the mind goes antagonizing on, and never prospers but by fits. We thrive by casualties. Our chief experiences have been casual. The most attractive class of people are those who are powerful obliquely and not by the direct stroke; men of genius, but not yet accredited; one gets the cheer of their light without paying too great a tax. Theirs is the beauty of the bird or the morning light, and not of art. In the thought of genius there is always a surprise; and the moral sentiment is well called "the newness," for it is never other; as new to the oldest intelligence as to the young child.[17]

The malleability and novelty-prone capacity of nature feeds the formulating and constructive powers native to the human imagination. Emerson, like James and Dewey, sees this transaction between the open nature of nature and the "active soul" as the necessary context for meaning. In his *Journals*, Emerson writes: "This power of imagination, the making of some familiar object, as fire or rain, or a bucket, or shovel do new duty as an exponent of some truth or general law, bewitches and delights men. It is a taking of dead sticks, and clothing about with immortality; it is music out of creaking and scouring. All opaque things are transparent, and the light of heaven struggles through."[18]

We should not mistake Emerson's position for a flight of fancy or for the poetic stroke in the pejorative sense of that word. Emerson is a hard-headed empiricist, reminiscent of the Augustinian-Franciscan tradition for whom the world was a temporal epiphany of the eternal implications and ramifications of the eternal ideas. For Emerson, "A Fact is the end or last issue of spirit."[19] Such facticity, paradoxically, comes to us only on behalf of our grasping and formulating the inherent symbolic features of our life.

> We learn nothing rightly until we learn the symbolical character of life. Day creeps after day, each full of facts, dull, strange, despised things, that we cannot enough despise—call heavy, prosaic and desert. The time we seek to kill: the attention it is elegant to divert from things around us. And

presently the aroused intellect finds gold and gems in one of these scorned facts—then finds that the day of facts is a rock of diamonds; that a fact is an Epiphany of God.[20]

The epiphanic, for Emerson, is not a result of human quietism. It is we who constitute these "facts" by our forging of relations. "Every new relation is a new word."[21] The making of words for Emerson, as for James, is the making of the world of meaning. Words are not simply grammatical connectors. As the embodiment of relations they do more than define. They make and remake the very fabric of our world as experienced. "The world is emblematic. Parts of speech are metaphors, because the whole of nature is a metaphor of the human mind."[22] This text mirrors the binary strands found in subsequent American philosophy: the idealist-pragmatic epistemology of James, Royce, Dewey, and Peirce, each with an original emphasis of one strand over another.

If we read the Emersonian project as one that focuses on the dialectic between the raw givenness of nature and the symbolic formulations of the human imagination, then we have a direct line of common interpretation from Emerson to the classic American philosophers. I grant that each of the American philosophers in question contexts this dialectic differently, yet even a cameo version reveals the similarity. The thought of Peirce, for example, exhibits a life-long tension between his acceptance of the irreducibly "tychistic" (i.e., chance-ridden) character of the world and of the inevitably fallibilistic character of human knowledge, and his extreme confidence in the method of science. And it is the tough-minded Peirce who writes that "without beating longer round the bush let us come to close quarters. Experience is our only teacher." And "how does this action of experience take place? It takes place by a series of suprises."[23]

The philosophy of John Dewey reflects a similar tension between a confidence in empirical method and the acknowledgment of novelty and unpredictability as indigenous to the history of nature. Dewey states that "Man finds himself living in an aleatory world; his existence involves, to put it baldly, a gamble. The world is a scene of risk; it is uncertain, unstable, uncannily unstable. Its dangers are irregular, inconstant, not to he counted upon as to their times and seasons. Although persistent, they are sporadic, episodic."[24]

Still, when faced with this extremely open and even perilous version of nature, Dewey calls upon philosophy to act as an intelligent mapping, so as to reconstruct, ameliorate, and enhance the human condition. Dewey's project is Emersonian, for the affairs of time and the activities of nature are the ground of inquiry, rather than the hidden and transcendent meaning of Being. Just as Emerson broke with the theological language of his immediate predecessors and many of his peers, so too did Dewey break with the ecstatic religious language of Emerson. This break in language should not hide from us that Dewey's understanding of the relationship that exists between nature and human life echoes that of Emerson: always possibility, often celebration, frequently mishap, and never absolute certitude.

As for an Emersonian analogue in Royce, readers of that indefatigable polymath know that cameo versions of any of his positions do not come easy. Nonetheless, Royce's long, speculative trek away from the absolute and toward a theory of interpretation, ever reconstructed by the community, echoes Emerson's emphasis on the conduct of life. Royce was forced to abandon the doctrine of the absolute mind because he finally accepted the judgment of his critics that he could not account for the experience of the individual on either epistemological or metaphysical grounds. In his last great work, *The Problem of Christianity*, Royce has come full circle and awarded to the individual the task of formulating the "real world" by virtue of the relationship between "self-interpretation" and the "community of interpretation." Emerson wrote that "we know more from nature than we can at will communicate."[25] Similarly, Royce writes that "the popular mind is deep, and means a thousand times more than it explicitly knows."[26] In my judgment, Royce's mature thought, under the influence of Peirce, structures philosophically the earlier informal approach of Emerson. Although the content is Emersonian, the following passage from Royce brings a heightened philosophical sophistication:

> Metaphysically considered, the world of interpretation is the world in which, if indeed we are able to interpret at all, we learn to acknowledge the being and the inner life of our fellow-men; and to understand the constitution of temporal experience with its endlessly accumulating sequence of significant deeds. In this world of interpretation, of whose most general structure we have now obtained a glimpse, selves and communities may exist, past and future can be defined, and the realms of the spirit may find a place which neither barren conception nor the chaotic flow of interpenetrating perceptions could ever render significant.[27]

It is with William James, however, that the Emersonian dialectic between the creative and constructive character of the human mind and the apparently intransigent character of the physical world most explicitly comes to the fore. James, like Emerson, holds to a relationship of congeniality between nature and human power. They both avoid the alternate interpretations, which, in turn, would stress either the complete objectivity of the meaning of nature or a completely subjective version in which nature has an existence only at the behest of the human, or failing that, the absolute mind. In some ways, James outdoes Emerson in his stress on the "powers" and "energies" of the individual, although we should remember that he also emphasizes "seeing and feeling the total push and pressure of the cosmos."[28]

William James is profoundly aware of these alternate versions of our situation and often evokes them in an extreme way. Two texts from *Pragmatism* stand out in this regard, and if we put them back to back, the poles of the Emersonian dialectic are thrown into bold relief.

> Woe to him whose beliefs play fast and loose with the order which realities follow in his experience: They will lead him nowhere or else make false connexions.[29]

> In our cognitive as well as in our active life we are creative. We *add*, both to the subject and to the predicate part of reality. The world stands really malleable, waiting to receive its final touches at our hands. Like the kingdom of heaven, it suffers human violence willingly. Man *engenders* truths upon it.[30]

Obviously, both of these texts cannot stand at one and the same time. James was very much aware of this conflict and continued to pose it, even though he was simultaneously working his way out of the dilemma. In an earlier entry in an unpublished notebook, he gives a reason for maintaining this conflict. "Surely nature itself and subjective construction are radically opposed, one's higher indignations are nourished by the opposition."[31] Emerson, of course, would approve of both the "indignation" and the "nourishment."

It should be noted, however, that James goes beyond Emerson at this point and develops his formal doctrine of radical empiricism to mediate this "opposition." The genesis and content of James's radical empiricism is a long and complicated story, but in his conclusion to his essay "A World of Pure Experience," James sets out the dramatic presence of the knowing self in a world both obdurate and malleable.

> There is in general no separateness needing to be overcome by an external cement; and whatever separateness is actually experienced is not overcome, it stays and counts as separateness to the end. But the metaphor serves to symbolize the fact that experience itself, taken at large, can grow by its edges. That one moment of it proliferates into the next by transitions which, whether conjunctive or disjunctive, continue the experiential tissue, cannot, I contend, be denied. Life is in the transitions as much as in the terms connected; often, indeed, it seems to be there more emphatically, as if our spurts and sallies forward were the real firing-line of the battle, were like the thin line of flame advancing across the dry autumnal field which the farmer proceeds to burn. In this line we live prospectively as well as retrospectively. It is "of" the past, inasmuch as it comes expressly as the past's continuation; it is "of" the future in so far as the future, when it comes, will have continued *it*.[32]

So much for the refractions of the Emersonian dialectic in some of the classical American philosophers. At this point, the reader may well ask why I have not cited these philosophers on this central theme in Emerson? The response, alas, is quite simple. Our philosophers did not write very much on Emerson and when they did, the focus was often on other, if related, themes. I turn now to James, Santayana, Royce, and Dewey on Emerson, directly.

II

At the age of three months, William James was visited by Ralph Waldo Emerson at the James family's home on Washington Square in New York City. This prepossessing and perhaps burdensome presence of Emerson lasted throughout most of the life of William James. In the decade following 1870, James read virtually everything Emerson wrote and at one point in 1873 made the following entry in his diary: "I am sure that an age will come when our present devotion to history, and scrupulous care for what men have done before us merely as fact, will seem incomprehensible; when acquaintance with books will be no duty, but a pleasure for odd individuals; when Emerson's philosophy will be in our bones, not our dramatic imagination."[33] Apparently, Emerson's thought had already reached the "bones" of James, for the above sentiment about the past is shared by Emerson. In "The American Scholar" he wrote that "I had better never see a book than to be warped by its attraction clean out of my own orbit and made a satellite instead of a system. The one thing in the world, of value, is the active soul."[34]

Some thirty years after his diary entry, in 1903, James was called upon to deliver the address at the centenary celebration for Emerson in Concord.[35] This occasion caused James to reread virtually all of Emerson's writings. Frankly, with regard to the question of the influence of Emerson on James, the address is disappointing. As one would expect, James is laudatory of Emerson's person and work.[36] And, as he often did in such pieces of encomium, the text is largely made up of long passages from Emerson. Despite these limitations, an important theme runs beneath the baroque prose of James and that of Emerson as selected by James. As we might expect, it is the theme of "possibility," of the hallowing of the everyday. James is struck by the radical temporality of Emerson's vision. He offers a brief collage of that attitude: "'The Deep to-day which all men scorn' receives thus from Emerson superb revindication. 'Other world! There is no other world.' All God's life opens into the individual particular, and here and now, or nowhere, is reality. 'The present hour is the decisive hour, and every day is doomsday.'"[37]

James cautions us that Emerson was no sentimentalist. The transformation of stubborn fact to an enhanced symbolic statement of richer possibility was an activity that James found very compatible with his own stress on novelty and surprise. Emerson had written, "So is there no fact, no event, in our private history, which shall not sooner or later, lose its adhesive, inert form and astonish us by soaring from our body into the empyrean."[38] On behalf of this and similar passages, James comments that Emerson "could perceive the full squalor of the individual fact, but he could also see the transfiguration."[39]

Aside from this important focus on Emerson's concern for "individuals and particulars," James's address is taken up with praise of Emerson's style as a literary artist. I note the irony here, for such praise of style is precisely what has taken up much of the commentaries on the thought of James, often to the detriment of an analysis of his serious philosophical intent. It is unfortunate that James never undertook a systematic study of Emerson, especially as directed to his notions of experience, relations, and symbol. James would have found Emerson far more "congenial"[40] and helpful than many of the other thinkers he chose to examine. A detailed study of Emerson as an incipient radical empiricist is a noteworthy task for the future.

The response of Santayana to Emerson's thought was more censorious than that of James and Dewey. On several occasions, James compared the thought of Emerson and Santayana, to the detriment of the latter. In a letter to Dickinson S. Miller, James comments on Santayana's book, *The Life of Reason*:

> He is a paragon of Emersonianism—declare your intuitions, though no other man share them; . . . The book is Emerson's first rival and successor, but how different the reader's feeling! The same things in Emerson's mouth would sound entirely different. E. receptive, expansive, as if handling life through a wide funnel with a great indraught; S. as if through a pin-point orifice that emits his cooling spray outward over the universe like a nose-disinfectant from an atomizer.[41]

We learn from a letter written by Santayana that James apparently had expressed similar sentiments to him as he had in the letter to Miller. Santayana was not pleased and in his response issues a devastating criticism of Emerson.

> And you say I am less hospitable than Emerson. Of course. Emerson might pipe his wood-notes and chirp at the universe most blandly; his genius might be tender and profound and Hamlet-like, and that is all beyond my range and contrary to my purpose. . . . What did Emerson know or care about the passionate insanities and political disasters which religion, for instance, has so often been another name for? He could give that name to his last personal intuition, and ignore what it stands for and what it expresses in the world. It is the latter that absorbs me; and I care too much about mortal happiness to be interested in the charming vegetation of cancer-microbes in the system—except with the idea of suppressing it.[42]

Although not quite so caustic as his rebuke to James, Santayana's writings on Emerson always had a critical edge to them. In an early essay, written in 1886, Santayana comments judiciously on Emerson's optimism, which he traces more to his person than to his doctrine. Yet, Santayana's sympathetic treatment of Emerson concludes with a damaging last line: "But of those who are not yet free from the troublesome feelings of pity and shame, Emerson brings no comfort, he is a prophet of a fair-weather religion."[43]

In 1900, as a chapter in his *Interpretations of Poetry and Religion*, Santayana published his best-known essay on Emerson. This piece has been frequently cited on behalf of those who are condescending to Emerson or severely critical of him. I believe this use of Santayana's essay to be a misreading. Certainly, Santayana was more indulgent of Emerson in 1900 than he was in 1911, when he published his famous essay "The Genteel Tradition in American Philosophy." In 1911, Santayana lumps Emerson with Poe and Hawthorne as having "a certain starved and abstract quality." Further, their collective "genius" was a "digestion of vacancy."

> It was a refined labour, but it was in danger of being morbid, or tinkling, or self-indulgent. It was a play of intramental rhymes. Their mind was like an old music-box, full of tender echoes and quaint fancies. These fancies expressed their personal genius sincerely, as dreams may; but they were arbitrary fancies in comparison with what a real observer would have said in the premises. Their manner, in a word, was subjective. In their own persons they escape the mediocrity of the genteel tradition, but they supplied nothing to supplant it in other minds.[44]

In 1900, however, when Santayana addresses Emerson's thought directly, his evaluations are more favorable. Admitting of Emerson that "at bottom he had no doctrine at all," Santayana writes that "his finer instinct kept him from doing that violence to his inspiration."[45] Santayana repeats his earlier contention that Emerson's power was not in his "doctrine" but rather in his "temperament" and that Emersonian temperament was, above all, antitradition and antiauthoritarian. Even though he was a classic instance of the "Genteel Tradition" and held many positions that were anathema to Santayana, Emerson nevertheless pleased Santayana by his refusal to professionalize and systematize his thought. Further, Santayana, with poetic sensibilities of his own, was taken with Emerson's style. He writes of Emerson: "If not a star of the first magnitude, he is certainly a fixed star in the firmament of philosophy. Alone as yet among Americans, he may be said to have won a place there, if not by the originality of this thought, at least by the originality and beauty of the expression he gave to thoughts that are old and imperishable."[46]

Still more to the point, and less known, is that Santayana shared Emerson's celebration and embracing of the "common." In 1927, as part of a chastising letter sent to Van Wyck Brooks, Santayana writes: "I therefore think that art, etc. has better soil in the ferocious 100% America than in the intelligentsia of New York. It is veneer, rouge, aestheticism, art museums, new theatres, etc. that make America impotent. The good things are football, kindness, and jazz bands."[47] It turns out that Santayana, like Whitman, learned something from Emerson.

Before examining John Dewey's essay on Emerson, I offer a brief interlude with a comment on Josiah Royce's assessment of Emerson. Although Royce was a voluminous writer[48] and ventured interpretations of an extremely wide range of problems and thinkers, he rarely spoke of Emerson. Yet Royce thought far more of Emerson than we could have divined from his publications. In 1911, Royce delivered a Phi Beta Kappa oration in honor of William James, who had died the previous year. The theme of Royce's essay was that James was the third "representative American Philosopher." It was in Royce's opening discussion of the first two candidates that his version of Emerson emerged:

> Fifty years since, if competent judges were asked to name the American thinkers from whom there had come novel and notable and typical contributions to general philosophy, they could in reply mention only two men— Jonathan Edwards and Ralph Waldo Emerson. For the conditions that determine a fair answer to the question, "Who are your representative American philosophers?" are obvious. The philosopher who can fitly represent the contribution of his nation to the world's treasury of philosophical ideas must first be one who thinks for himself, fruitfully, with true independence, and with successful inventiveness, about problems of philosophy. And, secondly, he must be a man who gives utterance to philosophical ideas which are characteristic of some stage and of some aspect of the spiritual life of his own people. In Edwards and in Emerson, and only in these men, had these two conditions found their fulfillment, so far as our American civilization had yet expressed itself in the years that had preceded our civil war. . . .
>
> Another stage of our civilization—a later phase of our national ideals— found its representative in Emerson. He too was in close touch with many of the world's deepest thoughts concerning ultimate problems. Some of the ideas that most influenced him have their far-off historical origins in oriental as well as in Greek thought, and also their nearer foreign sources in modern European philosophy, but he transformed what ever he assimilated. He invented upon the basis of his personal experience, and so he was himself no disciple of the orient, or of Greece, still less of England and Germany. He thought, felt, and spoke as an American.[49]

Again, we are left with a judgment as to Emerson's importance, notably in this case as a philosopher, but without subsequent or sufficient analysis. A search through the papers and publications of Royce does not cast much more direct light on this influence of Emerson. Royce's remarks do convince me, however, that Emerson wrought more in the lives of the classical American philosophers than written evidence can sustain.

Among the centenary addresses of 1903, we find another by an American philosopher, John Dewey. This essay sets out to rescue Emerson from the condescension implied when he is described as not a philosopher. Dewey complains that "literary critics admit his philosophy and deny his literature. And if philosophers extol his keen, calm art and speak with some depreciation of his metaphysic, it is also perhaps because Emerson knew something deeper than our conventional definitions."[50] The first of Dewey's complaints is now out of date, for Emerson is taken very seriously as a literary artist. The second complaint still holds, although with important exceptions as noted above in the work of Blau and Pollock.

In Dewey's judgment, Emerson has been misread and misunderstood. He takes as Emerson's project the submitting of ideas "to the test of trial by service rendered the present and immediate experience."[51] Further, Dewey contends that Emerson's method is consistent with this experimental endeavor. "To Emerson, perception was more potent than reasoning; the deliverances of intercourse more to be desired than the chains of discourse; the surprise of reception more demonstrative than the conclusions of intentional proof."[52]

It is intriguing that Dewey, whose own style is anything but oracular, would praise this approach of Emerson. One might rather expect this indulgence from those reared in the language of the existentialists or of twentieth-century religious thinkers, such as Buber, Berdyaev, and Marcel. A closer look at Dewey's text, however, provides some source of explanation. Similar to James's emphasis, Dewey states that the locus of Emerson's inquiry is the "possibility" inherent in the experience of the "common man." Against the opinions of other commentators, Dewey holds that Emerson's "ideas are not fixed upon any Reality that is beyond or behind or in any way apart, and hence they do not have to be bent. They are versions of the Here and the Now, and flow freely."[53] Dewey is especially sympathetic with Emerson's attempt to avoid the "apart."[54] And he is convinced that Emerson knew, as few others, of the enervating and diluting effect often had by theory on the richness of common and concrete experience. Dewey's text on this issue is crystal clear and can be read as well as a critique for much of what passes for philosophical discourse in our own time.

> Against creed and system, convention and institution, Emerson stands for restoring to the common man that which in the name of religion, of philosophy, of art and of morality, has been embezzled from the common store and appropriated to sectarian and class use. Beyond any one we know of,

Emerson has comprehended and declared how such malversation makes truth decline from its simplicity, and in becoming partial and owned, become a puzzle of and trick for theologian, metaphysician and litterateur— a puzzle of an imposed law, of an unwished for and refused goodness, of a romantic ideal gleaming only from afar, and a trick of manipular skill, of specialized performance.[55]

Dewey took Emerson's task as his own. Although his prose lacked the rhetorical flights so natural to Emerson, he too wrote out of compassion for the common man and confidence in the "possibility" inherent in every situation. By the time of Dewey's maturity, the world of New England high culture had passed. Dewey, despite being born in New England, was a child of industrial democracy. He alone of the classic American philosophers was able to convert the genius and language of Emerson to the new setting. John Dewey, proletarian by birth and style, grasped that Emerson's message was ever relevant. In the conclusion to his essay on Emerson, Dewey captures that message and carries it forward to his own time. I offer that we should do likewise.

To them who refuse to be called "master, master," all magistracies in the end defer, for theirs is the common cause for which dominion, power and principality is put under foot. Before such successes, even the worshippers of that which to-day goes by the name of success, those who bend to millions and incline to imperialisms, may lower their standard and give at least a passing assent to the final word of Emerson's philosophy, the identity of Being, unqualified and immutable, with Character.[56]

Notes

1. *American Philosophic Addresses*, 1700–1900, ed. Joseph L. Blau (New York: Columbia University Press, 1946); *Men and Movements in American Philosophy* (Englewood Cliffs, NJ: Prentice-Hall, 1952); "Emerson's Transcendentalist Individualism as a Social Philosophy," *Review of Metaphysics* 31, no. 1 (September 1977): 80–92.

2. Robert C. Pollock, "Ralph Waldo Emerson—The Single Vision," in *American Classics Reconsidered*, ed. Harold Gardiner (New York: Scribner's, 1958), 15–58.

3. George Herbert Mead tends to speak of Emerson only in the context of Concord transcendentalism. Ironically, in lamenting the failure of the transcendentalists to develop a distinctive doctrine of American self-consciousness, Mead overlooks the powerful voice of Emerson in precisely that regard. Mead, "The Philosophies of Royce, James and Dewey in Their American Setting," *Selected Writings*, ed. Andrew J. Reck (Indianapolis: Bobbs-Merrill, 1964), 377–78.

4. Charles Sanders Peirce, *Collected Papers*, ed. Charles Hartshorne and Paul Weiss, vol. 6 (sec. 101) (Cambridge: Harvard University Press, 1934), 86–87. Peirce also was fond of quoting and mocking Emerson's poem on the Sphinx, especially the

line, "Of thine eye, I am eyebeam," ibid., 1:153–54 (sec. 310), and 2:252 (sec. 404). Some unpublished material on Peirce's "boyhood impressions" of Emerson can be found in "Manuscript—296" as recorded in the *Annotated Catalogue of the Papers of Charles S. Peirce*, ed. Richard Robin (Amherst: University of Massachusetts Press, 1967), 31.

5. Ralph Waldo Emerson, "The American Scholar," in *The Complete Works of Ralph Waldo Emerson*, ed. Edward Emerson, vol. 1 (Boston: Houghton Mifflin, 1903–04), 86.

6. Ralph Waldo Emerson, "Nature," in *The Complete* Works, 1:3.

7. Ralph Waldo Emerson, "The Divinity School Address," in *The Complete Works*, 1:135.

8. Ibid., 151.

9. Emerson, "American Scholar," 1:95. The use of "he" and "man" in this text and in subsequent texts is to be read in the present chapter as referring also to "she" and "woman."

10. Ibid., 99.

11. Emerson, "Fate," in *The Complete Works*, 6:3. For a similar attitude, see William James, *The Varieties of Religious Experience* (New York: Longmans, Green 1902), 489. "Knowledge about life is one thing; effective occupation of a place in life, with its dynamic currents passing though your being, is another."

12. Texts in support of this position abound in the writings of John Dewey. Among others are Dewey, *Reconstruction in Philosophy*, vol. 12 (1982) of *The Middle Works* (Carbondale: Southern Illinois University Press, 1976–83), 132. "Experience carries principles of connection and organization within itself." And again, p. 134, "What Shakespeare so pregnantly said of nature, it is 'made better by no mean, but nature makes that mean,' becomes true of experience."

13. For a historical and philosophical treatment of the genesis of James's doctrine of radical empiricism, see John J. McDermott, "Introduction" to William James, *Essays in Radical Empiricism* (Cambridge: Harvard University Press, 1976), xi–xlviii. Dewey's doctrine of radical empiricism is best found in *The Influence of Darwinism on Philosophy and Other Essays in Contemporary Philosophy* (New York: Holt, 1910).

14. Emerson, "American Scholar," 1:111. For a richer description of the extreme variety of audience responses to Emerson's oration of 1837, see Bliss Perry, "Emerson's Most Famous Speech," in *Ralph Waldo Emerson: A Profile*, ed. Carl Bode (New York: Hill and Wang, 1969), 52–65. Oliver Wendell Holmes heard the oration as an "intellectual Declaration of Independence," and James Russell Lowell viewed it as "our Yankee version of a lecture by Abelard, our Harvard parallel to the last public appearances of Schelling."

15. Emerson, "American Scholar," 111.

16. Ralph Waldo Emerson, "Experience," in *The Complete Works*, 6:308 n. 1. "Everything in the Universe goes by indirection. There are no straight lines."

17. Ibid., 6:68. William James holds a similar position. "Notebook" entry of 1903 as found in Ralph Barton Perry, *The Thought and Character of William James*, vol. 2 (Boston: Little, Brown, 1935), 700 (cited above, pp. 15–16).

18. *The Journals of Ralph Waldo Emerson*, vol. 9 (Boston: Houghton Mifflin, 1909–14), 277–78.

19. Emerson, "Nature," 1:34.

20. Ralph Waldo Emerson, "Education," in *The Complete Works*, 10:132.

21. Ralph Waldo Emerson, "The Poet," in *The Complete Works*, 3:18.

22. Emerson, "Nature," 1:32.

23. Peirce, *Collected Papers*, 1:37.

24. John Dewey, *Experience and Nature*, vol. 1 (1981) of *The Later Works* (Carbondale: Southern Illinois University Press, 1981–), 43.

25. Emerson, "Nature," 1:31.

26. *The Letters of Josiah Royce*, ed. John Clendenning (Chicago: University of Chicago Press, 1970), 86.

27. Josiah Royce, *The Problem of Christianity* (Chicago: University of Chicago Press, 1968 [1913]), 86.

28. William James, *Pragmatism* (Cambridge: Harvard University Press, 1975), 9.

29. Ibid., 99.

30. Ibid., 123.

31. James Papers, Houghton Library, Harvard University (bMs AM 1092, box L, notebook N^2).

32. James, *Essays in Radical Empiricism*, 42.

33. Cited in Gay Wilson Allen, *William James: A Biography* (New York: Viking, 1967), 186–87.

34. Emerson, "American Scholar," 1:89–90.

35. William James, "Address at the Emerson Centenary in Concord," in *Essays in Religion and Morality* (Cambridge: Harvard University Press, 1982), 109–15. For a contrast of James's hagiographic approach to others more critical and substantive, the reader should consult two collections of essays: *Emerson*, ed. Milton Konvitz and Stephen Whicher (Englewood Cliffs, NJ: Prentice-Hall, 1962), and *The Recognition of Ralph Waldo Emerson: Selected Criticism since 1837*, ed. Milton Konvitz (Ann Arbor: University of Michigan Press, 1972). It is striking that in the vast secondary literature on Emerson, distinctively philosophical considerations are virtually absent.

36. James was not always complimentary to Emerson. In *The Varieties of Religious Experience*, for example, he criticized Emerson for tending toward "abstraction" on the religious question (32, 56). For a discussion of James's ambivalence on Emerson, see F. O. Mathiessen, *The American Renaissance* (New York: Oxford University Press, 1941), 53–54 n.

37. James, *Essays in Religion and Morality*, 114.

38. Emerson, "American Scholar," 2:96–97.

39. James, *Essays in Religion and Morality*, 114. The potential capacity for "transfiguration" of fact as subject to human will is not a strange contention for William James, as can be seen in his own doctrine of "The Will to Believe." Could it have some expressive origin in Emerson's "Nature"? "Build therefore your own world. As fast as you conform your life to the pure idea in your mind, that will unfold its great proportions. A correspondent revolution in things will attend the influx of the spirit" (*The Complete Works*, 1:76).

40. What could be more Emersonian than James's remark in his "Sentiment of Rationality" that "the inmost nature of the reality is congenial to powers which you possess" (*The Will to Believe* [Cambridge: Harvard University Press, 1979], 73). See also *The Writings of William James*, ed. John J. McDermott (Chicago: University of Chicago Press, 1977), 331. In preparation for his "Address," James did read Emerson, "volume after volume," but came away with "a moral lesson" rather than distinctive philosophical insight. Cf. *The Letters of William James*, ed. Henry James III, 3 vols. (Boston: Atlantic Monthly Press, 1920), 190.

41. James, *Letters of William James*, 234–35. For another contrast of Emerson and Santayana, see John Crowe Ransom, "Art and Mr. Santayana," in *Santayana: Animal Faith and Spiritual Life*, ed., John Lachs (New York: Appleton-Century-Crofts, 1967), 403–04.

42. George Santayana, *The Letters of George Santayana*, ed. Daniel Cory (New York: Scribner's, 1955), 81–82.

43. George Santayana, "The Optimism of Ralph Waldo Emerson," in *George Santayana's America*, ed. James Ballowe (Urbana: University of Illinois Press, 1967), 84. Another little-known piece of Santayana on Emerson is "Emerson the Poet," a centennial contribution of 1903. Although in this essay Santayana speaks of Emerson as often bland, he praises him for self-direction and a deep and unyielding sense of personal liberty. See *Santayana on America*, ed. Richard C. Lyon (New York: Harcourt, 1968), 268–83.

44. George Santayana, "The Genteel Tradition in American Philosophy," in *Winds of Doctrine* (London: Dent, 1913), 192–93.

45. George Santayana, "Emerson," in *Interpretations of Poetry and Religion* (New York: Scribner's, 1900), 218.

46. Ibid., 233.

47. Santayana, *Letters*, 225–26.

48. Ignas K. Skrupskelis, "Annotated Bibliography of the Publications of Josiah Royce," in *The Basic Writings of Josiah Royce*, ed. John J. McDermott, vol. 2 (Chicago: University of Chicago Press, 1969), 1167–226.

49. Josiah Royce, *William James and Other Essays* (New York: Macmillan, 1911), 3–4, 5–6.

50. John Dewey, "Ralph Waldo Emerson," in *Characters and Events*, vol. 1 (New York: Holt, 1929), 71.

51. Ibid., 74.

52. Ibid., 70.

53. Ibid., 75.

54. Dewey takes a similar position in *Art as Experience* (New York: Capricorn, 1958 [1934]), 11: "Theory can start with and from acknowledged works of art only when the esthetic is already compartmentalized, or only when works of art are set in a niche apart instead of being celebrations, recognized as such, of the things of ordinary experience. Even a crude experience, if authentically an experience, is more fit to give a clue to the intrinsic nature of esthetic experience than is an object already set apart from any other mode of experience."

55. Dewey, "Ralph Waldo Emerson," 75.

56. Ibid., 77.

Chapter 4

Teaching for Lustres

An Essay on the Emersonian Teacher

Arthur S. Lothstein

God's greatest gift is a teacher & when will he send me one, full of truth & boundless benevolence & heroic sentiments. I can describe the man, & have done so already in prose and verse. I know the idea well, but where is its real blood warm counterpart?
—*Emerson, Letter to his aunt Mary Moody Emerson, April 1833*

I take up in this essay Emerson's aesthetic pedagogy, centering on his normative concept of the teacher. His concept runs like a red thread through most, if not all, of his major writings, including his voluminous journal, yet it has been largely ignored in contemporary discussion of his work. As a result, a major aspect of Emerson's thought has been discountenanced or pitched in so low a key as to be effectively inaudible to most of his serious readers, including many of his most ardent promoters. In effect, the Emerson whom I address here is The Emerson That Almost Nobody Knows.

One of the principal attributes of the Emersonian teacher[1] is that he teaches primarily for lustres and only secondarily for argument. I have been lead to this conclusion by both personal experience and textual evidence. More than forty years of teaching philosophy and the humanities has persuaded me that education is what Emerson calls "the drawing out of the Soul," or what the ancients called "*psychagogia*"; and that teaching for aesthetic splendor (in addition to intellectual power and wisdom) is not pyrotechnical but existential and transformational. The Emersonian teacher teaches "as if for life," mindful of the fact that we live long before we logicize, and that "Life," as Nietzsche Emersonianly puts the point, "is not an argument." Like the three anarchic and experimental teachers celebrated in Peter Weir's and Nicholas Hyter's films *The Dead Poets Society* (1989) and *The History of Boys* (2006), and in Jonathan Kozol's extraordinary book, *Letters to a Young Teacher* (2007), the Emersonian teacher is a "Professor of the Joyous Science," an iconic embodiment of the medieval Provençal ideal of *"la gaya scienza."* "The Scholar" names such teachers as "detectors and delineators of occult symmetries & unpublished beauties, heralds of civility, nobility & wisdom, affirmers of the One Law, yet as ones who should affirm it in music or dancing." Indeed, two of the philosophical and pedagogical postures coronated by Emerson are those of the musician and dancer, both of which he likely inherited from ancient mythology and religious art, inclusive of the Dionysiac and Orphic cults and their respective iconographies, and from the Persian poet, Hafiz, who was a Sufi and thus a dervished descendant of Zarathustra. Other possible sources include Plato's myth of the cicadas in the *Phaedrus* (259C–D), Wordsworth's aeolian naturalism, and the American Shaker experience of dance and song. Both postures, especially that of the dancer, were philosophically reinherited by Nietzsche in *The Gay Science* ("I would not know what the spirit of a philosopher might wish more to be than a good dancer") and in *Thus Spoke Zarathustra* ("Only in the dance do I know how to tell the parable of highest things"). As Emerson journalizes (1841): "We wish to take the gas which allows us to break through your wearisome properties, to plant the foot, to set the teeth, to fling abroad the arms, and dance and sing."

What I find especially noteworthy here is that Emerson's tropings of dance and music suggest the singular importance of the foot and the ear as organs of abandonment and reception—two Emersonian "master tones" to which I shall return—and of the need for a fundamentally aesthetic approach to his writings, one that is centered on the educative values of dance and song.[2] Too much attention has been paid to "The American Scholar's" Rodinian image of "Man Thinking" and to its author's visionary and melioristic tropings of the eye and hand as pedagogical. By contrast, Emerson's aesthetic images of Man Dancing and Singing hardly have been given their due. As I read him, this second Emerson, who like Nietzsche's Zarathustra, has "an ear in his toe," is the more contemporary of the two Emersons. It is Emerson's aesthetic singer / dancer on the "feet of Chance," not the brooding Emerson nautilised in cognitive privacy, who is our most contemporary Emerson. This is the Emerson who says in "The American Scholar," "'Know thyself,' and the modern precept, 'Study nature,' become at last one maxim"; that "Thinking is a partial act," living "is a total act"; and that "the scholar loses no hours which the man lives." This is also the Emerson who is most consonant with a New Cosmos sensibility, one instantiated by the "continuous dance of cosmic energy" that the physicist Brian Greene describes as "the aeolian universe" of superstring theory, and that Frijof Capra calls "the Tao of physics." In the spirit of Deborah Digges's beautiful poem, "Dancing with

Mr. Emerson," which appears earlier in this volume, I offer that to read Emerson is to dance with him, perhaps not the genteel waltz imagined by Digges, but rather something more prankish, say, the tarantella, with jingling Zarathustran spurs on our feet.

To This New But Approachable Emerson the Tao of the human journey, "the true art of life," is to skate [or dance] across the glistering surface of experience with grace, speed, and ease. Or as Nietzsche poetically revises Emerson: Smooth ice / is paradise / for those who dance with expertise." Since "Nature is Becoming or Transition" and since every step we take "is an advance into a new land," the creation and negotiation of continuous transition, of "as much transitional surface as possible," is the emblem or signature of Emersonian power. As "Self-Reliance" dramatically puts the point: "Life only avails, not the having lived. Power ceases in the instant of repose; it resides in the moment of transition from a past to a new state, in the shooting of the gulf, in the darting to an aim." Revising Emerson, William James, one of Emerson's most seminal inheritors, speaks rather of living, "as it were, on the front edge of an advancing wave-crest," "our sense of a determinate direction in falling forward [being] all we cover of the future of our path." As James admonishes: "It is only by risking our persons from one hour to another that we live at all . . . be not afraid of life."[3] And indeed Emerson's "shooting of the gulf" is no cakewalk, no "sunny day's complete Poussiniana," in the phrase of Wallace Stevens. "Experience" says that "a man is a golden impossibility. The line he must walk is [but] a hair's breadth"; and, following "Self-reliance," the line, like "the voyage of the best ships, is a zigzag line of a hundred tacks." But as "abyss opens under abyss," the words "line" and "walk" hardly do justice to the perilsomeness of the journey, which is not a line dance or a walkthrough, but a long day's journey into night, one pockmarked by setback and mishap, be it a Trip to Bountiful, a Wisconsin Death Trip, or, as in Cormac McCarthy's post-apocalyptic novel, *The Road*, a trek across an "ashen scabland."

As the old blues song has it, it is all a matter of stepping up and going, of inch-meal reconnoitering, of taking the next step, in the hope that we will land on our feet and continue our journeying post-haste, notwithstanding the possibility of shipwreck in the abysmal "gulfs of space" surrounding the thin line that we tack. No matter the choreography, "the steps are actions, the new prospect is power." For the footloose and freewheeling, "life is a May game still." However, should "we lose our delicate balance," we may recover "the lost equilibrium not by abrupt and angular" movements, but by "gradual and curving ones," falling softly on our feet like cats. "Beauty" calls such recovery "the theory of dancing." In "Essential Principles of Religion" (1862), Emerson says that "to a good foot, no place is slippery." But, following Deuteronomy 32:35, every foot "shall slide in due time," including what the Psalmist calls "the foot of pride." Such is our metaphysical condition as "timed naturals." Yet, according to Emerson, "we stagger and grope," only "in our lapsed estate, resting not advancing," failing, as "Compensation" says, to slough off the snakeskin of "dead circumstances so as to renew our "raiment day by day." "Wisdom," on the other hand, "consists in keeping the soul [and body] liquid, or in resisting the tendency to too rapid petrifaction." Indeed, heroes for Emerson are those "who do not fix, but flow," "men of elastic . . . who . . . live in the moment and take a step forward." It is a view celebrated earlier in his famous essay "Nature": "As when the summer comes from the south, the snow-banks melt, and the face of the earth becomes green before it, so shall the advancing spirit create its ornaments along its path, and carry with it the beauty it visits, and the song which enchants it."

Honed thusly on a Tao of dance and song, the *telos* of Emersonian teaching is luminous self-becoming, not the delectative pleasures of the text or the niceties of logical analysis. The Eros of the Emerson teacher's poetic imagination is what lubricates and energizes such self-becoming, one that begins with the awakening of the self from its Oblomovian indolence, and from its disownership of its own repressed lustres. From Emerson to Martin Buber, from William James to John J. McDermott, dialogic conversation or encounter is what conduces to such self-recovery, not querulous and combative philosophical argument. As Emerson says in "Inspiration": conversation is "the right metaphysical professor . . . the true school of philosophy . . . the college where you learn what thoughts are, what powers lurk in those fugitive gleams, and what becomes of them; how they make history."

By contrast, argument is a poor man's lawyering, a bullring for show-boating and self-preening. At its worst, it is a cockfight, a bloodsport, in which the highest marks are awarded for supermasculine aggressiveness, pitbull tenacity, and peacock wit. Taking a cue from St. Augustine, Emerson says that he would rather wonder than wrangle, and warns the reader against the moral grotesqueries and logical seductions of combative argumentation. "A good symbol," for him, "is the best argument, and is a missionary to persuade thousands." Yet philosophical discussion nowadays, especially in Oxbridgean circles, is often an invitation to a beheading. The playfulness and *jeux d'esprit* that distingushed the ancient "agonistic aspirations"[4] has, alas, been transmogrified into a form of Grand Guignol, distinguished by supermasculine aggressiveness, envy, and *Schadenfreude*.

The texts that have drawn me to Emerson's normative notion of teaching for lustres are principally two; first, his claim in "The Poet" that "An imaginative book renders us much more service at first, by stimulating us through its tropes, than afterward when we arrive at the precise sense of the author. I think nothing is of any value in books excepting the transcendental and extraordinary"; and second, his assertion in "Nominalist and Realist" that he reads "for the lustres, as if we should use a fine picture in a chromatic experiment for its rich colors." The painterly reference to a "fine picture" should not surprise us, as Emerson says in a journal entry for 1843 that he is and always has been a painter. It is a self-representation borne out by a close reading of his numerous essays, sermons, journals, and poetry, all of which teem with painterly tropes. His use of the word "experiment" underscores the experimentalism that is endemic to Emersonian transcendentalism, specifically in "Circles," where its author describes himself as an unsettler of "all things" and, contrary to popular belief, finds hope only in such unsettlement: "I simply experiment, an endless seeker with no Past at my back," as if to disavow what Harold Bloom calls "the anxiety of influence." "Rich colors" call attention to the fact that Emerson's transcendentalism is not a "monochromatic," formlessly white painting, in the pejorative phrase of Hegel, but one that is colorfully dappled, like the sublime motifs of his contemporaries Albert Bierstadt and Thomas Cole. The context for Emerson's admission of his painterly arrogation of voice is his remarking on the false expectations of the people coming to his lectures. "They came," he says, "believing that I was to realize the Republic described, and ceased to come when they found this reality no nearer. But I paint on."

Note that both texts that I have cited are about reading, not teaching as such, although reading for Emerson is a kind of pupillage, as writing for him is a kind of teaching. Both texts should be read interlinear with a journal entry from 1859 in which Emerson says, "In a true time, I should never have written." Emerson's meaning, albeit hyperbolized, is that he wrote in order to help ameliorate or redeem the moral and spiritual destitution that he found everywhere regnant in contemporary American society. Indeed, the achievement of his morally, culturally, and spiritually unachieved country is one of the *teloi* of the Emersonian teacher.

More to the point, Emerson's writings are laced with passages that make direct reference to issues of pedagogy and that credentialize the Emersonian teacher as one who teaches primarily for lustres, not argument. These texts fall into two groups: the first group exalts what Emerson calls "*Whim*," which he says he writes "on the lintels of the door-post" as a kind of transcendentalist *mezuzah*, in the phrase of Stanley Cavell, one that emblemizes its author's allergy to and incapacity for system, methodical writing, and argument, although he hopes that "it is something better than whim at last, but we cannot spend the day in explanation." Relevant here is a journal entry from 1838: "I have always been from my very incapacity of methodical writing a chartered libertine . . . I could not give account of myself if challenged. . . . For I do not know, I confess, what arguments mean in reference to any expression of a thought. I delight in telling what I think, but if you ask me how I dare say so or why it is so I am the most helpless of mortal men."

The second group of texts speak specifically, if obliquely, to the issue of the medium and mood of Emersonian writing / teaching. For example,

"Self-Reliance," notes that imaginative teachers have learned "to detect and watch that gleam of light which flashes across (the) mind from within, more than the lustre of the firmament of bards and sages." "Let a Stoic [teacher] open the resources of man, and tell men they are not leaning willows . . . and that the moment he acts from himself, tossing the laws, the books, idolatries, and customs out of the window, we pity him no more, but thank and revere him—and that teacher shall restore the life of man to splendor." The beginning of "Nature" makes the same point when it damns the retrospectiveness of the present age and specifically its building of "the sepulchres of the fathers," and encourages its readers to "enjoy an original relation to the universe." "Why should we grope among the dry bones of the past, or put the living generation into masquerade out its faded wardrobe? The sun shines today also. . . . There are new lands, new men, new thoughts." Hence, "Compensation's" chastising of those who, eschewing the posture of onwardness, "walk ever with reverted eyes like those monsters who look backwards." "Fate" contrastively tropes the human journey as "the liberty and glory of the way," finding, as "Experience" also finds, "the journey's end in every step of the road." In other words, the journey is its own measure, or, following John J. McDermott, "the nectar of the journey" is in the journeying, in its en-route affairing, not the journey's end.

To Emerson, the priority assigned to anteriority or sedimented meaning over "enjoying an original relation to the universe" is evidence of experiential impoverishment, and is a profanation of "The voice of he Almighty [that] saith, 'Up and onward for evermore!'" It is also a tragic foretelling of our age of fissiveness and fragmentation, which, in at least its postmodernist incarnation, has ironically come to read the former not as facts to be mourned but as virtues to be promoted. Hence, the postmodernist coronation of Emerson as a Yankee theorist of The Fragment, and the egregious misreading of his writings as a farrago of dispersions, diffractions, effusions, and evasions, as a "glittering mosaic of disconnected apercus." Is this The New Yet Unapproachable Emerson That Nobody Knows, except perhaps for a self-benighted coterie of postmodernist readers?

A journal entry from 1834 says that "A poem is made up of thoughts each of which filled the whole sky of the poet in its turn with its lustre." Why should not a teacher's teaching also instantiate such coruscating thoughts, filling the "whole sky" of his and his students's minds with their gleaming lustres? If the reader "leaps to the trope," why should not the teacher's students not also leap to his scintillant and febrile poetic imagination? Moreover, if it is true, as Emerson journalizes (1845), that "the best part . . . of every mind is not that which [it] knows, but that which hovers in gleams, suggestions, tantalizing unpossessed before [it]," why should not teaching for lustres, which is the same as teaching aesthetically or for beauty, also be a desideratum of pedagogical experience? Emerson says as much, Platonically hyperbolizing "this dancing chorus" as "the quarry" of [a man's] future, as "his possibility," one that "teaches him that his life is of a ridiculous brevity and meanness, but that it is his first age and trial only of his young wings, [and] that vast revolution, migrations, and gyres on gyres in the celestial societies invite him." Teaching for lustres, then, would not only be nutriment for "the best part . . . of every mind." It would also be, like Platonic love, the flying fact of being and the lubricant of the mind's transcendental turn. In the language of "Spiritual Laws," the Emersonian teacher is a "photometer, the goldleaf, the irritable foil," one who is both aureoled in splendor and luminously self-reliant (due either to natural endowment or conversion), and who, as a result, is able to so lustre his students that, as John J. McDermott Emersonianly says, "out of the doom of obviousness and repetition shall come the light, a light lit by the fire of [their] eyes."

In "The Over-Soul" the cardinal attribute of the Emersonian teacher is the sacredness of his teaching; and the essay's central pedagogical thesis is that all sacred teachers "speak *from within*, or from experience, as parties and possessors of the fact"; whereas profane teachers speak "*from without*, as spectators merely, or perhaps as acquainted with the fact on the evidence of third persons." Herbert, Kant, Spinoza, and Coleridge are named as sacred teachers; whereas Pope, Locke, Paley, MackIntosh, and Stewart are reckoned "men of the world . . . accomplished talkers," anti-enthusiasts who, lacking in rapture and "that shudder of awe and delight with which the individual soul always mingles with the universal soul," are little more than "Reasoning Machines," technicians of the profane, who grind into a flinty grist the lushness of experience. In "Intellect" the *Trismegisti* are added to the list, inclusive of Hermes, Empedocles, Plato, Plotinus, and Proclus. Emerson refers to them as a "band of grandees," who are "so vast in their logic, so primary in their thinking, that it seems antecedent to all the ordinary distinctions of rhetoric and literature, and to be at once poetry, and music, and dancing and astronomy and mathematics." "I am present at the sowing of the seed of the world. . . . The truth and grandeur of their thought is proved by its scope and applicability, for it commands the entire schedule and inventory of things for its illustration." "The Over-Soul" claims that we "stand continually in the expectation of the appearance" of such a sacred teacher, but that "if a man [does] not speak from within the veil, where the word is one with what it tells of, let him lowly confess it." Why "lowly (shamefully?) confess it"? Because experience is pedagogical and because, as Thoreau says, "Wisdom does not inspect, but behold. We must look a long time before we can see. Slow are the beginnings of philosophy."[5]

Absenting "an original relation to the universe," one tutored by the fervency of visionary or poetic imagination, experience becomes ersatz and a shill, and is likely to conduce to and legitimize compulsory miseducation, or, worse, what Paulo Freire balefully describes as "poisonous pedagogy." In

"The Scholar," Emerson, sounding very much like the Kafka of *The Trial*, admonishes the profane teacher thusly: "For the sure months are bringing him to an examination-day in which nothing is remitted or excused, and for which no tutor, no book, no lectures, and almost no preparation can be of the least avail. He will have to answer certain questions, which, I must plainly tell you, cannot be staved off. For all men and women, Time, your country, your condition, the invisible world, are the interrogators. *Who are you? What do you? Can you obtain what you wish? Is there method in your consciousness? Can you see tendency in your life? Can you help any soul?*"

In the spirit of Emerson's Coleridgean description of the "strongest readers" as those of "the Golconda, who are sieves picking up the diamonds only," we may also think of teaching for lustres as teaching for diamonds in the sense in which that word is used by Emerson in "Education": "We learn nothing rightly until we learn the symbolical character of life. . . . And presently the aroused intellect finds gold and gems in one of these scorned facts,—then finds that the day of facts is a rock of diamonds; that a fact is an Epiphany of God." By contrast, profane teaching teaches for paste, for "Diamonique," a gaudy and tawdry simulacrum. "Spiritual Laws" says that we "measure . . . the accumulations of the subtle element" or "the authentic effects of the true fire through every one of its million disguises." Why should the Emersonian teacher teach for anything less that such luminous aesthetic measurement? "Self-Reliance's" way of making this point is to claim, "When private men shall act with original views, the lustre will be transferred from the actions of kings to those of gentlemen." I read "gentleman" as two words, whose self-reliance and enjoyment of intimate relations with the universe is a form of *potentia* or power, one that shines on brightly from afar, even in a morally and spiritually bedimmed age such as Emerson's or our own, in which the capacity for dreaming beyond brown-out has been trumped by cynicism, hopelessness, and the absence of a courage to be. I read the transferral of lustres from the actions of kings to those of gentle men as saying: "The King (of repression, of darkness) is dead. Long live the (unrepressed, illumined) kingly (Aboriginal) Self on which a universal reliance may be grounded." Emerson calls "this primary wisdom . . . Intuition, whilst all later teachings are tuitions"; adding: "In that deep force, the last fact behind which analysis cannot go, all things find their common origin." Emerson's (and transcendentalism's) code-word for this "primary wisdom" is "matutinal," as in "morning knowledge," or knowledge that is a fresh and original engraftment upon the world. Its antonym is "vespertinal," as in "evening knowledge," or knowledge that is moth-eaten or a sere remains.

"Fate" claims that "the great man, that is, the man most imbued with the spirit of the time, is the impressionable man;—of a fiber irritable and delicate, like iodine to light," the one who "feels the infinitesimal attractions," and whose "mind is righter than others because he yields to a current so feeble as can be felt only by a needle delicately poised." Thusly envisaged, we may speak of the Emersonian teacher as the impressionable man par excellence, for whom an Orphic / Taoist yielding and reception are two of the distinguishing marks of both his teaching and existential presence. "History" says that the soul's health "consists in the fullness of its reception,—call it piety, call it veneration." It is an Emersonian "master tone," one that is instantiated by the claim, "All I know is by reception" and that is exalted in the poetry and prose of transcendentalism. It is also an epistemological posture reinherited by the modern and contemporary Orphic poetic traditions, from Wordsworth to Rilke to Mary Oliver. Thoreau calls such reception "the law of obedience," and like Emerson, says that the man who is more obedient than he is to the law is his master or teacher. Abandonment is the dialectical sister of reception, and is epitomized by "Circles's" conclusion that "The way of life is wonderful; it is by abandonment." It is a "master tone" that is umbilically connected to Emerson's notion of the ecstasy of adverbial vision and to his promotion of unsettlement as a necessary condition of freedom. Its scriptual basis is his reading of Matthew 10:34 and 19:21, whose mandate of abandonment "Intellect" interprets as, "Who leaves all, receives more." "Self-Reliance's" version is patently autobiographical: "I must be myself. I cannot beak myself any longer for you," viz. father, mother, wife, brother friend. "Compensation's" reading, like that of "Intellect's," is more universal, but the words "new house" subtextually attest its author's domestic discomfiture and his desire for a new mode of inhabitation: "Every soul is by this intrinsic necessity quitting its whole system of things, its friends and home and laws and faith, as the shell-fish crawls out of its beautiful stony case, because it no longer admits of its growth, and slowly forms a new house." In the same spirit, "Nature" says, "Know then, that the world exists for you . . . build, therefore your own world."

Emerson calls the postures of reception and abandonment "manly," but neither posture sponsors a Promethean stance of aggressivity. Yet he not only has been accused of supermasculine bravado. He has also been charged with abrogating his masculinity by shunning rivalrous argument and by privileging a view of the mind that promotes effeminating dainties over virilizing contestation. Is this why he has little if any standing in the academic philosophical community? Is this why what Cavell calls Emerson's "philosophicality," what "perfectionists," he says, will always "find ways" to figure as an "untaken way of life," continues to be denied or ignored by university philosophy departments? Is this why Emerson's "call for philosophy . . . is not comprehensible as asking for guardianship by a particular profession within what we call universities"?[6] At the Emerson centenary celebration in 1903, Hugo Munsterberg, a member of the Harvard philosophy department, spoke of the funds being raised to erect a statue to Emerson's memory outside of the building (now Emerson Hall) where the Harvard philosophy department was (and still is) housed. What has happened since 1903 that would help explain Emerson's liminal philosophical status? William James wrote in his diary thirty years earlier that "an age will come when . . . Emerson's philosophy will be in our bones, not our dramatic imagination." That age has yet to arrive, though never was the need for Emerson as a "healing remnant" greater than it is today. Like so many other American literary and philosophical geniuses, Emerson has been canonized, anthologized, marginalized, and then shelved as an intellectual curio. Indeed, our cultural bones have become so osteoporosic that nothing seems to calcify or nutrify them. Instead, we proliferate pseudomorphic and travestied versions of our saving remnants, including Emerson, whom most American children and adults know, if they know him at all, only as the author of the patriotic poem "Concord Hymn."

As I write this, just four years after the Emerson bicentenary, to most Americans, including most American philosophers, Emerson is a repressed cultural memory, a disowned founding father, one who has been epigrammatized on greeting cards and rarely read except in bowdlerized quotation. Lady Amnesia and Professor Cooptation have relegated him to the status of a relic or ruin, of an old duffer on Golden Pond, one suckled in a transcendentalist creed long outworn. The most notable exceptions to our cultural refusal to possess him except as an Old Curiosity Shop, as a kind of Grandpa Moses, are our better poets, writers, philosophers, and artists who continue to draw inspiration and sustenance from him, inclusive of the poets and philosophers assembled in this volume, and of Emerson inheritors from Charles Ives and the Emerson String Quartet, to W. E. B. DuBois and Martin Luther King.

Yet most Anglo-American philosophers generally have no philosophical use for poets, including poetic philosophers, whom they regard as intellectually soft or *infra dig*. Both a poet and a philosopher, Emerson believed the opposite, holding that "to the poet, to the philosopher . . . all things are friendly and sacred, all events profitable, all days holy, all men divine." The passage is quoted by Nietzsche, himself both a poet and philosopher, on the title page of the first German edition of *The Gay Science* (1882). But what happens to philosophy when it is disenchanted and debased into scientism and semantics, into an empiricidal empiricism and an obscurantist rationalism; when its most celebrated academic practitioners are sledge-hammering kill-joys born with knives in their head who "murder to dissect"? And what happens to poetry when, like philosophy, it becomes so seduced by the illusion of technique that it devolves into visionless meter-making and academic formalisms? Where, then, as Bloom provocatively asks, "shall wisdom be found"? And who shall be its lovers? Or as Thoreau, at the conclusion of his first book (1849), pedagogically asks: "But where is the instructed teacher? Where are the *normal* schools?"

Mindful of Emerson's prolific use of the language of fire and specifically of his reference to us as "children of the fire" and as "torches in the wind," and mindful also of the semantic association of lustres with fieriness, teaching for lustres may be taken to be the same as teaching flammeously, meaning teaching for color, shining, and resplendence. Commenting on the obligation of colleges "to teach elements," "The American Scholar" says colleges "can only highly serve us, when they aim not to drill, but to create; when they gather from far every ray of various genius to their hospitable halls, and by their concentrated fires, set the hearts of their youth on flame." Or, as Yeats revises Emerson: "Education is not the filling of a pail, but the lighting of a fire." By contrast, "apparatus and pretension avail nothing." "Among the multitude of scholars and authors we feel no hallowing presence; we are sensible of a knack and skill rather than inspiration; they have a light, and know not whence it comes, and call it their own; their talent is some exaggerated faculty, some overgrown member, so that their strength is a disease." As Emerson admonishes: "The spirit only can teach. Not any profane man, not any sensual, not any liar . . . but only he can give, who has; he can only create, who is. The man, on whom his soul descends, through whom the soul speaks, alone can teach. Courage, piety, love, wisdom can teach . . . But the man who aims to speak as books enable, as synods use, as the fashion guides, and as interest commands, babbles. Let him hush." "We do not wish to make believe [that we are] instructed, we wish to be ravished, inspired, and taught." But "instead of Man Thinking, we have the bookworm" and the glossator, "the restorers of readings, the emendators, and bibliomaniacs of all degrees." By contrast, "the teacher of the coming age must occupy himself in the study & explanation of the moral constitution of man more than in the elucidation of difficult texts. He must work in the conviction that . . . as long as the heart & the mind are illumined by a spiritual life there is no dead letter but a perpetual Scripture." As Emerson journalizes (1834): "When anyone comes who speaks with better insight into moral nature, he will be the new gospel . . . from one the constitution of man may be got better teaching still." Following Cavell, "constitution" should be read here, as elsewhere in Emerson, politically as well as personally: "The endlessly repeated idea that Emerson was only interested in finding the individual should give way or to make way for the idea that this quest was his way of founding a nation, writing its constitution, constituting its citizens."[7] In other words, moral and political issues of democracy and education serially entwine and feed one another in Emerson, as they also do in his most seminal pragmatic inheritors, from John Dewey to John J. McDermott.

In "Celebration of Intellect," Emerson breaks his lance against colleges and universities that have betrayed their public trust, sacrificing education on the altar of political sycophantry. In a text that is remarkably contemporary in its condemnation of the bureaucratization of so-called "higher education," Emerson offers: "'Tis because the college was false to its trust, because the scholars did not learn and teach, because they were traders and left their altars and libraries and worship of truth and played the sycophant to presidents and generals and members of Congress, and gave degrees and literary and social honors to those whom they ought to have rebuked and exposed, incurring the contempt of those whom they ought to put in fear, then the college is suicidal; ceases to be a school; power oozes out of it just as fast as truth does; and instead of overawing the strong, and upholding the good, it is a hospital for decayed tutors." In a journal entry from 1834, Emerson speaks of American colleges and universities as having become a duncedom: "A young man is to be educated & schools are built & masters brought together & gymnasiums erected & scientific toys & Monitorial Systems & a College endowed with many professorships & the apparatus is so enormous & unmanageable that the e-ducation or *calling out of his faculties* is never accomplished, he graduates a dunce," short on experience and dumb as a post, and doomed to occupy a permanent "freshman's seat in the world." "Spiritual Laws" puts the point somewhat less acidulously: "What we do not call education is more precious than that which we call so . . . We pass in the world for sects and schools, for erudition and piety, and we are all the time jejune babes." "The University, as it is ludicrously called," has scandalously betrayed its pedagogical duty to remove "all obstructions" to the student's "genius, or his nature, or his turn of mind." Almost without exception, it has metamorphosized into a deadening and grey-domed bureaucracy whose chief functions are economic and political; and for whom the "leading out of the Soul" is hubristically shelved as a Platonic anachronism. As the author of *Walden* revises Emerson: ". . . that economy of living which is synonymous with philosophy is not even seriously professed in our colleges." *Plus ça chance, plus c'est la même chose.*[8]

In claiming that the sacred teacher sets aflame the hearts of his students, Emerson wants us to understand that the beginning of wisdom is inspiration, and that sacred teaching is an act of love, of Eros, which in inflaming the affections emblazes and draws out the "active soul," "the one thing in the world of value." In other words, sacred teaching is cardiological, whereas profane teaching is merely logical or propositional. The following passage from "The Over-Soul" is quintessential Emerson: "When we have broken our god of tradition, and ceased from our god of rhetoric, then may God fire the heart with his presence. It is the doubling of the heart itself, nay the infinite enlargement of the heart with a power of growth to a new infinity on every side." The infinitized heart is a cardiological revision of "Nature's" innumerably sided "absolute *Ens*," and is a fiery foreshadowing of Emerson's "central doctrine," which he defines in a journal entry from 1840 as "the infinitude of the private man." I read the doubling of the heart as affectively co-extensive with the ecstatic experience of the world, and I connect the heart's doubling to Emerson's doubling of the self-God relationship and to his finding of the sublime in the ordinary. The heart's doubling should not be read as Hallmark kitsch, but as a metaphysical birthmark of our human mode of inhabitation, one that underscores our limitless capacity for loving and caring, for service and compassion; and note, in this connection, that Emerson calls the American scholar "the world's heart." "Treat men as pawns and ninepins," "Compensation" warns, "and you shall suffer as well as they. If you leave out their heart, you shall lose your own."

In a destitute time, such as Emerson's was, such as our own is, whole-heartedness or "the doubling of the heart" is redemptive, if not salvific. Say it is "the heart-by-heart resuscitation" of our moral, cultural, and spiritual heart-lessness, whose symptoms include what Dewey, revising Emerson, calls "the humdrum; slackness of loose ends . . . rigid abstinence, coerced submission, tightness on one side to dissipation, incoherence, and aimless indulgence on the other."[9] For the ontologically disheartened, ordinary experience "doesn't sing, it spits," in the more colloquial idiom of John J. McDermott. Hence, the anaesthetic drifting and "snatching at distractions" of the disinheartened, and their ritualized cultivation of exotica, esoterica, and narcotica as substitute gratifications. Having lost the capacity to take heart, theirs is a catch-as-catch-can culling of ersatz satisfactions, from "intoxicants and anodynes to mild sprees and saturnalia." For the Miss Lonely Hearts of the world, "the plain sense of things" becomes, under such circumstances, an unhealable "malady of the quotidian," one stigmatized by "artificial stimulation" and the "subconscious nursings of festering sore spots."

The cardiological coefficient of Emersonian teaching is indebted to both Augustine's exaltation of "good fire" as the catalyst of the soul's journeying to God, and, less belatedly, to Jonathan Edwards's "inward ardor and burning of heart" as the gestation of "new appetites, and a new kind of breathings . . . and groanings that cannot be uttered," ones that he also calls the "sweetnesses and delights" of the heart's "circumcision." Everything else, for Edwards, is "mere flowers." The Emersonian teacher is able to set hearts aflame, to teach for lustres, because he is a mind on fire, one who is himself lustred and "loaded with life." No wonder we continually and anxiously await the advent of such a sacred teacher, whom "The Poet" calls "the timely man . . . the reconciler." For not only is his aesthetic presence a shimmering and a hallowing; the central task of his teaching is to transform our "spotted," "cribbed," and "maudlin(ly) agglutinated" lives into a forever-younged New Morning of wakeful and numinous selfhood. As Emerson journalizes (1841): "I think that only is real which men love and rejoice in—not the things which starve & freeze & terrify them." "Whilst we converse with what is above us," "Self-Reliance" says, "we do not grow old, but grow young. Infancy, youth, receptive, aspiring . . . counts itself nothing and abandons itself to the instruction flowing from all sides . . . [Let] "the man and woman of seventy . . . who have outlived their hope and talk down to the young be lovers; let them behold truth; and their eyes are uplifted, their wrinkles smoothed, and they are perfumed again with hope and power. This old age ought not to creep on a human mind. In nature, every moment is new."

What Emerson calls "perpetual" or "perennial" youth—a theme that is repeatedly explored in his writing—is an affective quality of body / mind / spirit, which presumably is catalyzed by a radical shift in angle of vision, from the "wrinkled calculator" of the Understanding to the "leaping lightning" of Reason or Poetic Imagination. The experiential context for such a shift in consciousness is not a room of one's own, but the great American outdoors, from the pinewoods to the stars. Relevant here is a journal entry from 1839, in which Emerson describes "the substance of [his] shrift" as inviting men and women, "drenched in Time," "to recover themselves and come out of time, and taste their native immortal air." Note that Emerson's invitation is gustatory, not visual, as if coming out of time were both a nectaring of the spirit and an inoculation against the prose of the world. But how, we may ask, is such a transcendentalist turn of consciousness possible for Jane and John Doe in an age of wing-clipped "Commodity"? Is Emerson's invitation so irresistible as to rouse the Does from their indolence or sleep? Or switching metaphors, is, as Thoreau believes, the mellifluous crowing of a transcendentalist "chanticleer standing on his roost" sufficient to awaken the Does from their metaphysical slumbering? Will chanticleer's lusty cock-a-doodle-doing be enough to slip them from their moorings and carry them into empyrean? Both Emerson and Thoreau obviously think so. The upshot of the Does's journey is that they will be forever-younged, and, *a fortiori*, will change their lives accordingly. Moreover, their bloom and splendor is likely to be contagious, spreading to their neighbors and beyond. As a check against the possibility of their backsliding, Emerson expresses the hope (half-seriously?) that "a time will come when there will be a telescope in every street," in order to provide a permanent visual reminder to the Does of their cosmic bearings, and of their ontological need to hitch their unlustred wagsons to the blazing furnaces of the stars. He is not asking them to become transparent eyeballs or "debauchees of dew," whose heads, like that of the mad transcendentalist poet Jones Very, "run up into a spire." He is asking them rather to acknowledge the cosmic setting of their lives from which the "poor-spirited age" has cut them off experientially. He rephrases the point pedagogically and aesthetically in a journey entry for 1865: "Of all tools, an observatory is the most sublime . . . What is so good in a college as an observatory? The sublime attaches to the door & to the first stair you ascend, and this is the road to the stars." The wedge that turns into a rocket here is the visual and gustatory experience of the beauty and "immortal air" of American cosmic nature. Later, we shall see evidence of a slightly different Emerson, one for whom the wedge-cum-rocket is auditory, not visual or gustatory, and one that is energized by "the call" of cosmic beauty. In both cases, the affective is the effective, although the meaning of the word "effective" in the second case seems to be more socially consequential, as it presumptively leads to the consciousness "of [a] force to shake the world."

In "Experience," Emerson's most philosophical essay and a rewriting of Montaigne's essay by the same name, he analogizes man to "a bit of Labrador spar, which has no lustre as you turn it in your hand until you come to a particular angle; then it shows deep and beautiful colors." In *A Pluralistic Universe*, William James revises Emerson's trope, substituting the language of extrication for that of turning: "Everything is smothered in the litter that is fated to accompany it. Without too much you cannot have enough, of anything . . . The gold-dust comes to birth with the quartz-sand all around it. . . . There must be an extrication. . . . The clay matrix and the noble gem must first come into being unsifted. . . . Once extricated, the gem can be examined separately . . . but this process of extrication cannot be short-circuited—or if it is, you get the thin inferior abstractions which we have seen . . . instead of the more living divine reality." Placed in the tuition of an Emersonian teacher, our lackluster selves are made to shine with a radiance and splendor that is an efflorescence from the deep inner hollows of our bodies, as when we fall in love and, shucking off our larval cerements, we experience ourselves as silver-shod astronauts of Eros who "sow the sun and moon for seeds." Hence, the lovers' all-over bodily joy after a long night's sweet comminglings from head unto feet. Thusly aglow, everything seems illuminated to our hypothetical lovers / students, as in Mark Strand's magnificent poem "The Continental College of Beauty," which is reproduced in this volume. In his poem a city is awash and ablaze with beauty, is an environ of "angelic surprise, of impalpable chance. . . . nothing but lustre washing the streets, . . . the prose of everyday life . . . turning to gold." Like Emerson's poet, Strand has "turned the world to glass," showing us "things in their right series and procession." And as if by wizardry, what seemed to have been a dun sparrow has metamorphosized into a great speckled bird with a Whitmanesque "similitude [interlocking] all."

There is no richer description anywhere in Emerson's writings of the methodology of the Emersonian teacher than that contained in the "Labrador spar" passage that I have quoted from "Experience." The phrase "beautiful colors" conjures Emerson's painterly or aesthetic account of his reading for lustres, in which, to repeat, he asks us to imagine him (ourselves) using a text as if it were "a fine picture in a chromatic experiment" that he (we) are exploring "for its rich colors." But the key words in the Labrador spar passage are "angle" and "turn." "Angle" calls attention to Emerson's perspectivism ("What is there but the angle of vision"?), a doctrine that is epistemologically inherited by Nietzsche, William James, and G. H. Mead, among others. The word "turn" is a philosophical inheritance of Plato's use of the word in the cave parable in Book 7 of *The Republic*. It also evokes Martin Buber's use of the Hebrew word *teshuvah* or turning in his analysis of the silent existential movements of genuine dialogic encounter, as, for example, may happen between a master teacher and a receptive student. As Emerson perceptively notes: "There is no adaptation or universal applicability in men, but each has his special talent, and the mastery of successful men consists in adroitly keeping themselves where and when that turn shall be oftenest to be practiced." I read Emerson as saying that the self is a kaleidoscope, which in the soft and deft hands of a lustred teacher will experience "lush (Stevensian) chorals" spiraling through its fire. Bloom nominates this discovery as "the first principle for Emersonian genius," and correctly sees that the principle is not simply a literary one, but one that "transcends reading and indeed is transcendence itself." But he fails to see the pedagogical application of the principle. Specifically, he fails to see the powerful enactment of this stance of transcendence by both the Emersonian teacher, who is an *Überleser* and *Übermensch*, and by his students who, once awakened from their indolence, will find that their pyrite has been transmuted into gold; and that, contrary to Robert Frost, their gold will stay. Relevant here is Emerson's first sermon, "Pray without Ceasing" based on 1 Thessalonians: 5:17, in which he warns his congregants: "Beware, (if it teach nothing else let it teach this) beware of indolence, the suicide of the soul, that lets the immortal faculties, each in their orbit of light, wax dim and feeble, and star by star expire." For indolence eats up our "giant energies," and transmogrifies us into moral dwarves, "puny suffers[s] tottering, ill at ease, in the Universe."

In a more optative mood, Emerson journalizes (1831): "Were you ever instructed by a wise and eloquent man? Remember then, were not the words that made your blood run cold, that brought the blood to your cheeks, that made you tremble or delighted you—did they not sound to you as old as yourself? Was it not truth that you knew before, or do you ever expect to be moved from the pulpit or from man by anything but plain truth? Never. It is god in you that responds to God without, or affirms his own words trembling on the lips of another." Hence the claimed existential transfusiveness of Emersonian teaching: "There is no teaching until the pupil is brought into the same state or principle in which you are; a transfusion takes place; he is you and you are he; then is a teaching, and by no unfriendly chance or bad company can he quite lose the benefit."[10] Of course, should such transfusion so blur the difference between teacher and pupil as to problematize their individuality, then you have, as in transference-love gone awry, pathological merger not authentic self-becoming.

Four years later, the hyperbole of transfusion gives way to the more cautious language of diagonality: "There is never a coincidence, but always a diagonal line drawn partaking of the genius of the tutor & the genius of the pupil . . . two precious madmen who cannot conspire." Why "madmen"? What has happened to account for such a radical shift in authorial mood and conviction? Perhaps the answer lies in Emerson's reiterated use of the language of diagonality in his essay "Solitude and Society," wherein he notes that "our safety is in the skill with which we keep the diagonal line" between the self and society. If no diagonality, then possible coincidence, and if coincidence, then not merely bereaved self-reliance, but worse, possible emasculation. As "Self-Reliance" famously says: "Society everywhere is in conspiracy against the manhood of every one of its members. "Members," of course, is a double-entendre, connoting both the political and the phallic. Hence, "no covenants but proximities"; hence, the Emersonian self as porcupine, as "infinitely repellent orb." Note here the semantic kinship between "conspire" in the journal entry from 1845 and "conspiracy" in the earlier passage from "Self-Reliance." And note the triple-entendre of "conspire," as in conspiring against, but also as in having to do with, and more primally as in having to breathe with, as if the incapacity for the second is a function of the deoxygenated state of the third; and as if diagonality, not coincidence, is the aversive self's best defense against the conspiracy of society to devirilize or dismember it. Pedagogically translated, the teacher and student walk a dangerous tightrope between the transfusion of blood-making marrow and their mutual abrogation of self-reliance, or what is the same, their mutual unmanning. "He is you and you are he" is *Wuthering Heights* or The Beatles at their psychedelic worst. "I am me and you are you, and we are sometimes both together" is anthemic Yankee horse-sense.

William James's formulation of the teacher / student relationship in *Talks to Teachers on Psychology* avoids all the issues raised by Emerson, and, more significantly, is dead-on pedagogically: ". . . you must simply work your pupil into such a state of interest in what you are going to teach that every other object of attention is banished from his mind; then reveal it to him so impressively that he will remember the occasion to his dying day; and finally fill him with devouring curiosity to know what the next steps in connection with the subject are . . . divination and perception, not psychological paedagogics or theoretic strategy are the only helpers here."

The words "old as yourself" in the 1831 journal entry conjure what Stevens calls the rediscovery of a "lost nakedness," a trope that I am led to connect to Freud's notion of the effulgence of infant being, and to the left-wing Freudian notion of the possible recuperation of the all-over lustred condition of infant being as a paradigm of post-repressive cultural experience. Ever the cultural conservative, Freud could only find in mystical experience the possibility of such recuperation, although his ascription of a seamless, "all-embracing feeling" to infant being, of which our "present ego-feeling" is but a shrunken residue," is an incisive, albeit belated, inheritance of Emerson's analogous depiction of our contemporary fall into fraction. In "Nature," Emerson's Orphic poet proleptically instructs him that the contemporary self has "shrunk to a drop"; and taking up this line of thought from "Nature," "The American scholar" speaks of the the human condition as "spilled into [ungatherable] drops," entymologizing this strewn spillage as grub like, as "bugs" and "spawn."

But "Nature" contrastively salutes "Infancy (as) the perpetual Messiah," as an antidote to such shrinkage and spillage; and six years later (1842), we read Emerson hailing "the child, the infant" as "a Teacher" "who charms us all." Indeed, many of Emerson's writings are redolent with references to infancy that Wordsworthianly celebrate "The Child (as) Father of the man," a text that Freud also belatedly appropriates in his privileging of childhood as the paradigm for human self-development. As the soul is "a jet of light," so infancy is a stream of luminosity; and "The child, the infant is a transcendentalist *in statu nascendi.*" Revising Freud's discussion of the polymorphously perverse condition of infant being, we may describe the Emersonian teacher's mode of embodiment, his existential presence, as suffusively erotic and aesthetic. Like Thoreau's red maple, he is "full of ripe juices, from lowest to topmost spire, all aglow. . . . Visible for miles, too fair to be believed." More significantly, its brilliantly hued fluttering leaves "teach us"—better than Plato or Montaigne, two of Emerson's "representative men"—"how to die."[11] So astonishingly lustred are these electrically colored naturalistic teachers that "even the truants are caught and educated the moment they step abroad." The radical empirical assumption upon which this existential wisdom rests is that we are not outsiders or self-encapsulated egos sealed in the calcium of our skulls, but insiders, uterinely and metabolically wedged into nature's tissue structure, not different in this respect from the soil of a forest or the surface of a pond. In the biophysical and gastronomic idiom of John J. McDermott, "we are floating, gestating organisms eating all the while"; "livering" permeable membranes, not linguistic condoms.[12]

A wheel on fire himself, the teacher is also a "conductor of the whole river of electricity," one who is both electrified and electrifying. His Romantic burning after the "*aliquid immensum infinitumque*" (something unlimited and boundless), coupled with "the fiery grain" in his authorial voice and the "pencil of fire" in his writerly hand, fill both his presence and page with forked lightning; and finding yourself in his tuition, you know in an instant that "you must change your life," and that you must do so "immediately, flamboyantly. No exceptions." Greened by the Emersonian teacher's constant gardening, you come to believe, as William James says Emersonianly in *The Varieties of Religious Experience*, that "[k]nowledge about life is one thing; effective occupation of a place in life, with dynamic currents running through your being, is another." Call this James's (and Emerson's) existential pragmatism, the posture of which is dynamically occupational not epistemically voyeuristic. Or as Emerson puts the point in "Circles," "the coming only is sacred. Nothing is secure but life, transition, [and] the energizing spirit."

But suppose your burning is not as flammeous as your teacher's, but is rather a hard gemlike one, or one that is a slow smouldering. Isaiah 33:14 wisely asks: "Can anyone live in endless burning"? Nietzsche notwithstanding, the answer to Isaiah's question is, for most of us, a resounding "No," even for those "few persons of purer fire," that happy few of "exciters and monitors, collectors of the heavenly spark, with power to convey the electricity to others"; those "rare and gifted men, [who] compare the points of our spiritual compass, and verify our bearings from superior chronometers" whom Emerson calls "transcendentalists," and for whom, following Emily Dickinson, the flaming redheaded Belle of Amherst, "A Lightning in the Germ" is not enough. They, she assures us, "demand the Flame." For these "exacting children" and "novices," "their heart is the ark in which the fire is concealed which shall burn in a broader and universal flame." The conclusion of "The Transcendentalist" finds its author surprised by "the largeness of the (Movement's) effect," having (falsely?) seen "how little kernel there was to that comet which had shed terror from its flaming hair on the nations, how few and what cinders of genius." But before the reader can bat an eye Emerson's surprise turns into "a favorable inference about the intellectual and spiritual tendencies of our people." In other words, the little kernel has swelled into a diapason of hopefulness, as its cinders of genius have fanned into flame the possibility of the nation's constitutional self-recovery. "The Young American" says hope is "the prolific mother of reforms," and in a destitute time, such as our own, such as Emerson's was, the continual deferral of hope, especially among the young, undercuts the possibility of such cultural self-recovery, and in so doing sickens the heart, including the heart of the country.

In *Touched with Fire*, a study of manic-depressive illness and the artistic temperament, Kay Redfield Jamison persuasively argues that a "mind on fire" may be as psychologically dangerous as it is spiritually emancipating. She specifically claims that Emerson's mental inflammability and his self-confessed incapacity to "farm" his contrarian moods are evidence of clinical bipolarity, a diagnosis born out by a close reading of his voluminous journal. But were Emerson simply a "cheerful monist" who always saw one not two, were he to have had no tragic sense of life, no "thorn in the flesh," he would indeed have been the woolgathering Pollyanna whom his most unsympathetic critics have taken him to be. Moreover, it is the "wounded warrior" in Emerson that causes us, his post-Freudian, post-Holocaustic, postexistentialist readers, to resonate powerfully with his writing. Indeed, plagued by our own considerable mishaps and misadventures, we take heart in a man who is not merely open about his own "dark spots" and misdemeanors but who also knows how to use them pedagogically and in a way that is both cheering and transformational. Is not this why we are magnetically drawn to the Emersonian teacher as filings to a lodestone? Why he is the lodestar of our journey, the polestar of our mental gaze? Why, following "The American Scholar," we repair to his lamp "when the intervals of darkness come, as come they must"? Why we follow him adoratively in the jingle jangle New Morning of our numinous self-quickening? For he is our soul-food, our nectar and ichor, and we are his care-kin, starvelings in search of calories or sustenance, clipped buds who, if unnourished by his nectaring, may die on the vine of our rubicund youth.[13]

Unfortunately, Emerson does not make the etymological and semantic connection between lustres and lustration. But his requirement of a "collyrium" that would wash the mud of egotism at the bottom of the eye, and, *mutatis mutandis*, cure us of our "opthalmia," is an optical analogue of the ceremonial washing and purification that defines a lustration. Moreover, "Education's" lament over our "uneducated bodies" and its celebration of their anointment by poetic lustration, by a kind of *mikvah* or ritual bathing, may be read as a brightening by washing of our whiter shade of pale. William Carlos Williams's plainer version goes to the heart of the matter: "BRIGHTen / the cor / ner / where / you / are!" In *Agon*, Bloom makes the connection that Emerson ignores, linking the word "lustre" to Walter Benjamin's "aura," Longinus's "*hupsos*" (the sublime), Ralph Cudworth's "exposition of the astral body," and finally to the Kabbalistic "*zelem*" (ethereal or subtle body). In a more recent book on the subject of genius, Bloom interprets lustres as referring "to the condition of shining by reflected light, the gloss or sheen that one genius imparts to another, when juxtaposed in my mosaic." In the spirit of Bloom's reading of lustres, I am led to think of Emerson's own "mosaic" of pedagogical geniuses, the ones pantheonized in "Representative Men" and elsewhere, as instantiating such a condition of mutual shining by "reflective light." Is not this how we should understand the community of Emersonian American scholars? In a sermon entitled "This Do in Remembrance of Me," based on Luke 22:19, and delivered on September 26, 1829, when Emerson was but twenty-six, he makes the same point pedagogically and peripatetically: "The results of an old philosopher are the elements of his pupil. Their harvest is our seed. . . . I think . . . the conversation of a wise man or the study of a good book or anything else that has a tendency to excite the affections or impart light . . . will teach us to walk in the world as having received the light of another."

If, as Bloom says, we should think of lustres as "gestures of freedom," then it follows that to those "strong originals" who have delivered us from what Stevens calls "the rotted names," the severest criticism is due, lest in swooning at their feet we extinguish our own spark of radiance by sycophantic imitation. Call this the exaltation of the Student's Sublime, and say it is also the Emersonian teacher's sublimest bequest to his students. As Whitman instructs us in "Song of Myself": "[Y]ou shall listen to all sides and filter them through yourself"; "all I mark as my own you shall offset it with your own." Or more succinctly, in an 1861 "Unpublished Introduction" to *Leaves of Grass*: "[Y]ou must do the work"; meaning, "you must find out for yourself"; "not the book so much needs to be the complete thing, but the reader of the book does." And, following John J. McDermott following Martin Buber, "You are really able!"[14]

But suppose that we do not think of lustres as stances of freedom or self-cultivation but as tropes of aesthetic delight. In other words, suppose that teaching for lustres is interpreted tropologically not ontologically and that, thusly refigured, aesthetic delectation not numinous self-becoming is its *modus vivendi*. In other words, suppose that the *telos* of reading / teaching for lustres is "delectative duration" or *juissance* (as opposed to intellectual power or wisdom), especially if the text is a marbled iridescent one, such as, say, Emerson's is. Surely one can imagine "moods" in which we (and Emerson, whose writings are a veritable bouillabaisse of moods) find ourselves reading / teaching for tropes not power. But if such a mood were ritualized in our reading / teaching, if we mainly or, worse, only read / taught for tropes, this would imply, as Bloom correctly says, our assigning "a priority to figurative language over meaning," an assignment ardently promoted by the most solipsistic members of "the tribe of Waldo," from Richard Poirier to William Gass.

But our human condition is not merely a "habitation of words." Contrary to Stevens, the "words of the world" are not coterminous with the "the life of the world"; and life does not merely consist "of propositions about life." Whatever propositions may be—and there is considerable philosophical disagreement about their logical and ontic status—it seems clear that experience is richer than our most seminal wording of it. Indeed, the most that we can ever hope to bring home from its moveable feast are linguistic crumbs, as the James brothers, William and Henry, repeatedly remind us. If language is primarily a form of life or conduct, and only secondarily a purple trope to be privately and lubriciously savored, how can we not grizzle at Stevens's glossing of the relationship between language and life? Could the author of *The Conduct of Life* really have meant to be understood as defending an effete aestheticism, according to which reading / teaching for lustres is synonymous with the solipsistic belief that all that there is is metaphor? Clearly not, as the text quoted earlier from "The Poet" speaks only of being stimulated "through tropes" and "afterward . . . [arriving] at the precise sense of the author." Moreover, "The Poet's" promotion of "meter-making argument" over "the finish" of verses makes it tolerably clear that it is meaning not varnishing that Emersonian poetry exalts. A journal entry from 1839 enjoins us to "Treat all things poetically," from the most sundry to the most sublime, saying that "we must have fire under the Andes at the core of the world." Orphically rephrased, Emerson's is an aesthetic imperative to live or dwell poetically, and is more or less congruent with both Rilke's and the late Heidegger's ontologizing of poetry as a mode of inhabitation. Corollary with the latter is the view that language originates in hearing not speaking, a view that is inextricably connected to Emerson's aeolian metaphysics and to what he calls "the doctrine of perpetual revelation," by which he means to celebrate the instructiveness of every moment.

As "The Poet" intones: "poetry was written"—meaning inscribed into the nature of things—"before time was"; it is "a sort of tomb of the muses," as language itself is "fossil poetry." The "men of more delicate ear . . . can penetrate into that region where the air is music . . . and write down more faithfully the cadences" miraculously tissued into nature. Vis-á-vis Plato, for whom philosophy is a talisman against the bewitchments of poetry, Emerson ascribes to poets, not philosophers, the pedagogical role of human liberation. Calling them "the children of music" and "liberating gods," through whom the divine *aura* breathes, it is the sacred transcendentalist poet, not the idealist philosopher-king, who unlocks our chains and leads us out of our caves or cellars into "the open air." In an earlier journal entry (1834), Emerson draws the pedagogical conclusion of the poet's emancipatory practice: "The whole secret of the teacher's force lies in the conviction that men are convertible. And they are. They want awakening. Get the soul out of bed, out of her deep habitual sleep, out into God's universe, to a perception of its beauty, and hearing of its call, and your vulgar man, your prosy, selfish sensualist ["Mr. Prose & Mr. Hoarse-as-Crows"] awakes, a god, and is conscious of force to shake the world." Albeit overwritten, the last clause of this journal entry gives a kind of pragmatic tensility to the claimed awakening of the "prosy selfish sensualist" by the call of cosmic beauty. Here the agency of awakening is auditory not visual; and, *a fortiori*, the awakened soul seems to be a divinized meliorist, "conscious of force to shake the world." Or does "shake" here not mean remake, but merely "*épater le bourgeois*"? Emerson looks "in vain for the poet" he describes, observing that "we have yet had no genius in America, with tyrannous eye, which knew the value of our incomparable [poetic] materials," of our ample and dazzling geography. In *Songlines*, Bruce Chatwin says, "an unsung land is a dead land"; and indeed Emerson calls his America "a dead pond," one stacked with "snivelling nobodies," all "dying of miscellany," yet all choking on tropes. Time may have bequeathed to America "many gifts, but not yet "the reconciler, whom all things await. It is the same point that Whitman will powerfully remake twenty-one years later in the *Preface* to *Leaves of Grass*.

In other words, the poet of whom "The Poet" speaks futuristically is the quintessential teacher, in the most elastic sense of the word. It is for him "we all stand waiting, empty" and "at the side of road," as if he were a slow train coming. From where? From out of the wilderness with locusts and honey in his mouth, as Thoreau had imagined? From the journalistic bowels of Brooklyn, out of which Walt Whitman would emerge with a twirling tongue, claiming its encompassing of volumes of worlds? "Shall not a poet redeem us from . . . idolatries, and pale their legendary lustre before the fires of the Divine Wisdom which burn in his heart"? "Circles" says that when the poet / teacher comes he will "convert the statues into fiery men, and by a flash of his eye [will] burn up the veil which shrouded all things"; and, anticipating the Rilke of the Ninth "Duino Elegy," "the meaning of the very furniture, of cup and saucer, of chair and clock and tester, [will become] manifest." And when he comes, he will come as "the fuller minstrel," one who will "ring out, ring out the mournful rhymes," and ring in the "*ascension* or the passage of the soul into higher forms." To those so aggrieved by "the dwarfishly Actual" as to seek abroad "the exorbitant Idea," Emerson avuncularly advises: "Best swallow this pill of America, which fate brings to you & sing a land unsung. Here stars, here birds, here trees, here hills abound and the vast tendencies concur of a new Order." The American landscape painter, Asher Durand, agreed, writing home after making the "grand tour" of Europe in 1840 with his fellow painters Casilear and Kensett: ". . . for real and unalloyed enjoyment of scenery, the rocks, trees and green meadows of Hoboken will have a charm that all Switzerland cannot boast."[15]

The poet's advent, Emerson says, as if clapping his hands "in infantine joy and amazement," will be better than the day of his own birth. For the poet / teacher will come as a singer / dancer, as a celebrant of "a new and excellent region of life," one that Emerson analogizes to the discovery "in flashes of light" of an environ of "profound beauty and repose," as if the clouds that covered it parted at intervals and showed the approaching traveler the inland mountains, with the tranquil eternal meadows spread at their base, whereon flocks graze and shepherds pipe and dance." "Young with the life of life . . . what a future it opens! I feel the new heart beating with the love of the new beauty. I am ready to die out of nature and be born again into this new yet unapproachable America I found in the West," the America unveiled by Lewis and Clark, paradisiacally painted by Albert Bierstadt, and celebrated in a nearly liturgical mood by Emerson in "Experience," by Thoreau in "Walking" and by Whitman in *Democratic Vistas*.

As the poet Rilke ontologizes Emerson: "*Gesang ist Dasein*," Song is Reality. "The Poet's" version of this Orphic wisdom is that "the soul of the thing is reflected by a melody. The sea, the mountain-ridge, Niagara, and every flower-bed pre-exist, or super-exist, in pre-cantations, which sail like odors in the air." In other words, the universe is a tuning-fork, one that is permeatively, homeopathically, and opalescently dosed with spirit and melodious song. Analogously, America's hills are alive with the sound of music, but, alas, are blighted by the "young scholars" who devastate them unreligiously." "Blight" calls the latter "thieves and pirates of the universe," fragmentists of a fragmented world, from whom are withheld the "nectar and ambrosia"; and who "shut out / Daily to a more thin and outward rind, / Turn pale and starve," or like Emerson himself at the poem's beginning, "die of inanition." Emerson, we know, placed an aeolian harp in the window of his study so that he could hear nature caroling the songs of herself to him as he read and wrote. His final words on the subject are *non pareil*: "But life is good only when it is magical and musical, a perfect timing and consent, and when we do not anatomize it. You must treat the days respectfully, you must be a day yourself, and not interrogate it like a college professor . . . Cannot we be a little abstemious and obedient? Cannot we let the morning be?"[16]

As I understand it, teaching for lustres conduces to self-electrification leading to self-fecundation leading to self-recovery. But "Love" says that beauty, including the beauty of self-sparkling, is as unapproachable as rainbow-like "opaline doves-neck lustres, hovering and evanescent"; and "Nature" (1844), generalizing about the "referred existence" or "absence" that stigmatizes both "men and women" and "the silent trees," asks whether beauty is so horsed on the Proteus as to be effectively ungraspable. Does Emerson's troping of truth as a "fly-away," a "slyboots," imply that the self quickened and gemmed by lustres is also unapproachable, including to itself? If so, would not such epistemic unapproachability be incompatible with education, with "the Drawing out of the soul"? If lustres are thusly construable, how do teachers and their students ever learn anything except how to savor the succulence of tropes, even if the savoring is a honeyed torah on the tongue? Moreover, would not such an over-aestheticized troping of lustres likely conduce to a decadent "superfineness" and "delicatesse," one arrogated to an *aristoi* of aesthetic snobs and mandarins? On this accounting, teaching for lustres would hardly be an acceptable strategy or goal of a democratic pedagogy, and would more likely be associated with an aristocratic arrogation of voice, such as that of a T. S. Eliot, who thought Emerson "already an encumbrance," one that the New Criticism had to jettison as a condition of its instauration.

But Emerson has no use for the jaded self-indulgence of "parlor or piano verse" that prefers effeminating "dainties," "enamelling," and "upholstery" to grand, virilizing Pindaric strokes. Plato's *Gorgias* (485a–486d) interprets lustres as dainties, and claims that privileging them is the same as taking the side of the lisping, childlike *kinaidos* against the heavily armed hoplite. For Plato, whom Emerson calls "The Philosopher," adopting the posture of the *kinaidos* is but another way of shunning dialectical and combative philosophical argument. In *Paideia: The Ideals of Greek Culture*, the Greek scholar, Werner Jaeger, has shown that Plato's whole pedagogical project, including his denunciation of the posture of the *kinaidos*, needs to be understood in the context of his attempt to reviralize Athenian culture in the aftermath of the Peloponnesian War. In this same spirit, we may ask what would the shunning of argument mean for the Emersonian project of the "upbuilding" of American culture?

Are there perhaps two antithetical Emersonian moods here that do not believe in one another: one, the Promethean voice of manly upbuilding, and the other, the Orphic voice of an effeminated aestheticism? If so, should we not, mindful of Emerson's bipolar angle of vision, view their relationship as poetically agonistic and not as logically self-contradictory? Emerson says that "the ground" of his "hope" lies in his "adverting to the doctrine that man is one," a thesis that he ontologically hyperbolizes as the claim that "we are all bones of the same body." Journal entries for 1842 and 1843 depict a "highly endowed man with good intellect and good conscience" as a Man-Woman, claiming that the Aristophanic vision of the androgynous self enshrined in Plato's *Symposium* is "the symbol of the finished soul." Is this a Swedenborgian atavism? Or Jungian prescience? Or is it possibly evidence of a flirtational neurosis, one that Roland Barthes claims is a necessary condition of all seductive reading / teaching?

In *Manhood and the American Renaissance*, David Leverenz asks whether Emerson's plumping for "initiative, spermatic, prophesying man-making words" is tantamount to asking for perceivers of gleams, as opposed to ardent proponents of agonistic argument. In pressing this issue, Leverenz takes up the same question that I have begun hypothetically to ask here about whether teaching for gleams or lustres is in fact as self-awakening and self-engendering as Emerson thinks that it is. The answer to this question, I would offer, turns on how we understand what Emerson means by power or *potentia*. Levrenz claims that the dispossessive Emersonian self of ecstatic abandonment is, in its imperious nonchalance, incorrigibly powerless. Emerson, on the other hand, asserts, "[T]he true romance which the world exists to realize will be the transformation of genius into practical power," and "The sentiment never stops in pure vision, but will be *enacted*." Emerson's promotion of an easefully Orphic mode of inhabitation as quintessentially healthy and heroic is premised on the anti-Lockean notion that "Life is ecstatical," and that "Nothing great was ever achieved without enthusiasm." Viewed thusly, lustres are tendentiously softening, but are as far a cry from self-immolation as they are from brimstoning about the fire next time.

If the *telos* of Emersonian teaching is not to drown in lustres, but to be luminously transfigured by them, then teaching for lustres would not only not be a retreat from *potentia* but an heroic actualization of it, creating what Shelley calls "a being within our being"; in other words, the lineaments of a post-repressive selfhood. Transforming adverbial vision into power or *potentia*, specifically the power of cultural upbuilding, means disavowing meaning as implying stasis or permanence and, concomitant with this, taking up the *agon* enacted by poetic genius as a prologue to pragmatic self-creation.

Bloom calls this the "agonistic Sublime" and asks if "this cost (is) too high"? But if the cost of self-authoring is too dear, how much more costly would be the self-destitution implied by its refusal?

Still there will be those who will insist that the equation of the "best part" of the mind with abandonment to visionary gleams unduly solipsizes and aestheticizes the self. Such critics will also want to claim that the Emersonian self's relishing of its unsettlement or dislocation is dishabilitating, as it deprives the self of a sense of being-in-place and hence a sense of being at-home-in-the-world. If "Nothing is got for nothing," perhaps Emerson's much-underplayed *Unheimlichkeit* is the ontological price he has to pay for his visionary skylarking and solipsistic aestheticism. Is the acknowledgment of this cost unconsciously coded into the question about a "great soul" pressed by "The American Scholar": "[D]oes he lack organ or medium to impart his truths"? Could teaching for lustres do anything but worsen this blighted condition? Is momentary self-enchantment, or episodic participation in *le marveilleux* or in a Bachelardian "existentialism of the fabulous" the most that can be hoped for from such reading / teaching? If so, should we not then interpret reading / teaching for lustres as an aesthetic antidote—call it a "refugee idealism" or "inner-worldly aestheticism"—to both the dark side of Emerson's transcendentalist moon and to what he calls "the badness of the times"? Is Emerson's journalistic claim (1840), "If I am true, the theory [of self-reliance] is, the very want of action, my very impotency, shall become a greater excellency than all skill and toil," a persuasive answer to these questions? Surely the shunning or refusal of "dirty hands" is not evidence of *potentia* or power, especially for a writer / teacher for whom "the thumb of practice" is as educative as "the anointed eye," for whom "the inward analysis must be corrected by rough experience."

A close reading of Emerson demonstrates, however, that wisdom lies in hermeneutic transformative practice, not in a retraction into self, which Emerson clinicalizes as "tumor and disease." I mean by hermeneutic not interpreting a text but being interpreted by it; or put differently, deconstructing reading and teaching as "a process of being read," of subjecting oneself to legibility and therefore to intelligibility. If this is what we mean by reading and teaching, then its requirements "are equivalent to those of possessing a self," including perhaps the self of a nation or its constitution. The latter, I presume, is what Cavell, following Emerson and Thoreau, means by "peopling" a text or finding it as "founding." "Self-Reliance's" claim that we are all texts, that who and what we are is written over all our persons and is emitted as "virtue or vice" by our breath "every moment" of our lives, would then be the underlying semiotic assumption of our liability to such legibility.

But if teaching for lustres is what Emersonian writing mandates, how shall we understand "Art's" assertion that all pictures should be domesticating, not dazzling, that they "must not be too picturesque"; and that "nothing astonishes . . . so much as common-sense and plain dealing"? The answer to this question is two-fold: first, for Emerson, as for the ancient Greek Hera- clitus, the way up (the transcendent) is the way down (the incendent) and vice- versa; second, nothing finally is more lustrous for Emerson than the ordinary sublimed, the diurnal transcendentalized, the commonplace transfigured. Indeed, the celebration of a patinaed Quaker / Shaker plainness is a cardinal pedagogical tenet of the Emersonian teacher, and has filiation with the plain- ness of presence of the Taoist master, who is "radiant, but easy on the eyes," who does not try to shine and hence "people can see his light," who "does not glitter like a jewel . . . [but is] as rugged and common as a stone." Does this filiation entitle us to speak of the "Tao" of Emerson?[17]

Emerson's celebratory finding of the sublime in the pedestrian has been acknowledged and saluted as an essential feature of his leftwing democratic posture by a number of his American philosophical and literary inheritors, from Walt Whitman to William Carlos Williams to Wallace Stevens; from William James to John Dewey to John J. McDermott. It is a philosophical posture that needs to be repeatedly underscored in light of his adoption by his rightwing betrayers, who have essentially misconstrued his doctrine of self- reliance as sponsoring both sloth and possessive individualism. Were they correct, Emersonian self-reliance should be read as presaging "the culture of narcissism" and "the fall of public man," in other words, as implying a "ragged" (because ostriched) bourgeois individualism. In "The Sovereignty of Ethics," Emerson strongly disavows this misreading of his doctrine as "small, liliputian, full of fuss and bustle." "Not insulation of place, but independence of spirit is essential." In this context, we should recall Emerson's paen to "the plain old Adam, the simple genuine self," "The Over-Soul's" glossing of both God and the soul as "plain," and "Immortality's" detheatricalizing of post- mortem experience: "My idea of heaven is that there is no melodrama in it, at all, that it is wholly real." Consider also "Demonology's" claim (repeated nearly verbatim in "New England Reformers") that "One moment of a man's life is a fact so stupendous as to take the lustre out of all fiction." Or as Whit- man revises Emerson: "As soon as histories are properly told there is no more need of romances." In a more oxygenated mood, Bloom speaks of "the Emer- sonian Dionysiac, returning to the commonal."[18]

"The Poet's" assertions that "the poet's habit of living should be set on a key so low that the common influences should delight him," and that "the ground-tone of conventional life" should be heard all through his "varied music" have been interpreted as entering a claim on behalf of Emerson's "quest for the ordinary." But Emerson's monumentalizing of the ordinary, of what he calls "the titmouse dimension," to which, he says, "to be valiant, / [men, cowardly "overgrown"] must come down," is not so much a quest as it is a finding, except where the squalor of the ordinary requires aesthetic or moral transfiguration.[19] Say, following Stevens, that it is a finding of "the particulars of a relative sublime," of a "diviner health disclosed in common forms," or of what Emerson himself oxymoronically speaks of as "the transcendentalism of common life." It is in "The American Scholar" that this posture of obedience to the ordinary is most poignantly expressed: "Life is our dictionary. . . . The literature of the poor, the feelings of the child, the philosophy of the street, the meaning of household life, are the topics of the time . . . I embrace the common. I explore and sit at the feet of the familiar, the low. . . . What would we really know the meaning of? The meal in the firkin; the milk in the pan; the ballad in the street; the news of the boat; the glance of the eye; the form and the gait of the body;—show me the ultimate reason of these matters; show me the sublime presence of the highest spiritual cause lurking, as always it does lurk, in these suburbs and extremities of nature." Call this Emerson's "secular liturgy," his epistemology of the diurnal, and note that by the low and familiar Emerson does not mean a vanilla monism, but a pistachioed pluralism, one "thick with impasto and strewn with pentimenti," in the wonderful painterly phrase of Peter Gay. And following John J. McDermott, note also that we walk a "thin line [here] between the rich deposits of the ordinary and the equivalent characteristic of a frequenting numbing repetitiveness. . . . The first dulls, the second can flash."[20] And note finally that Emerson's posture is one of natural piety, of humble pupillage, of sitting reverentially and petitionally "at the feet of the low," "as someone who serves, to win the confidence of what seems poor," in the formulation of Rilke.

The Aurelian metaphysics of relations enshrined in Emerson's major essays and epitomized by the notions that the energies of the universe are *solidaires*, and that "relation and connection are not somehwere and sometimes, but everywhere and always," leads Emerson to speak of the teacher / scholar as a "university of knowledges." But the latter's mental capaciousness and his extraordinary capacity for analogy-making, for joining "contrary and remote things [that] cohere, and flower out from one stem," should not cause us to soft-pedal the proletarian and sacramental bottom of his pedagogy, what "Experience" calls its "respect to the present hour" or what "The Over-Soul" refers to as "the earnest experience of the common day." But saying that the "present hour" is pedagogical is not to mark or exalt its knife-edge transience and effulgence. Rather it is to call attention to its experiential lushness and to the radical empirical fact of "continuous transition," which, to repeat, is, for Emerson, "the attitude of power." What we want are not fugitive sparkles from the wheel of experience but "an astronomy of Copernican worlds." As Emerson journalizes (1854): "If Minerva offered me a gift & option, I would say give me continuity. I am tired of scraps." Or, as John Dewey gerundively rewrites Emerson: "Perfection means perfecting, fulfillment, fulfilling, and the good is now or never."[21]

Such processualism is not only a forerunning of Jamesian radical empiricism. It is also a philosophical signature of the Emersonian teacher, whose teachings are not dime-store wisdom, but blood-making marrow. Like Cavell, I am led to speak of Emerson's privileging of continuous transition as his philosophical "hoboism," one that presciently anticipates, in its notions of onwardness and waying, the ontological nomadism endemic to Jamesian radical empiricism, which is epitomized by the claim, "Life is in the transitions as much as in terms connected; often, indeed, it seems to be there more empatically." Cavell connects "the religious idea of the Way," the Tao, with the onwardness of thinking, of knowing how to go on philosophically. But Emerson's hoboism ("Everything good is on the highway") is not primarily a way of troping the capacity for philosophical onwardness. It rather images for the weary and the woebegone a way of carrying on in a world gone miserably wrong. It also telescopes "the Genius or Destiny of America," which "is no log or sluggard, but a man incessantly advancing," not because of its Faustian restlessness or imperial or hegemonic ambition, but because of its continual essaying to be.

In *Principles of Psychology*, William James refers to "the higher poets," all of whom he says "use abrupt epithets, which are alike intimate and remote, and, as Emerson says, sweetly torment us with invitations to their inaccessible homes." In taking up the Emersonian notion of teaching for lustres, I have resisted the temptation to read "lustres" as an abrupt epithet that sweetly or otherwise torments us with its inaccessibility. To read / teach for lustres, I have wanted to say, is to exalt what "Self-Reliance" calls "the one fact the word hates," namely aversive "essaying to be," which Joel Porte correctly identifies as the "fundamental conceit of this greatest of American essayist."[23] If there is a key that turns all the locks to Emersonian writing / teaching, it is that everything for Emerson is "ever, not quite," meaning that there are no Circles, only arcs, no Frames, only edges. "Compensation" says this straight out, claiming that its author would be "happy beyond my expectation if I shall truly draw the smallest arc of this circle." Like the world itself, which is an unfinished multiverse, Emerson's work, I would offer, is a kind of continual sculpting in snow, comparable in its incompleteness, to Cezanne's late *non finito* watercolors or to Lawrence Durrell's n-dimensional novels, which it is the viewer's / reader's task to refashion creatively in aesthetic imagination. Hence, Whitman's reference to Emerson as "the giant [who] always destroys himself"; and hence Emerson's journalistic "boast that I have no school & no follower." "Circles" says, "every man believes that he has a greater possibility," and John J. McDermott hits it off exactly when he says in this volume that "the central theme of Emerson's life and work is that of *possibility*." It is a theme sanctioned by the experience of an open universe "in which we seem in the bosom of all possibility," and by an America in which, geographically if not socially, "the theme is creative and has vista," in the phrase of Whitman.

Analogously, Emerson's strongest readers must continually reinvent him into the teeth of their own historical circumstances. In a journal entry from 1844, Emerson instructs us that "the book must be good, but the reader must also be active." By "active" he means "spermatic," not mendicant, original, not quotational. One must be an inventor to read well . . . there is creative reading as there is creative writing," says "The American Scholar." Or, as Bloom revises Emerson: "Reading is a heuristic process, a path-breaking into inventiveness."[24] Strong reading is not for the pleasures of the text alone, but also for meaning, for intellectual power, which is always aversive and revisionist. "Quotation and Originality's" way of making this point is to ask, "But what can we read but ourselves"? This is not readerly solipsism, but rather existential self-reliance. As Emerson journalizes (1838), he hopes for "a reader and an age that will justify [his context]"; and personal transfiguration and cultural reconstitution—not emotional captivation and entrancement—is, I am persuaded, the best justification of his context. "I would have my book read [like] the sight of a new landscape on a traveler." I read "landscape as a double-helixed inscape / outscape, the former spiritually expansive, the latter culturally emancipatory. Whitman's advice is unimprovable: "Read all the Emerson you can—it is the best preparatory soil. Emerson is not conclusive on all points, but no man more helps to a conclusion."[25]

This is not to imply, however, that Emerson is a literary and philosophical Alice's Restaurant in which you can get anything you want, from Gnosticism to neo-pragmatism. It is simply to observe, consistent with his tendentious radical empirical stance, that he is an action painting, not a still life. He cannot be pinned like a butterfly to a board or analyzed without remainder into an ism or ology. What we want is the leap of the salmon ("a living, leaping Logos"), not what the poet Archibald MacLeish pejoratively calls "a plank of standard pinkness in a dish." Switching metaphors, I would ask you to think of Emerson as a Penelopean web that requires continual reweaving, and not as a bronze statue in a cultural Cooperstown that commemorates for spectating passersby his enshrinement as a Great American. For, as Nietzsche presciently observes, Emerson "simply does not know . . . how young he is going to be."

As a teacher, I have always tried to be obedient to Emerson's instruction to "be an opener of doors for such as come after thee," and not "to make the universe a blind alley."[26] It is an instruction repeatedly underscored in Emerson's writings, and one that is mark and criterion of the Emersonian teacher. Let John J. McDermott, whom I have described elsewhere as the quintessential American scholar and Emersonian teacher,[27] have the last word here: "No matter the intellectual disagreements and the ever-tightening noose of bureaucracy, teaching remains a hallowed calling. To teach is to help others move through the vestibule into the feast. The generational continuum of teacher and student is an ennobling lifeline and perhaps, at times, a lifeboat on a fractured, contentious planet earth."[28]

Notes

1. Although based on a plethora of texts on teachers and teaching, the normative concept of teaching for lustres is my construct not Emerson's. It is a spectrum concept encompassing what "Self-Reliance" calls "guides, redeemers, and benefactors obeying the Almighty effort advancing on Chaos and the Dark"; and is also instantiated by sacred poets and philosophers, visionaries, prophets, saints, seers, adepts, geniuses, heroes, public intellectuals, and educators. Emerson never nominates himself (or any other American) as "the teacher of the coming age," and it is an essential misconstrual of his discussion to read it as an *apologia pro vita sua*. In a journal entry from "New Year's Eve," 1843, he says, "The Universal Genius beckons [him] to the redeemer's office." But his journals are filled with self-nihilizing remarks about his physical constitution, his myriad "dark spots," and his intellectual impoverishment ("I am a dwarf and will always remain a dwarf'; "I am a bard least of bards"), all of which, taken together, presumably disqualified him, in at least his own mind, as "the teacher of the coming age." I say "he" because Emerson always says "he." However, my understanding of the concept of the Emersonian teacher is gender-neutral.

2. See Richard M. Griffith, "Anthropodology: Man A-Foot," in *The Philosophy of the Body: Reflections on Cartesian Dualism*, edited by Stuart Spicker (Chicago: Quadrangle Books, 1970), 273–292. I say "ear" rather than "mouth," because the language of music for Emerson is more auditory than vocal.

3. *The Writings of William James: A Comprehensive Edition*, edited by John J. McDermott (Chicago: The University of Chicago Press, 1977), 206. See also *The Will To Believe and other essays in popular philosophy* (New York: Dover, 1956), 59, 62.

4. See Johan Huizinga, *Homo Ludens: A Study of the Play Element in Culture* (Boston: Beacon Press, 1962), 146–157.

5. *The Portable Thoreau*, edited by Carl Bode (New York: Viking Penguin, 1982), 56.

6. Stanley Cavell, *Conditions Handsome and Unhandsome: The Constitution of Emersonian Perfectionism* (Chicago: The University of Chicago Press, 1990), 62.

7. Stanley Cavell, *This New Yet Unapproachable America: Lectures after Emerson after Wittgenstein* (Albuquerque: Living Batch Press, 1989), 93. On the question of the erosion of moral sensibility and its cultural and other consequences, see John J. McDermott, "'Turning' Backward: The Erosion of Moral Sensibility," *Alice McDermott Memorial Lecture in Applied Ethics*, VIII (1998), pp. 1–15.

8. Actually, things have not stayed the same. See Andrew Delbanco, "Scandals of Higher Education," *The New York Review of Books*, LIV, 5 (March 9, 2007), 42–47.

9. *The Philosophy of John Dewey* (Chicago: The University of Chicago Press, 1981), 559–635.

10. Ralph Waldo Emerson, *Essays: First Series* (Boston: Houghton Mifflin, 1903), 152.

11. Henry David Thoreau, *Wild Apples and Other Natural Essays*, edited by William Rossi (Athens: The University of Georgia Press, 2002), 117, 125.

12. John J. McDermott, *Streams of Experience: Reflections on the History and Philosophy of American Culture* (Amherst: The University of Massachusetts Press, 1986), 131.

13. Much of the previous paragraph first appeared in my "No Eros, No Buds: Teaching as Nectaring," *Experience as Philosophy: On the Work of John McDermott*, edited by James Campbell and Richard E. Hart (Fordham University, 2996), 178–210.

14. Ibid., 237–271.

15. Cited by Joel Porte, in *Representative Man: Ralph Waldo Emerson in His Time* (New York: Oxford University Press, 1979), 39. Durand's letter is cited by Barbara Novak in *American Painting of the Nineteenth Century* (New York: Praeger, 1969), 83–84. The words "fuller minstrel" and "ring out, ring out [the] mournful rhymes" are from Alfred Lord Tennyson's poem, *Ring out, Wild Bells* (1850), published as part of *In Memoriam*. William James quotes them, without attribution, at the end of *A Pluralistic Universe* (1909).

16. Ibid., 371. On Emerson's American version of Orphism, see R. A. Yoder, *Emerson and the Orphic Poet in America* (Berkeley: University of California Press, 1978).

17. See Richard Grossman, *The Tao of Emerson* (New York: Random House, 2007).

18. Harold Bloom, *Agon: Towards a Theory of Revisionism* (New York: Oxford University Press, 1983), 331.

19. See the "Address of William James" in *The Centenary of the Birth of Ralph Waldo Emerson* (Concord: 1903), 76. "He could perceive the full squalor of the individual fact, but he could also see the transfiguration."

20. *Experience as Philosophy: On the Work of John J. McDermott*, edited by James Campbell and Richard B. Hart (New York: 2006), 262. I owe the phrase "secular liturgy" to John J. McDermott. The citation from Peter Gay is taken from his book *Art and Act: On Causes in History—Manet, Gropius, Mondrian* (New York: Harper & Row, 1976), 32.

21. John Dewey, *Human Nature and Conduct* (New York: Henry Holt, 1930), 290.

22. Stanley Cavell, *This New Yet Unapproachable America*, 116. See his essay "Thinking of Emerson," in *The Senses of Walden: An Expanded Edition* (San Francisco: North Point Press: 1981), 136.

23. *Representative Man*, 153.

24. *Agon*, 238.

25. Cited in Robert D. Richardson Jr., *Emerson: The Mind on Fire* (Berkeley: University of California Press, 1995). 529.

26. *Emerson in His Journals*, selected and edited by Joel Porte (Cambridge: Harvard University Press, 1982), 328.

27. See my "No Eros, No Buds: Teaching as Nectaring."

28. *Experience as Philosophy*, 271.

The Continental College of Beauty

Mark Strand

The city was flooded with light
that burrowed through mist and morning cloud-cover,
giving the lordly rivers their samite robes.
Out to The Narrows the weather was all arranged.
Tugs, gilded and sleek, in the harbour were stitching the glitter
and graveyard grass, littered with bottles and ash,
glowed as it did in pure wilderness days.
Down in the subway, somebody said,
'Longing is turned into fullness transparent as sunlight.'
Everyone clapped and rose to street-level where the blaze
of tenement windows, of storefront glass was blinding.
This was the time of angelic surprise, of impalpable chance.
Baskets of pears, boxes of plums, racks of oranges gleamed.
Counters of cheese, aisles of meat went pink in the glare.
The shawls of the poor were suddenly mended, the glazed
faces of sleepers rose from the pitch of their personal lives.
The Continental College of Beauty had opened its doors.

For a minute no one would die.
Each eye was a window through which an invisible energy poured
and the flash and flare of truth leapt from the language
that mourned for itself the night before.
Words of the bright mid-morning had risen
into the fuming air. Somebody climbing the steps to his house
looked to the city and said, 'A great similitude spans all.'
And somebody else looked up from her book that sang
the unguarded night of stars and saw that the moon,
stone pillow of angels, had gone, and saw nothing but lustre
washing the streets, and stacks of fuel-fed roses
burning at the city's edge. The armies
of students and drifters that had circled the globe for years
heard a voice from a radio buried in leaves
say that the prose of everyday life was turning to gold.

Over crescents of worried water
flotillas of swans, unaging, paddled
and in the park's tall elms desire flared.
A man raking leaves, who knew he was dying said,

'The wind of heaven wheels round and everything shines.'
The flags of sorrow had been shredded by furious gusts.
Bones long stiffened under the gowns love wore, a woman's
oval face, an old man's golden hair, glowed in the fabulous instant.
And the girl was freed who grieved windswept guitars,
O heart, unwedded, on lonely shores. The rain's monotonous pounding
had come to an end. It was a day of glory wherever you were.
The wind was in flames, was everywhere circling the towers,
the high glass houses, the streaming halls, the painted floors.
Even the fields of sleep were filled with fire
because suddenly out of the blue
the Continental College of Beauty had opened its doors.

Chapter 5

Emerson at *The Gates*

David LaRocca

The world is all gates,—all opportunities,—strings of tension waiting to be struck.

> —*Emerson, "Resources"*

A heterogeneous population crowding on all ships from all corners of the world to the great gates of North America, . . . quickly contributing their private thought to the public opinion, . . . it cannot be doubted that the legislation of this country should become more catholic and cosmopolitan than that of any other. It seems so easy for America to inspire and express the most expansive and humane spirit; new-born, free, healthful, strong, the land of the laborer, of the democrat, of the philanthropist, of the believer, of the saint, she should speak for the human race. It is the country of the Future.

> —*Emerson, "The Younger American"*

*I*n the cold midseason of winter, when the trees have stood with bare branches for months, and the fallen leaves are nearly emulsified into the soil below, there is an interstitial span of time when things seem quieter; the wind slows, nearing stillness. After new snow, the frozen white tarp covers all evidence of human action on the surface of the world, and dampens whatever sounds remain above that shimmering layer. Ralph Waldo Emerson relates an experience from a similar scene: "Crossing the bare common, in snow puddles, at twilight, under a clouded sky, without having in my thoughts any occurrence of special good fortune, I have enjoyed a perfect exhilaration. I am glad to the brink of fear."[1] In New York City, where the flux of light and life is said never to cease, one cannot help witnessing this calm center while walking the pedestrian pathways of the city's great, sprawling heart: Central Park. In its midregions, away from the rush at the edges—the friction of tires on the road, the construction clanging, the horns and voices and engines surging and falling—one can hear birds singing, see an opalescent half-moon set against the violet haze of low clouds, and feel entirely solitary as if walking through woods three hundred miles away in the Adirondacks. In such a season, in fact, in February 2005, the artists Christo Javacheff and Jeanne-Claude Denat de Guillebon, a husband and wife partnership of familial and creative energies for nearly forty years, achieved what they had been planning from the late 1970s: a series of gates spread intermittently throughout the pedestrian pathways of Central Park.[2] This installation, like many of Christo and Jeanne-Claude's other works, became an object of international awe, confusion, celebration, and ridicule, drawing visitors and art enthusiasts from around the world. Much of the process of realizing *The Gates* had a sensational quality: the decades of planning, the extent of drawings and drafts representing what the project might look like, the fundraising (largely by means of selling the drawings and drafts), the quantity of raw material needed to build *The Gates*, and the political, social, and aesthetic debates surrounding its development (including decades of negotiation with the City of New York and the New York State Parks Commission). As I walked Central Park in February, the day before the opening (or "unfurling of the cocoons"), and for a few days afterward, when the saffron drapes of fabric had been released, I began to see another sensational aspect to the work: that the thinking (or methodology) of Christo and Jeanne-Claude's project contained strong lines of continuity with things Ralph Waldo Emerson had written on the role of the artist, the nature of art, the daring required for artistic creation, the relationship between art and nature, elitism and democracy, process, politics, the experience of the ordinary, walking, inhabiting private and public space, performance art and institutional art, and the undeniably familiar feeling of existential impermanence. In the present essay, I take the occasion of the realized project *The Gates*, to suggest some ways it reflects, or returns us to, Emerson's ideas and, conversely, the way some of Emerson's ideas lend insight into the nature of Christo and Jeanne-Claude's method as artists. In this mood, where I find myself in a series of thoughts stimulated by walking the paths of Olmsted's park, through Christo and Jeanne-Claude's gates, I am, as much, perambulating Emerson's prose— his sentences like pathways demanding one step at a time, and a destination in every step. The topics I wish to address, then, seem truly topographical: suddenly the park, *The Gates*, and the pages all appear in three dimensions and reveal themselves as part of a singular project, each meditating on the same *topos* from one or another angle of vision, or rather that the topos just *is* the project underway, namely, that Christo and Jeanne-Claude like Emerson (as much like Olmsted), are engaged in establishing conditions for the possibility of experience.

I

"Valor," Emerson writes, "consists in the power of self-recovery, so that a man cannot have his flank turned, cannot be out-generalled, but put him where you will, he stands. This can only be by his preferring truth to his past apprehension of truth."[3] Valorous thinking acknowledges that the self is not a totemic insularity, an enduring element, but a "stupendous antagonism" that resists any will to isolation and durability.[4] Recovering one's self demands a willingness to go on from it—to let go of what one imagines it to be, while imagining what it might become. One must move ahead into an unknown while leaving familiar ground behind. With each advance, one witnesses new relations and sees anew one's former associations. One must live with the "intrepid conviction that his laws . . . may at any time be superceded and decease."[5] This kind of skepticism guards against the false rigidity of an "established" self. A valourous skepticism reminds us that any story of an ossified self is a threat to growth, innovation, and insight. There is no greater challenge to well-being than stagnation, no greater offense to self-creation than the conceit that the self is *already* created. When doubt is transformed into the condition of experience one develops a willingness to be unsettled. Doubt is no longer an obstacle, but an invitation to thinking. It allows whatever truth there may be in a situation to emerge from it. "No truth so sublime but it may be trivial to-morrow in the light of new thoughts. People wish to be settled; only as far as they are unsettled is there any hope for them."[6] Valor in one's thoughts and actions comes to light when the process of vision and revision is embraced, when the sequence of things is not just manifest but a perceived accomplice in the project that lies at our feet, in our hands.

The 7,532 "gates" that lined the twenty-three miles of pedestrian pathways in Central Park were, despite differences in width, fundamentally the same. The name "gate" intentionally alludes to Olmsted's naming the entrances to or exits from Central Park "gates" (e.g., Artist's Gate, Scholar's Gate, Children's Gate, Woman's Gate). Christo and Jeanne-Claude's gates were all constructed of the same materials and painted the same color— so-called saffron (a color described by attendees in radically different ways: as referencing the spiritual significance of a Buddhist monk's gown or the ubiquitous, yet still eye-catching construction cone). A single gate, admired on its own, is an interesting enough object: a rectangular metal frame with wide, steel supports, it clearly defines a "this side" and a "that side," and the flowing curtain, hanging down to about six feet above the ground creates associations to a half dozen pleasant experiences of moving fabric (a drape in the wind, a dress around striding legs, a blanket tossed up to be spread out, a sail let out, a flag caught in a wind current, laundry on the line, a curtain pulled back at performance time, and so on). While Christo and Jeanne-Claude's name for the project acknowledges Olmsted's description of his design, it is to Stonehenge that the gates bear a more pronounced structural resonance. The "hanging stones" (*stanhen gist*), like the gates, outline a space of transition or conversion, especially because of the dominant sense of vertical coverage—on Salisbury Plain in the form of a monolithic cap-stone; in Central Park by means of a flowing sheet of vibrantly colored fabric. There is a mythos in this simple architecture; like the door, it seems the very icon of "going through to the other side." Alone, taken one at a time, a gate stimulates a multitude of engaging questions about the nature of entry and exit, and the way we approach interstitial spaces (such as the space between rooms, thresholds that may amount to no more than the few inches of a door-jam). Some critics noted the odd success of setting up several thousand gates in a city known as a gateway to American immigrants somehow did not stimulate worries about immigration, and at a time when airport security checkpoints have made passing through gates a tedious, awkward, and anxious experience.[7] The unexpected fact here, though, is that the single gate is immediately and identically repeated (that is, with a duplicate). There is a first gate, and then another. And so an entry and an exit is followed, some twelve or so feet later, by another entry and exit. But then there is another, and another, and another. The feeling of entering and exiting, of preparing to leave one space, trading through an in-between, and emerging in a new venue, is repeated in a seemingly endless series. There is no way, it seems, to cease this processional experience: going in and coming out, all the while mesmerized by the sight, sound, and texture of the curtains. There is a rare power here: not just the iteration of some dramatic element, but the radical repetition of that same dramatic element—at twelve-foot intervals for twenty-three miles. In that repetition, the drama of the structure magnifies and diminishes: at once revealing a grandness of scope, and showing that there is nothing particularly special about any given gate. Is not this just like our experience of the everyday in our days? Each subsequent day seems possessed of a miraculous potential, yet it gets lived in a sequence of intimate, earthly engagements.

The well-traveled still live within the confines of provincial life: there is food and water, walking and rest, a demand for basic care of domestic and professional life, and some engagement with others. In fact, travel, for all it is supposed to offer in the way of "new" experiences, actually intensifies the degree to which we attend to the most fundamental aspects of our everyday lives: food, shelter, transportation, safety, and human, cultural engagement. At home, the discrete elements of life—the look of the neighborhood, the details of a friend's face, the lines of one's car, the content of one's personal library—diminish. One becomes blind to what is right there. Commuting home from work, lost in thought, one cannot recall what happened on the way. But in traveling sensorial sensitivity is enhanced. Every mundane detail holds worlds of charm and interest. The errands that distract and exhaust when at home become exhilarating adventures worthy of journal entries and letters home.

Over time, "the new day" loses its mystique.[8] It ceases to be the grand field of potential we may have once thought it was. And that can be a relief. In that state where nothing seems special or demanded, the day is free to have us dwell at a different level—call it the level of the familiar or ordinary. Here, our dearest habits and tastes develop; in them, we recognize attributes of our best character. In the everyday, faced with the repetition of elements (the same kitchen table, the same view, the same desk, the same routes, etc.), we are freed to go further into the space of our day. Unlike the traveler, we are not preoccupied with the discovery of a new kind of life, nor are we overwhelmed with novel impressions from another world. The book is where we left it. The car is in the driveway. The clocks are set to local time. We can go on—into conversation or work—without attention to the things that persist around us. We take them for granted. They can be relied upon.

So it is with *The Gates*. Repeated to the horizon in all directions, lining the pathways, swaying and swerving, from the inside to the edges of the park, there is less and less demand to dwell on the particulars of any given gate. At first a marvel, the gates as structures recede from dominance, giving us a chance to have a new perception of the park itself or the city just behind or above its border; or another reminder of the fact of the park's presence *in* the city, striking because the park's uncanny location and scope can still claim and compel special attention. A tree, a bridge, a wall, a building that have stood in a place for a decade, for a century, now seem like novel members of a new order. *The Gates* juxtaposed beside them kindle a new glimpse of proportion, color, and shape. At first a bold, bright, to some brazen, interruption of an established space, the gates cease, over time, to demand the attention one assumes for the spectacle. They become, mainly due to their extensiveness and repetition, an expected element of the scenery—something against which we measure our view of the world. As a frame reveals new things about what is framed, as a new wall color makes exterior patterns align differently and interior objects stand in a different relation to the wall, the iteration of gates, like the repetition of our days and the things and habits that define them, transforms them from objects demanding our attention to objects that make us look or think elsewhere. They are not the point. What lies between them or through them, or around them: that is the point. So *The Gates* becomes a condition for the possibility of experience. Because of the gates we inhabit a new world, that is, the same old world, but in a new day, from a new position, with a new sense of orientation and perspective.

The Gates itself is a remarkable metaphor for valor in thinking: making oneself available to new truth, and being in a position to accept it—that is, to move on from past truths. The Gates, like the doors in our homes, enables a constant entering and exiting, a continual shift in location (where one stands, where one looks out from). Like windows or camera lenses, they frame the world again and again. But we must have legs to carry us through this procession and eyes to see what lies there before us. "All I know is reception," Emerson writes.[9] As with a book, The Gates in Central Park, draws one in and lays out a pathway through words—sentence by sentence. While reading, while walking, there is an initial sense of how to go on, where the sentences might lead, where the pathways could take us. But along the way things change. Each subsequent sentence, like each gate, positions us anew to see the world, to see ourselves. The process of reading the lines of prose, or walking the pathways in the park, is like the process of thinking. It is always a project of getting one's bearings—finding where one is, and finding how to go on from there. Consider Emerson writing at the commencement of "Experience," as if he were entering Central Park, passing beneath a first gate: "Where do we find ourselves? In a series of which we do not know the extremes, and believe that it has none."[10] Reading, walking, thinking all have this quality about them: they are processes of orientation and disorientation, experiences that demand and reward essaying and experiment, and resist passive prediction in lieu of deliberate risk. "If any of us knew what we are doing, or where we are going, then when we think we best know!"[11] The fact is: we do not know such things from a fixed standpoint, but by means of a process, what Emerson calls "onward thinking": "Every thing the individual sees without [that is, outside of] him corresponds to his states of mind, and every thing is in turn intelligible to him, as his onward thinking leads him into the truth to which that fact of series belongs."[12] In this series, there are only new things—old things are found again and again—but no fixed or settled things. Not knowing the extremes, but availing oneself to thinking onward—word by word, step by step, gate by gate—truth manifests itself, and we are ready when it does. Being "in a series of which we do not know the extremes" (a terse summary of the human condition?) requires valor, requires a spirit of movement in the direction of what draws us in, and provokes our thinking. To speak into the world a rough or fine truth, one must be receptive to the world one addresses. What interests us? What captivates our attention? And how does that interest prepare us for the thinking that Emerson calls "a pious reception"?[13]—By maintaining a brave commitment to the idea that at once unsettles us and calls us forth.

II

Composed of so many creative elements, *The Gates* is not clearly aligned with a specific form of art; some critics and spectators went beyond subcategorical distinctions to simply ask the more general question: "Is it art?" Arguably, identifiable attributes from several fields of art are manifest: over the course of its thirty-year vetting, there are scores of hand-drawn illustrations of the proposed installation; then, once materialized in Central Park there are the flowing fabric drapes suggesting fashion design, the metalwork some strain of installation art and architecture, the color a possible link to a populist marketing campaign or political ascription, and the brief duration of the installation drawing the work into the realm of performance art or theater. *The Gates* thrives by associations and allusions. Yet, far from being a spectacle that obscures context, *The Gates* leaves the viewer or pedestrian perambulator wondering about the many ways it points outward to the world—not drawing attention to itself, but from itself. As vast as this installation was, as sweeping its vision and the human imaginative and physical resources needed to realize it, it is a remarkably humble work. *The Gates*—as gates can be made to do— welcomes visitors to the park, guides them around, frames the natural environment, and sets the city's flora, architecture, and skyline into new patterns of relation, and then transforms into gracious modes of egress so that one can return to the streets of the city. Considering the many realms and practices of art involved in the project, and the generous presence of *The Gates* itself, the work can feel like the precipitate of a dozen unlikely analogies and metaphors. The viewer seems to see more than is there, that is, more than an artwork, but something like an installation as a condition for experience, for example, establishing a space for conversation, photography, drawing, and criticism.

In the essay "Art," from *Society and Solitude*, Emerson writes about how art does its work in the world, in particular, how great works become either translucent (so we can see through them to the world we inhabit) or reflective (so we can be given back to ourselves anew and find where we are in the world in the wake of such perceptions). *The Gates* stands as a candidate of his description:

> Proceeding from absolute mind, whose nature is goodness as much as truth, the great works are always attuned to moral nature. . . .
> Herein is the explanation of the analogies, which exist in all the arts. They are the re-appearance of one mind, working in many materials to many temporary ends. . . . The laws of each art are convertible into the laws of every other.
> Herein we have an explanation of the necessity that reigns in all the kingdoms of Art. Arising out of eternal Reason, one and perfect, whatever

is beautiful rests on the foundation of the necessary. Nothing is arbitrary, nothing is insulated in beauty. It depends forever on the necessary and the useful.[14]

Consider this an aesthetic reading of the first line of prose from Emerson's first essay in his first book of essays, written three decades earlier: "There is one mind common to all individual men."[15] The work of art, then, is the expression (the *ex*-pressing, the pressing out) of this mind into forms available to other minds, minds that, by virtue of their own possession of this common mind, can recognize the truth it contains. Christo and Jeanne-Claude coalesced a number of striking features from a variety of art forms (illustration, fabric design, metalwork, landscape architecture, and so on) and displayed the resultant combination in such a way that the installation raises a number of questions about those forms, for instance: about public versus private art, the institutional value of an artwork, the public and pedestrian experience of art (as something that includes or excludes membership in a community), the effect of scale in art, the effect of duration in displaying it, the relationship between architecture and sculpture, the question of purpose or usefulness in an artwork (and whether this relates to it being privately or publicly funded), and, perhaps most strikingly, a model for an unselfconscious and unpretentious ethical method for the creation of art. What then are the "temporary ends" that *The Gates* exists to show us? What sort of "analogies" does the installation create? There are several worth dwelling on.

In the literal sense, *The Gates* is a remarkably accessible work. It is both public and free. The gates, then, are truly open to whomever wishes to see them or walk through them. A gate in York, England, or in a score of Italian cities, such as Sienna or Montereggio, is meant to establish a boundary between the outside and inside, the protected and the vulnerable, the native and the foreign. The "gates," in these historical instances of architectural defense, establish a limit, declare where the "outside" begins, and locate where the outsider stands. Here, in Central Park, the gates are always open, free, welcoming. Since there is not one but more than seventy-five hundred gates, walking the pathways reinforces the fact that we are continually being invited and then guided through a sequence of portals. It is hard not to feel at home with such attractive and genuine solicitations—the series of insistent greetings dissolves apprehensions about being or belonging there. Is this a seduction? Can one help but be drawn into the energy and emotion of the event? A familiar walk under these new circumstances allows one to feel the personal hospitality of the gates and the stately formality they evoke; the strolling pedestrian feels special enough to receive the glory of a dignified entrance and a graceful exit at every step in a progress through the vast Central Park, all the while remaining anonymous. A passage across the park from the west side to the east side of the city, a common traversal, becomes an unexpectedly grand transition. One emerges on Park Avenue feeling escorted, step by step, in the most intimate yet bold manner.

The Gates is not sponsored by a museum, school, government, business, or charity. In fact, it has no sponsors of any kind. The work has none of the peculiar institutional or corporate aura that turns a dirigible into the Goodyear blimp or Candlestick Park into Monster Park. *The Gates* is unencumbered by this kind of association, so the visitor is freed from associating the installation with some institution, business, product, or service. In a period when being "underwritten" by a corporate sponsor means having the name written over the experience (from the US Postal Service sponsoring the US team at the Tour de France to Target and Tide sponsoring cars at the Indianapolis 500, from the JVC Jazz Festival to ExxonMobil Masterpiece Theatre), *The Gates* presents a unique model of a public work that is privately funded. We are not required to purchase an admission ticket, still less are we relentlessly pursued to buy t-shirts and posters and books commemorating the event, nor are we pitched the virtues of some new product or useful service.[16] We are left alone, free to roam the park and navigate its thousands of gates, perpetually unobstructed by fee or franchise.

Because of this unusual circumstance, namely, of a major installation unconstrained by an institutional sponsor or corporate benefactor, we participate in what can seem both an extremely democratic project and the most elitist. It seems democratic for obvious reasons: the free and open access, the central metropolitan location, and the topographic extent of the installation. But elitist as well? If the project is not funded by the public (as, for example, the construction of Central Park was), or by a corporation (as the architectural design for the new World Trade Center is), then what sort of power in judgment is at work here? Even after *The Gates* was approved for implementation by New York City's Mayor Michael Bloomberg,[17] there is the overt fact that the project is strikingly the work of a two-person team, Christo and Jeanne-Claude. *The Gates* can then seem like the public manifestation of a private fantasy, the flourish of someone with the inspiration to create the project and the skill to muster necessary political, social, economic, and material support for its implementation. In terms of vision, then, *The Gates* is entirely inaccessible to the public; there is no town meeting held or public opinion poll conducted to help decide the details. Unlike the proposals for the rebuilding of the World Trade Center site, where public opinion is a limited if crucial part of the process (for example, especially with regard to the families of September 11 victims and the memorial planned in their honor), *The Gates* is offered up as a work by Christo and Jeanne-Claude. A competition for an installation in Central Park was not announced, entrants were not solicited. Christo and Jeanne-Claude had a vision, drafted it, proposed it, and waited and worked to bring it off. They advocated on behalf of their idea. And while concessions were made along the way (to address concerns raised variously by politicians, attorneys, parks commissioners, public works officials, and the like), the implemented Gates bears undeniably close resemblance to the sketches they made in the late seventies. Christo and Jeanne-Claude did not significantly revise their plan in the light of public pressure, economic limitation, or political intimidation.

A lack of revision does not necessarily bespeak an intransigent and stubborn artist, but someone who has already integrated ideas from a wide spectrum of positions. Christo and Jeanne-Claude's intervention at Central Park is similar in spirit to Olmsted's shift "away from [Calvert] Vaux's narrow conception of landscape architecture as art."[18] Olmsted came to believe that a park in the midst of a dense urban environment could have, as Witold Rybczynski describes it, a "curative power."[19] For Olmsted, there was artistry in landscape architecture, "but it was combined with city planning, urban management, public education, and public health."[20] Christo and Jeanne-Claude, like Olmsted, do not condescend to different parts of a project's development (valuing the drafting, for example, more highly than metal craft, shipping procedures, or assembly). They spread widely their artistic interests and activities; for this, there is little chance to disparage them for doing something other than their work when they are choosing fabric, inspecting metal seams, or timing routes for delivery. Every element and aspect of their work reflects their artistry.

If there is concern that Christo and Jeanne-Claude got their way, and if such leverage and execution is an offense—some of the visitors I spoke with in the park complained that the money could have been spent in better ways (on the city, some suggested; on themselves, said others)—take seriously the scope of Christo and Jeanne-Claude's claim on our time and the space of the city. In a way, they did ask for Central Park. But in a limited way. They requested use of the park for sixteen days, and they promised that the park would remain open throughout the event, and that nothing physical in the park would be damaged by the installation. Once removed, *The Gates* would leave no physical trace of having been there. *The Gates* as inhabitant of the park for 384 hours would become ghostly—specters of a pedestrian's memory or reconstituted imaginations of what was there based on photographs, sketches, and stories told. And, not incidentally, Christo and Jeanne-Claude said they would pay for everything themselves: no municipal funds would be used.

Unlike the ambitions of those redesigning and reconstructing the World Trade Center site, Christo and Jeanne-Claude's intention was not to establish a permanent memorial, but to enact a temporary provocation to perception. *The Gates* is not conceptual art, but art that makes new conceptions possible. In this delimited perimeter of the city—in Central Park—a pair of artists made a space and a time available to others as a basis for thinking, what could be regarded as the democratic aspiration and achievement of *The Gates*. There is nothing didactic about Christo and Jeanne-Claude's installation (they never presume to say what the project "means"). It is just there, for us (like a gift, like a child).[21] So it becomes a platform and a pathway for our thinking: in the moment and beyond it, to the next, step-by-step, in a series of which we know not the extremes.

Speaking to the "necessity" of *The Gates*—its conception, its planning, its implementation—the scale of the project becomes immediately over-whelming: 5,290 US tons of steel (equal to two-thirds the steel in the Eiffel Tower); 315,491 linear feet of vinyl tube; 165,000 nuts and bolts; 116,389 miles of nylon thread extruded in saffron color, woven into 1,067,330 square feet of fabric, cut and hemmed into 7,532 discrete fabric panels; with 640 paid assembly workers. All this material and labor—not to mention Christo and Jeanne-Claude's thirty years on the job—for only sixteen days of display at a cost of $21 million? The impressive magnitude of the instal-lation, rather than stoke a conservative reaction (calling for restraint) further complements the kind of valor in thinking, the kind of art of necessaries that Christo and Jeanne-Claude's work exemplifies. Raising the money for the project, gathering the materials and support to create it, and hiring people to install it are part of the work.[22] Negotiations between artists and politi-cians, the use of commerce and the organization of workers and materials, as well as visionary illustration and design form the biography of *The Gates*. The life of the work did not begin on February 12, 2005; it began in the late 1970s. The sixteen days in February formed the denouement of an impres-sive decades-long undertaking. A witness at *The Gates* or a viewer of pho-tographs from the installation saw the coalescence of grand elements of a theoretical and practical nature. The event itself can seem like a brief forum on how things come together and separate again. Sixteen days measured against thirty years can seem like the time between the Big Bang and the formation of a galaxy. Yet every day—from conception to implementation to recovery—became a necessary portion of the whole.

III

"Art," wrote Emerson, "is the path of the creator to his work."[23] For an artist, the work of his or her art is more than the art work he or she produces; it is his or her method as well. With Christo and Jeanne-Claude, their method may, in fact, supercede the finished work in boldness of vision, and novelty of style. This suggestion may relieve a reader concerned, even preoccupied, with having "missed" seeing *The Gates* in New York, or any of Christo and Jeanne-Claude's other installations—a concern that the work is somehow in-tellectually or aesthetically inaccessible without firsthand experience. To this worry, I ask: What if Christo and Jeanne-Claude's most interesting, alluring, even pioneering creative offering is not their finished work but their process of creating it, their method? If so, we can apprehend their critical importance from any location, at any time. We do not have to understand Christo and Jeanne-Claude's method in order to understand their completed work. Rather, Christo and Jeanne-Claude's method may simply be more philosophically daring and fecund than the finished work (which is the customary locus of critical interpretation). The present concern, then, is not with the "meaning" of *The Gates*, still less the significance of their installations in general (though I do not wish to disparage those worthwhile intellectual pursuits). We then wish to dwell on how Christo and Jeanne-Claude move from an idea to an installation, that is, to study the nature of this movement. The work that occupies the space between conception and inception can be called their "method," and will now become the site of attention while considering their contribution to our thinking about how art gets made, and how Christo and Jeanne-Claude's method—as a style of thinking—establishes new conditions for experience.

A criticism of art relies, with an overt or a surreptitious admission, on the principle that context and content affect one another, which is to say that *we* change because of their relationship. Like performance art or a political rally, a Christo and Jeanne-Claude piece depends heavily on the place and time of its materialization. For this reason, with Christo and Jeanne-Claude's work, selecting a site for an installation can seem almost *more vital* than the work itself. As has been the case throughout their career, the grounds they choose to build on become the grounds for thinking. Yet, instead of "establishing" something, their kind of installation unsettles. *The Gates*, for example, does not reinforce a standing notion of Central Park, or the experience of a public green space in a vast and vibrant metropolis, but instead creates a space and time for considering (or reconsidering) what one believes given these novel conditions.

Emerson describes a fundamental connection between what a man is and what he does, between the character of his imagination and the nature of the thing he manages to create because of that vision. In "Spiritual Laws," he writes: "A man's genius, the quality that differences him from every other, the susceptibility to one class of influences, the selection of what is fit for him, the rejection of what is unfit, determines for him the character of the universe. A man is a method, a progressive arrangement; a selecting principle, gathering his like to him, wherever he goes."[24] And in the same book, this time in the essay "Intellect," he tactfully equivocates between "mind" and "man": "Each mind has its own method. A true man never acquires after college rules. What you have aggregated in a natural manner surprises and delights when it is produced. For we cannot oversee each other's secret."[25] Frederick Law Olmsted says something similar about landscape architecture: "The best concepts of scenery, the best plans, details of plans—intentions—the best, are not contrived by effort, but are spontaneous and instinctive."[26] In "Powers and Laws of Thought," Emerson writes, "Every man is a new method and distributes things anew";[27] and "Every creation, in parts or in particles, is on the method and by the means which our mind approves as soon as it is thoroughly acquainted with the facts; hence the delight."[28] Emerson's sense of an abiding connection between personal constitution and method remains an ongoing topic in his writing, appearing in a later essay such as "Perpetual Forces," where he says: "Every valuable person who joins in any enterprise, . . .—what he chiefly brings, is, not his land, or his money, or bodily strength, but his thoughts, his ways of classifying and seeing things, his method."[29]

One of the conspicuous attributes of Christo and Jeanne-Claude's work is the extended duration of creative incubation and development. In the case of *The Gates*, the process began in the late 1970s. *Wrapped Trees*, in Riehan, Switzerland, began in 1966, and took thirty-two years to complete. Political negotiation (for use of land and other resources) coupled with the financing for installing the work require great spans of time, especially when the primary content of the work is not up for vote or veto. Clearing difficult proposals through elaborate bureaucratic systems and raising vast sums of money is not the usual domain of the independent artist, but Christo and Jeanne-Claude believe that this work is part and parcel of their occupation as artists. Though it would be a challenge, it is not unthinkable—and is certainly customary—for an artist to seek out the patronage of private donors and institutions. With a patronage approach, a project such as *The Gates* might be proposed to a large foundation or trust (the Bill and Melinda Gates Foundation?), to some group that has both the authority and fiscal capability to support a major installation. In such cases, money would be pledged, land contracted, and the work assembled. How long might this take? Who would be authorizing the process and authoring the work?

For *The Gates*, Christo and Jeanne-Claude resolved to create the work solely for New York City's Central Park, and appropriately so: the title, and the inspiration, were drawn from the park they lived by since moving to the city in 1963. No alternative space was considered. This is understandable. The idea that a piece of installation art is site-specific—where a single place holds the only chance for fulfilling the vision of the artist— is not rare, or unreasonable. Deciding to create a work in Central Park is simply ambitious, but not intellectually or creatively unintelligible.

What is exceptional—and boldly so—is Christo and Jeanne-Claude's decision to self-fund the proposal process, installation materials, and labor costs. Unlike celebrities who might use money earned from movies or music to support an art or humanitarian project (and thereby use income from one field of life to sustain a different field), Christo and Jeanne-Claude created a linear sequence between what they did to raise the money and what they did to spend the money. Christo and Jeanne-Claude drew sketches, painted paintings, and created collages of *The Gates* project, then sold those sketches, paintings, and collages. The proceeds from those sales, accumulated over time, became the sole source of financing for mounting the $23 million installation New Yorkers perambulated through in February 2005. Here we find artists who sell their art to make more art. Or, more specifically: we find artists who sell representations of a specific vision of an artwork in order to accumulate sufficient money to transform the vision into an actuality. The oddity of this model, and the rare achievement it reveals, can be glimpsed by considering what it would be like for a novelist to sell a précis or drafts of his prospective novel in order to have money enough to write a full, finished book. Just like a summary that might describe what the novel would be "about" (if it were written), Christo and Jeanne-Claude's sketches are drafted before there is any "thing" there to sketch. The more intuitive parallel is between Christo and Jeanne-Claude's sketches and an architect's drawings: the architect draws as a means to construction; his art lies principally beyond the sketch; a drawing is a guide to make something else. For Christo and Jeanne-Claude, each drawing is a possibility. It depicts "what might be" given the right conditions. The art buyer then acquires a representation and a hope (perhaps even a hope masquerading as a promise; is this an illicit implication in all of Christo and Jeanne-Claude's sketches—that one wants to believe more is being offered than a drawing? Maybe a prediction? Maybe a vision of the future?). Regardless, buying the sketch (or painting or collage) is an act that creates a further condition for the possibility that what the sketch depicts will be made manifest. This is a unique inversion (or conversion) of a patronage model of support: with Christo and Jeanne-Claude, the patron does not buy a work of art in the hope that the artist will create more art, and still less does not give away money before there is art to buy (even in the hope that the artist will create because of the support). No. Here, the patron buys a bona fide artwork (single unto itself, independent of what may or may not "follow" it). It is a question, though, whether the thing represented will, at some future time, be more than represented there. Christo and Jeanne-Claude implant this curious and profound economy into every transaction of their work: the collector buys both actuality and possibility, engages in a trade (e.g., exchanging money for a sketch), and implicates herself in the conditions for extending the scope of the thing depicted. The prospective buyer of Christo and Jeanne-Claude's art possesses a unique incentive: buying the work can change its value (since the nature of the thing represented can change because of the purchase), and can change the nature of the material world (since the proceeds can be used to finance another phase of creative activity).

Beyond this already interesting model for creating art, there is the sequence of further commitments—having to do with the creation of art and the use of monies gained by its sale—that further elaborate a portrait of Christo and Jeanne-Claude's method. First, that once Christo and Jeanne-Claude raise sufficient funds for installing a project, they cease to create sketches of it. Thus, Christo and Jeanne-Claude only draw things that do not yet exist. Their work is entirely speculative. As if they were conjurers, the moment the thing they have drawn appears, they stop engaging it as a possibility—for it is, by its very presence an actuality. The sketches, then, can never be regarded as a commemoration of their "finished" (installed) work, but only a record of their imaginings in the direction of its realization. Their art, then, is spared any chance of being degraded by accusations of nostalgia or sentimental distortion. Even after the work is installed, the sketches remain in a perpetual state of "what could be." And the counterpoise is equally as important: the installed work is given its unique time and space to flourish on its own terms. With *The Gates*, the varied materials, the logistical demands of using massive quantities of steel and fabric, the enormous physical scope of the installation, the need for an extensive and capable labor force, and the severely limited duration of its tenure in the park create the context for experiencing the realized work. *The Gates* installed in the park is meant to be engaged as a work of presence—of what is. No longer speculative, it is immediate.

Just as the sketching ceases when the exhibition is mounted, so do the elements of the exhibition terminate when the exhibition is completed. Christo and Jeanne-Claude did not sell off the seventy-five hundred saffron colored gates and curtains. Disbanded, there were enough of them to supply one to every major gallery and museum in the world, or scores of private gardens and sculpture parks, and even front and back yards. Instead of these outcomes, which must also include the ways *The Gates* would achieve a kind of cultural saturation (and so become both cliché and intellectually and visually fatiguing), and suffer from gradual physical deterioration (thus tarnishing one's memory of *The Gates* as it appeared in the park), every single steel column and base and run of fabric was recycled. Once the materials were reclaimed, there was no physical trace of *The Gates*. In the aftermath of the disassembly and destruction, there are two primary fields of experience that remain: the sketches (as representations of what could be), and our memories (of what was). The sketches become artifacts of Christo and Jeanne-Claude's imagination for what *The Gates* might become if installed in Central Park; our memories of *The Gates* installed in Central Park become artifacts of our imagination as witnesses to the full realization of their vision (in a temporary state); photographs and drawings made by the witnesses fold into the experience of memory, sometimes reminding us what was seen, other times creating what we did not see or recreating what we could not. *The Gates* resembles the process associated with an elaborate feast: recipe, preparation, enjoyment of the prepared things, digestion, and remembrance. In the end, only the recipe and remembrance remain.

If as Emerson postulates, "a man is a method," how then are Christo and Jeanne-Claude a method? From what I have detailed about their method, including strategies and commitments, for creating art, there is no appeal to their personal or private life. Reasons and causes for their method—whether they wish to proclaim political or religious doctrines, or compensate for a long-standing grudge against an art patron who did them wrong—are quite incidental, and perhaps worse: distracting and distorting. A search for method is not a search for causes; this is no genealogy. Rather, the methodological nature of Christo and Jeanne-Claude's project—its principles of creation and action—resemble what Emerson referred to as "the conduct of life," having to do, in particular, with our responses to the question, How shall I live?[30] As independent artists, Christo and Jeanne-Claude exemplify the way a person can be a "a progressive arrangement; a selecting principle, gathering his like to him, wherever he goes." Beyond this, their manner of creating work insinuates an ethical dimension, perhaps allowing us to say that their method has a moral nature.

IV

I do not suggest that Christo and Jeanne-Claude's artwork is moral, worse still that it has some lesson to teach; it neither has a moral, nor is it moralistic. Rather, intrigue lies in the question of a moral quality to his method. I ask, then, about the moral nature of action, not the moral value of an artifact. The artwork deserves attention for its aesthetic merits or faults, while the artist stands in the light of moral judgment. Given the celebrity nature of *The Gates* project—largely derived from the duration of the planning and the extent of the installation both in cost and in materials—and given the social and political remarks that the project possessed some sort of regenerative power for the city of New York in the years following the terrorist attacks downtown, there is a temptation to associate *The Gates* with a kind of goodness. It was an artwork that seemed to catalyze positive regard from the public by virtue of its exuberance. This was mislaid praise since *The Gates* was not created as a memorial to the dead of September 11, or to serve as a political exigency for an ambitious mayor, or to promote the economic viability of a tremulous marketplace. It may have become those things to people who wanted to see them, and it is part of *The Gates'* legacy that the timing of its installation enabled such readings. But the *goodness* of *The Gates* must be seen as a reflection of anachronism and sentimental judgment. My interest in a moral quality in an artist's method is not for parsing the moral (or, as noted earlier, meaning) of her work, but instead, for discerning the characteristics of human action that lead to artistic creation, and whether those characteristics bear the weight of moral assessment. The focus, then, is on the power that an artist can reveal by how she works out and through her ideas. When the idea takes hold of the artist, the artist rightly takes her place as its minion; she serves it.

> And so, one step higher, when he comes into the realm of Sentiment and Will,—he sees the grandeur of Justice, the victory of Love, the eternity that belongs to all Moral Nature,—he does not then invent his sentiment, or his act, but obeys a pre-existing right which he sees.
>
> We arrive at virtue only by taking its direction, instead of imposing ours. And the last revelation of intellect and of sentiment,—namely, that of, in a manner, severing the man from all other men, and making known to him that the spiritual powers are sufficient to him, if no other being existed;—that he is to deal absolutely in the world, as if he alone were a system and a state, and, though all should perish, can make all anew,—that no numbers and no masses are any reason for sacrificing a right. 'Tis like the village operator who taps the telegraph wire, and surprises the secrets of empires as they pass to the capital. So is this child of the dust throwing himself by obedience into the circuits of the heavenly wisdom, and sharing the secret of God.
>
> The forces are infinite. Every one has the might of all; for that is the secret of the world,—that its energies are *solidaires*; that they work together on a system of mutual aid, *all for each, and each for all*; that the strain made on one point bears on every arch and foundation of the structure; that is to say, every atom is a little world, representing all the forces. But if you wish to avail yourself of their might, and, in like manner, if you wish the force of the intellect, and the force of the will, you must take their divine direction, not they yours. Obedience alone gives the right to command.[31]

The artist's commitment to the idea does not belittle him but aggrandizes his service to it, and opens a field of possibility: how will he serve his idea through his conduct of life? By what means? A method must be developed in order to honor the commitment. In the creation of a method an artist predicates his aesthetic view on moral action, and becomes a representative of it, for it. His work is the culmination of the applied method, regardless of its claim for praise. An unattractive or unappealing work remains an artifact of action; it may not receive our praise, but for our disregard it is no less the manifestation of an artist's effort.

The work of an artist is first perceptual: she must sense what there is to do. Once she is gripped by an idea, she can then consider how she is going to effect it. In her mature state, the artist is a representative for the idea she has seen. In time, her work becomes the representation of that idea. The representative artist shows us a new method, that is, a new way to realize the world of thought. Because of her—her method, her artwork—we see things differently, we think differently, we live differently.

Christo and Jeanne-Claude are representative artists for this reason: they show us that the ideas that compel them are not understood after they are realized in an artwork, but throughout the process of their service to them, prospectively. In short, we cannot understand what kind of thing Christo and Jeanne-Claude are trying to show us—in their work—unless we understand the method they devise in bringing it to final form.[32] Sentimental readings of their work (as an inspiration to depressed New Yorkers in the middle of winter, in the aftermath of September 11, etc.) move us away from their method and toward something like the symbolic meaning of the completed installation. It is hard to fathom that the finished work (i.e., the gates installed in February) should be our primary concern, first because they draw our attention only to then help us look past them (as if to see the city and park anew), and second, because their completeness does not seem to crystallize the significance of Christo and Jeanne-Claude's methodological efforts to understand the nature of processes and relations. As Christo and Jeanne-Claude note: "We have completed 18 projects and have failed 37 projects."[33] Abandoning two-thirds of their proposals before they were installed reinforces the suggestion that the representative methods here do not depend on the work being finished. In fact, the opposite may be true: with a majority of projects going unfinished, incompleteness seems a significant attribute of Christo and Jeanne-Claude's legacy. And given that the third that make it to completion are recycled, emphemerality may be counted another attribute of their approach. More crucially, though, *The Gates* is not a sign of a method; it is a method. Reading *The Gates* symbolically makes it stand for something other than itself (hope, community, hospitality, freedom, affluence); but we should prefer that it stand for itself. And it does. Consider the Golden Gate Bridge, which has profound symbolic significance as, among many other things, a gateway from the Far East into the American West. Yet its genius as an artifact comes in the actual and literal achievement of connecting people. The compelling quality of the object as an icon of emotional attribution follows after the brilliance of the idea to build a bridge at that place, and the skill employed to design and construct it. Though not practical in the same way as the Golden Gate Bridge, the genius of *The Gates* remains its capacity to connect people—to themselves, to each other, to the park, to the city. The color of the fabric and the height of the gates are almost incidental to the way the culminated project enables us to experience the nature of our presence and our relation to what lies beyond it.[34] As its own representative, *The Gates* reveals the idea that gripped Christo and Jeanne-Claude and summoned a power in them sufficient to serve and manifest it. To recognize the idea, one may have to look through the gates. It is the idea that an artwork can provide conditions for the possibility of thinking, conversation, and transformed perception. One goes to *The Gates*, one walks through the gates, in order to know where one stands, and to see how to go on from that place.

Notes

1. Ralph Waldo Emerson, "Nature," *The Complete Works of Ralph Waldo Emerson*, 12 vols. (Boston: Houghton Mifflin, 1903–04), 1.9.17.

2. In the present essay, I refer to the artists as "Christo and Jeanne-Claude" instead of "Christo," adhering to a rubric the artists have established. Because they have taken care to name themselves in a special way, and because their reflections on this matter may help us to understand the meaning of creation and authorship in their work, I quote them at length below. In a response to James Pagliasotti on January 4, 2002, they explain the evolution of their naming practice:

> Jeanne-Claude and I have been working together since our first outdoor temporary work: "Dockside Packages, Cologne Harbor, 1961." The decision to use only the name "Christo" was made deliberately when we were young because it is difficult for one artist to get established and we wanted to put all the chances on our side. Therefore, we declared that Christo was the artist and Jeanne-Claude was the manager, the art dealer, the coordinator and the organizer. And, this served us very well for many years.
>
> Of course, all our collaborators always said, "Christo and Jeanne-Claude," but for the public and the media, it was "Christo." By 1994, though, when my hair had turned gray and Jeanne-Claude's hair had turned red (laughter), we decided we were mature enough to tell the truth, so we officially changed the artist name "Christo" into the artists "Christo and Jeanne-Claude."
>
> All works created to be indoors, from 1958 until today, such as Wrapped Objects and Packages, drawings, collages, scale models and lithographs are works by "Christo." All works created to be outdoors, and the large scale indoor temporary installations, are works by "Christo and Jeanne-Claude." (<http://christojeanneclaude.net/eyeLevel.shtml>)

3. Ralph Waldo Emerson, "Circles," in *The Complete Works*, 2:309.

4. Ralph Waldo Emerson, "Fate," in *The Complete Works*, 6:22.

5. Emerson, "Circles," 2:309.

6. Ibid., 2:320.

7. Hal Foster, "In Central Park," *The London Review of Books* 27, no. 5 (March 3, 2005). This article is available online at <http://www.lrb.co.uk/v27/n05/fost01_.html>.

8. Ralph Waldo Emerson, "Self-Reliance," in *The Complete Works*, 2:57.

9. Ralph Waldo Emerson, "Experience," in *The Complete Works*, 3:83.

10. Ibid., 3:45.

11. Ibid., 3:46.

12. Ralph Waldo Emerson, "History," in *The Complete Works*, 2:23.

13. Ralph Waldo Emerson, "Intellect," in *The Complete Works*, 2:328.

14. Ralph Waldo Emerson, "Art," in *The Complete Works*, 7:51.

15. Emerson, "History," 2:3.

16. Jok Church summarizes some of the details of Christo and Jeanne-Claude's business ethics/etiquette at <http://christojeanneclaude.net/faq.html>: "Hand-signed

prints [of drawings of *The Gates* project] are now available from the not-for-profit, Nurture New York's Nature (associated with the Carriage House Center for Global Issues Foundation). Christo and Jeanne-Claude do not receive payment of any kind from these sales. . . . All proceeds benefit New York's nature and arts. Christo and Jeanne-Claude offer the prints to Nurture New York's Nature as one of their donations to New York City [<http://www.40yearsofpublicart.org/>]. . . . Christo and Jeanne-Claude earn the money [for their projects] by selling Christo's preparatory drawings and collages as well as early works from the fifties and sixties. They will not accept grants, or money for books and movies. The money for the project comes only from the sale of preparatory art of that project. . . . Christo & Jeanne-Claude pay the entire cost of the artworks themselves. . . . They do not accept grants or sponsorships of any kind. They do not accept donated labor (volunteer help). They do not accept money for things like posters, postcards, books, films, T-shirts and mugs or any other products at all. *None.*"

17. Hal Foster voices cynicism about the political incentive Michael Bloomberg may have redeemed in green-lighting this languishing proposal: "Out of one eye, then, I saw an enjoyable mass art event; out of the other, a telling instance of high kitsch in the Bloomberg-Bush era, a cross between the Yellow Brick Road and a grand opening where the packaging was literally all" (Hal Foster, "In Central Park," *The London Review of Books* 27, no. 5 [March 3, 2005]).

18. Witold Rybczynski, *A Clearing in the Distance: Frederick Law Olmsted and America in the 19ᵗʰ Century* (New York: Simon and Schuster, 1999), 364.

19. Ibid., 363.

20. Ibid., 364.

21. Reflecting on the parallel between creating *The Gates* and creating a child, Jeanne-Claude has said: "It is a little bit (like) on a human level . . . if you compare our work, let's say, a father and a mother are walking down the street and they are holding the hand of their little child, and someone stops them and says, 'Oh, what a beautiful child!' Of course, the father and the mother are very happy, but everybody knows that they didn't create that child so that people will enjoy it" (<http://christojeanneclaude.net/eyeLevel.html>).

Jok Church has also invoked this parallel: "[T]here is no money back, much like bringing up a child in that the rewards are not tangible" (<http://christo jeanneclaude.net/faq.html>).

22. Jok Church has written: "How [Christo and Jeanne-Claude] make the money for an artwork is part of the art" (<http://christojeanneclaude.net/faq.html>).

23. Ralph Waldo Emerson, "The Poet," in *The Complete Works*, 3:38.

24. Ralph Waldo Emerson, "Spiritual Laws," *The Complete Works*, 2:144.

25. Emerson, "Intellect," 2:330.

26. Witold Rybczynski quoting Frederick Law Olmsted in *A Clearing in the Distance*, 186.

27. Ralph Waldo Emerson, "Powers and Laws of Thought," in *The Complete Works*, 12:29.

28. Ibid., 12:4.

29. Ralph Waldo Emerson, "Perpetual Forces," in *The Later Lectures*, 2:295. A variant of the selected quotation appears in *The Complete Works*: "Every valuable

person who joins in an enterprise, . . .—what he chiefly brings, all he brings, is not his land or his money or body's strength, but his thoughts, his way of classifying and seeing things, his method" (10:77).

30. Emerson, "Fate," 6:3.

31. Emerson, "Perpetual Forces," in *The Later Lectures*, 2:297–98.

32. The order of my claim here, I see, inverts the order Stanley Cavell proposes in the first paragraph of *The Claim of Reason*: "that the way this work [i.e., Ludwig Wittgenstein's *Philosophical Investigations*] is written is internal to what it teaches, which means that we cannot understand the manner (call it the method) before we understand its work" (Oxford: Oxford University Press, 1979/1999, 3). I do not think this means I disagree with Cavell's reading, but that, perhaps, the order applies to Wittgenstein where it does not to Christo.

33. <http://christojeanneclaude.net/faq.html>.

34. Hal Folster, for example, cheerfully considered other color options: "[T]he hue was off, at least to my eyes: the light orange was too close to both the bleached green of the grass and the smoky grey of the trees to make for a vivid contrast. Sometimes the banners did catch the light or the breeze to flow like veils or shimmer like kites, but often the nylon hung rather dull and limp like big tarps or giant laundry. Red would have been better, or black or white" (ibid.)

Chapter 6

Taking Emerson Personally

John Lysaker

I am drawn to Emerson by self-culture, the project of cultivating a personal life, one that I have in some sense fashioned and that eloquently expresses my character in its diversities and my coherencies, to the degree that they exist. Self-culture is a watchword of the nineteenth century that freely translates the German *Bildung*. We might just call it "culture," as many did and do, Emerson included, were it not that the English term now denotes little more than the social fabric backgrounding and foregrounding human life, thus eliding a crucial aspect of *Bildung*: it is a project at which one can fail.

The ambiguity is nothing new. Even Emerson suffered the problem as he notes in a journal of 1837: "Culture—how much meaning the Germans affix to the word & how unlike to the English sense." For clarity then, and to acknowledge my inheritance of a project that captivated nineteenth-century America, "self-culture" orients these reflections.

Self-culture is a theme that runs through Emerson's writings, from the 1830s into the 1860s. And it is not just an incidental theme, as this passage from "The American Scholar" makes plain in its negation and affirmation. "Men such as they are, very naturally seek money or power; and power because it is as good as money. . . . And why not? for they aspire to the highest, and this, in their sleep-walking, they dream is highest. Wake them, and they shall quit the false good and leap to the true. . . . This revolution is to be wrought by the gradual domestication of the idea of Culture. The main enterprise of the world for splendor, for extent, is the upbuilding of a man." Nor is self-culture—the prefix "self " beginning a domestication of *Bildung*, bringing it within the province of *a* person, as opposed to some wave of a figure, like society, race, or nation—merely a topic that Emerson addresses, say in the "Introductory" to his *Human Culture* lectures, or in the "Culture" essay that one finds in *Conduct of Life*. Self-culture is also a matter that

Emerson's writings express and perform. As many have noted, Emerson's texts, whether journal entry, public address, or essay, enact the declaration from "literary ethics" with which Emerson elevates himself to the ranks of Plato, Shakespeare, and Milton: "I will also essay to be." That is, Emerson's writing is Emerson elaborating himself, practicing self-culture on the page, in the sentence, with the word, "building up a force of thought which may be turned at will on any subjects," to rely on Emerson's contemporary William Ellery Channing.

By temperament and training, both philosophical, I am rarely able to leave well enough alone. As soon as I found myself turning toward issues of self-culture in Emerson (and I need you to hear the word *issues* at least twice), I began to worry about what it meant to work with Emerson. What haunted me was not the question, What is a philosopher doing reading Emerson? Matters of philosophical import are everywhere in his work. Moreover, I am not without role models in this regard, most notably Stanley Cavell, though there are others such as Cornel West. Rather, my perplexity was that of an obsessive who returns to what seems secure, even legitimate, and frets: "But do you really know what's going on here?" There is something neurotic in this kind of revolution, this incessant turning back upon oneself. But can one bent on self-knowledge do otherwise, at least every now and then, particularly when the luster of our inspirations fade, in what Emerson would term our "idle hours"? I doubt it, particularly if Emerson is right when he insists, repeatedly, that there is nothing mean in nature, or more elaborately, in "Spiritual Laws," "Human character evermore publishes itself. The most fugitive deed and word, the mere doing of a thing, the intimated purpose, expresses character."

I confess to this compulsion because it makes evident that my turn to Emerson, my reading him, my writing about him is part and parcel of my own self-culture, that more is going on here than a gathering of signs to render "Emerson" transparent. In fact, in addressing you I am also offering your self-culture something to take or leave, in part or whole—for now, consider it a way of a reading, one that takes Emerson personally, as if, in a sense I will try to specify, our lives were at stake in his address and the ways in which we receive it.

When a philosopher frets over reading, you might suppose the concern will be primarily epistemological. But my fuss is less a matter of insuring accurate readings than of examining reading as a practice that manifests my character. I am thus more concerned with how and why we read than with arming myself with a purported method. In fact, I am rather distrustful of the language of method and what it seems to promise.

Rhetorically, "method" suggests something secure, a mode of engagement that is particularly appropriate to the matter at hand, that has secured a kind of privileged access, something in virtue of which one's reading would be more than a series of fallible steps along paths opening within hermeneutic circles. But one cannot elude such circles, and thus reading is always a matter of double reading, of reading a text against a previous construal, be it one's own, another's, or the prereflective construals that one's sociopsychological background conditions instantiate. Epistemologically speaking, then, philosophy—or more generally, theory—has nothing particularly insightful to offer interpretation.

For those who find this glib, let me add the following. A text is readable only on the basis of certain preconditions—in the least, literacy, cultural associations, and an implicit or explicit theory of textuality, one that delimits meaning with reference to elements such as authorial intent, unconscious projections, class struggles, genres and forms, literary devices like enjambments, and so forth. Given those conditions, we proceed by tracking the interplay of textual elements, whether formal, thematic, or performative, until a meaning becomes apparent—ubiquitous and unstable metaphysical oppositions, Plato's esoteric doctrine, or Nietzsche's self-overcoming inquiry into truth. Some meaning in hand, one then compares one's efforts with those of others, real or imagined—activities suggesting that reading is, at least formally, a communicative act. So one continues until one thinks one has it well in hand.

As I see it, interpretations clash when they track differently or disagree about what elements delimit the meaning of the text, and an interpretation succeeds to the degree that it shows how some set of elements combines to present certain meanings rather than others. In either case, the proof is in the putting, that is, as Adorno insists in "Lyric Poetry and Society," all readings, even sociological readings, must vindicate claims in and through the text. I stress this because ascertaining a context is not the same as interpreting a text, just as looking up a word in a dictionary is not the same as tracing its meaning within a poem. This is not to say that texts generate their own meaning. Nor is it to say that the text is a fixed playing field. Rather, my insistence is that whatever meaning is *found* there, whether it involves class struggle, sublimated desire, authorial intent, or language speaking itself, must be found *there*.

Now, if one could secure from the outset the propriety of those conditions that make a text readable in the first place, which include the elements whose interactions produce meaning, one might imagine the process of vision and revision coming to an end. But those initial steps are part and parcel of the interpretation, and thus equally susceptible to revision. Said otherwise, every interpretation, even a long-standing one, may find itself in the scene that opens Emerson's "Experience":

> Where do we find ourselves? In a series, of which we do not know the extremes, and believe that it has none. We wake and find ourselves on a stair:

there are stairs below us, which we seem to have ascended; there are stairs above us, many a one, which go upward and out of sight. But the Genius which, according to the old belief, stands at the door by which we enter, and gives us the lethe to drink, that we may tell no tales, mixed the cup too strongly, and we cannot shake off the lethargy now at noonday. Sleep lingers all our lifetime about our eyes, as night hovers all day in the boughs of the fir-tree. All things swim and glimmer. Our life is not so much threatened as our perception. Ghostlike we glide through nature, and should not know our place again.

Because this fate might befall any interpretation at any time, it strikes me that philosophy will never convincingly lay hold of criteria, say on the basis of a theory of textuality, that will categorically distinguish better from worse readings, and thus it has little to offer interpretation by way of epistemic insight. One would do better to take to heart, and repeatedly, questions such as, Now where and how does it say that? As Emerson tells an audience in 1837: "I acknowledge that the mind is also a distorting medium so long as its aims are not pure. But the moment the individual declares his independence, takes his life into his own hand, and sets forth in quest of culture, the love of truth is a sufficient gauge. It is very clear that he can have no other."

But more than epistemic questions arise as we read. In taking Emerson's texts into my own go at self-culture, I have come to regard him as a peer of sorts, as someone with something to tell me about how I might cultivate my life. But his texts are old, their author dead. So what kind of reading is this? How am I receiving this pile of texts signed "Emerson"?

Let me begin by way of negation. In reading Emerson through self-culture, I am not involved in source criticism. My concern is not Emerson's sources, whether within his corpus—tying together journal, lecture, and essay passages—or without,—determining what precisely Emerson drew from Coleridge, Kant, and de Stael regarding genius. Nor am I much concerned with Emerson's influence on later thinkers, for example, Nietzsche, as great or slight as it may be. I admire such work, but after awhile, it makes me impatient. I want a reading eventually to ask: "Should I think and/or act in this way? What claim does it have upon me?" Source-critical treatments of a text stand aloof from such questions, however. Instead, they regard the text as a function in a causal series and work to locate that text's contributions to the series, discerning contingencies and effects—for instance, Emerson got that from William Ellery Channing, and William James took this from Emerson.

The essays of self-culture are also not principally comparativist, and for a similar reason. While it is genuinely instructive, for example, to compare how Emerson and Thoreau received the *Bhagavad Gita*, unless we eventually champion or descry aspects of the how and what of their reception, we are left with artifacts whose place in self-culture is merely ornamental. Again, valuable work, but not the work of self-culture, and thus not the kind of work I want my reading of Emerson to do.

Without much precision, I would say at this point that I am hoping more to work with Emerson than to talk about him. I am thus not all that concerned with what one might call Emerson's "considered views" on matters of long-standing philosophical concern, such as freedom and determinism. I am mistrustful of the authority of so-called considered views. As readers of extant work, authors are just that, readers, and not necessarily the best. Focusing upon a supposedly considered view might very well obscure thoughts and/or implications whose brilliance eluded the author's considerations. I prefer to focus on problematics, not theses or views. What grabs me is that to which a text or corpus responds, what Heidegger would term its "*Sache.*" My principal concern is what to think about the matter at hand, not which view Emerson eventually elected.

But what, one rightfully asks, does it mean to attend to the matter at hand while interpreting a text? Emerson's feel for Shakespeare gives us the beginnings of an answer: "[T]he Genius draws up the ladder after him, when the creative age goes up to heaven, and gives way to a new, which seeks the works, and asks in vain for a history." But what does this entail, and must any such reading prove ahistorical? I think not, but it will take some time to show you why.

In seeking works instead of authors, I am not supposing that works simply await our gaze. I concur with Emerson's assertion in the *English Literature* series of 1835–36: "Reading must not be passive. The pupil must conspire with the Teachers. It needs Shakspear, it needs Bacon, to read Shakspear and Bacon in the best manner." As Heidegger will say about a hundred years later, preparing his students for an encounter with Hölderlin, reading is a struggle against ourselves, a "*Kampf gegen uns*," one in which we attempt to translate ourselves into the fundamental sensibility and mood in and with which a work addresses us. Emerson offers us a similar though differently mooded thought in *Representative Men*. "Shakspeare is the only biographer of Shakspeare, and even he can tell nothing except to the Shakspeare in us, that is, to our most apprehensive and sympathetic hour." Odd thoughts. Let us see if we cannot position ourselves so as to apprehend their claim.

In comporting myself toward Emerson's texts through something like the Emerson in me, I am approaching them as their secret addressee, to invoke a figure offered by Osip Mandelstam in 1916. This is not narcissism. I am not presuming that Emerson wrote with me in mind. Rather, to engage a text as its secret addressee is to respect a dimension of its performativity. Every speech act, no matter its content, no matter its form, has a second-person facet: it is addressed to another. So too the essay and the lecture; just like the poem. Mandelstam on his mind, Paul Celan writes in 1958: "The poem can be, because it is a manifestation of language and thus dialogical by nature, a letter in a bottle sent with the faith—certainly not always full of hope—that it might sometime and somewhere wash ashore, perhaps on the land of the heart."

Let this be a first designation, then. When I say I am taking Emerson personally, this is to say that I hear or read him interpersonally, that I am reading a speaker as his or her addressee, or to defer to a figure from his journals: "Happy is he who looks only into his work to know if it will succeed, never into the times or the public opinion; and who writes from the love of imparting certain thoughts & not from the necessity of sale—who writes always to *the unknown friend.*" Emerson's texts are thus not merely outcroppings on the mountain of objective spirit, although they are certainly that insofar as they are part and parcel of our cultural record. But they also address us with a second-person liveliness, and our reception of them should register that, just as one should acknowledge a friend's criticism as a criticism and not simply as the product of sociopsychological forces.

You may be thinking: "Shouldn't a philosopher be concerned with Emerson's claims?" I am. I reject Emerson's recurrent theodicy, his belief that a divine being orders history in a way that is ultimately and thus persistently just. "What can be more sublime," he tells an early audience, "than this doctrine that the soul of the world does impregnate every atom and every spirit with its omnipotent virtue, so that all things are tuned and set to good. Evil is merely privative not absolute." And I am cheered by and would defend his insistence that self-culture is intrinsically dependent upon enabling conditions: "You cannot have one well-bred man without a whole society of such." But a claim is not merely some proposition floating in a space between our ears, ascribing predicates to subjects or offering predictions. Nor is it simply a premise or a conclusion, a logically determinate rung in the ladder of an argument.

I am not suggesting that Emerson fails to offer arguments, or that his claims do not have what has come to be called "propositional content." He has arguments, and his remarks refer to states of affairs: emanations, intuitions, and moods. My point, rather, is that Emerson's claims are not reducible to that content or the logical forms in which they are presented. Moreover, any reading that proceeds by way of such reductions misreads the claims that Emerson advances, ignoring both the intersubjectivity of Emerson's address and other performative dimensions opening within the genres of the lecture and essay.

Much has been said about the genre of the essay, from its individuality to its spontaneity to its fragmentary nature, and much of that discussion applies to Emerson's own essays. What I would stress here, however, is that Emerson's essays are concentrated versions of his lectures. This is not to remind us of the obvious, namely, that many of Emerson's essays had their first run at the lectern. Rather, my point is that what Emerson sought in his lectures, "an eloquence that can agitate," also orients his essays. In a journal of 1839, Emerson writes: "Is it not plain that not in senates or courts or chambers of commerce but in the conversation of the true philosopher the eloquence must be found that can agitate, convict, inspire, & possess us & guide us to a true peace? I look upon the Lecture room as the true church of today." To my ear, this passage holds a key to the door through which we might responsibly receive Emerson's claims.

Emerson's essays and lectures are agitating in the broad sense. They start us thinking, in irritation or excitement. They thus not only ruminate, as William Gass has suggested, but nip and gnaw at what passes for truisms—that consistency is a virtue, that Jesus was an unsurpassable moralist, or that an exemplar cannot be great and flawed. Not that they tell us to be agitated, or give us imperatives, although at times they do. Rather, they are agitating performances, rhetorically provoking us, say with the kind of overstatement we just witnessed. "Is it not plain that not in senates or courts or chambers of commerce but in the conversation of the true philosopher the eloquence must be found that can agitate?" But such a matter is far from plain. In fact, coming as it does from one who holds self-reliance in such high esteem, I find the appeal more like bait dangling before me, bait that if taken, forces me to determine the matter for myself.

Emerson's writings are also full of accusation—for example, "We are afraid of truth, afraid of fortune, afraid of death, and afraid of each other." Such remarks convict us directly, driving us to recall (or hope for) postures that rise above the cower of cowardice. At times we find ourselves convicted less directly, however, and often in the passages we find most inspiring. "What is it we heartily wish of each other? Is it to be pleased and flattered? No, but to be convicted and exposed, to be shamed out of our nonsense of all kinds, and made men of, instead of ghosts and phantoms. We are weary of gliding ghostlike through the world, which is itself so slight and unreal. We crave a sense of reality, though it come in strokes of pain." Here Emerson is baiting us with our own desire to grow, to improve, to leave dross and moss behind. And while I thrill to the thought—and I do, even now—I realize that most of the time I do not desire this, at least not strongly, but live "afraid of truth, afraid of fortune, afraid of death, and afraid of others." And so, in my affirmation of that with which Emerson tempts me, shame rises as I realize how often I do not live the life I really want. In passages such as these, therefore, it is less that Emerson accuses me than that he enables me to accuse myself, thus drawing out of me what he so often demands of me: self-reliance.

While provocative, Emerson's lectures and essays ultimately resist indoctrination. In "Considerations by the Way," he writes: "Although this garrulity of advising is born with us, I confess that life is rather a subject of wonder, than of didactics." And as he tells an audience in a better-known passage: "Truly speaking, it is not instruction, but provocation, that I can receive from another soul." Socratic rather than encyclopedic in their orientation, Emerson's remarks thus seek to "possess" their addressees with something other than doctrine.

But what else is there?

Consider the essay "Experience." It opens with a manifold realization that the steps that have brought us here are not what we took them to be, while the steps that lie ahead may buck and sway and topple us should we attempt to ascend them on the basis of what we know. Perhaps our theories may fall flat. Or, more powerfully, our children might perish, and leave us both empty across years we imagined would be full, and guilty that we were able to live on without them. Full in the swim and glitter of this uncertainty, the essay proceeds to probe and test the "lords of life" whose march the prefatory poem marks as defining moments of a day, and all in the hopes of securing a foothold. But Emerson's reckoning, speculative and incisive as it is, fails to call these lords to order—among them, illusion, temperament, surface, and surprise. Instead, in the third to last paragraph, he confesses, "I know better than to claim any completeness for my picture. I am a fragment, and this is a fragment of me." And he accepts, in both a theoretical and practical way, the moral this insight imposes: "I know that the world I converse with in the city and in the farms, is not the world *I think*. I observe the difference, and shall observe it." The essay thus fails to overcome the impasse with which it began. This is not to say the essay fails, however. It seeks an "eloquence that agitates." Thus, if it brings us to this step and leaves us there (and it leaves us there in the speaker's commitment to an almost ritualistic observance of the difference between appearance and reality), then the essay succeeds insofar as it prods us to determine for ourselves, in and through our observances, what we need in order to move on, to ascend the steps of experience, to pursue the "true romance which the world exists to realize . . . the transformation of genius into practical power," to cite the essay's cheering, inspiring final line.

A proper reception of Emerson's texts thus not only requires an acknowledgment of the challenges they pose—challenges to our beliefs, habits, and character—but also a willingness to assume the tasks they set, conclude them as we will. *Conduct of Life* is thus not simply the title of one of Emerson's late collections; it names that which his claims consistently invoke as a matter in question for both speaker and addressee. In reading Emerson, then, one should be drawn to the etymological roots of "claim," the Latin *clamare*, to call or shout out. An Emersonian claim calls out, shouts even, in order to compel us to take it to heart and adjust our lives accordingly.

In stressing the performative aspects of Emerson's texts, I am not suggesting that their claims are provocations without content, as if we could translate each into one stern command such as, "Think for yourself."

Emerson's lectures and essays offer numerous thoughts purporting to be insights. And while he never systematically binds them together, this does not mean that they are offered ironically. When Emerson tells us, "In our way of talking, we say, 'That is yours, this is mine;' but the poet knows well that it is not his; that it is as strange and beautiful to him as to you," he is offering a phenomenologically astute account of thought. Likewise, anticipating what Heidegger later termed "*Geworfenheit,*" throwness, he aptly describes in "The Over-Soul" our more general condition: "Man is a stream whose source is hidden. Our being is descending into us from we know not whence." Emerson's claims thus not only seek to possess us with the problems they set before us, but also with touchstones from which we might address those problems, touchstones we might ourselves essay, that is, make an experiment of, try out, venture.

I have been outlining what Emerson would regard as a "manner," a way of behaving, a way of reading, of receiving and responding to claims and provocations. At this point I need to add that Emerson's claims are not offered on their own behalf, as if some person "Emerson" were trying to convince us of something in order to have convinced us, in order to have won some argument or even a convert. Instead, they seek our attention on behalf of some matter that has compelled them. Their so-called propositional content is something to which they have been driven to bear witness, and our reception of them is lacking if we overlook this responsive pathos, one quite evident in Emerson's feel for lecturing: "But only then is the orator successful when he is himself agitated & is as much a hearer as any of the assembly."

By tuning the notion of claim with the notion of witnessing, I am underscoring the debt that any claim owes to that which is witnessed. What goes by the name of propositional content is neither the possession of an Emersonian claim nor something entirely produced by an Emersonian text. Rather, Emerson's claims are responses to what has been given to them, made evident. One could state it this way: it is not that an Emersonian remark lays claim to the matter at hand, but that it is claimed by that matter. In still other words, Emerson's claims become such because they have been called as witnesses for some matter. Taking Emerson personally is thus not only a matter of receiving his claims as provocative interpersonal addresses, replete with tasks, but also one of attending to the witness and testimony at work in those addresses, and all in order to bring it to the shorelines of one's heart, that is, to receive it as having the potential to claim one as well.

A passage from "New England Reformers" should help us here. Emerson writes: "As every man at heart wishes the best and not inferior society, wishes to be convicted of his error, and to come to himself, so he wishes that the same healing should not stop in his thoughts, but should penetrate his will or active power." This is a remarkable line, the kind Stanley Cavell has helped make legible, one that sketches a landscape that readings should traverse if they wish to join Emerson in pursuit of self-culture. At its close, the line suggests that we keep the company we do (including collections of essays, I would think), because it promises a deepened self-knowledge whose translation into practical power provides a life more fully lived, that is, one with richer and deeper relations. To his readers, then, Emerson seems to be saying, "Isn't this why you are here, to come to yourselves?" And "Aren't these the stakes of your reading—a kind of healing, even empowerment?" We need not agree with the assertions embedded in these rhetorical questions; but in receiving them we are nevertheless driven to consider why we have sought the company of this text, and that seems Emerson's deeper concern—that we engage him on terms we have thematized and chosen, that we know why we are here, reading, reflecting.

Consider next the opening moments of Emerson's sentence: "As every man at heart wishes . . ." In venturing a description of what goes on in our hearts, the line provokes the reader to search out his or her heart, to pose a similar question, less "Why am I reading this?" than "What do I really believe?" In other words, Emerson is indirectly insisting, as he does at the end of the line, "You'd better be taking this personally," and rhetorically provoking us to do so.

As it continues, the passage also predicts what one will find in one's heart: a wish for good, ennobling company. For now, my concern is not whether this thought, one recurrent throughout Plato's early dialogues, merits our assent. Rather, I want to direct your attention to how Emerson figures the heart: with a wish, a longing for what is not in our control. In Emerson's implicit instruction to consult our hearts, this figure of the wish instructs us on how to consult our hearts. Our concern should not simply be what we are willing to defend in an agon of debate. Rather, he directs his readers to those matters that have claimed them, those matters on whose behalf they might bear witness, say through an argument. In his claim about what lurks in our hearts, therefore, Emerson is also tuning his predictive assertion with what we could call the "terms of the heart," with the wish, an inclining toward something that has claimed us and has drawn an emphatic response.

Oddly, even surprisingly, I think we are now at a point to make better sense of Emerson's claim that the best reader of Bacon needs Bacon, that one should approach Shakespeare from the Shakespeare within. I think we find the Shakespeare within when we personally attend to the matters to which Shakespeare's claims bear witness and to the tasks those claims initiate, for then we begin to see what it would mean to think in this way, what it might mean to be Bacon, to be Shakespeare, to be the bearer of these thoughts, which is not to say their creator, but one who takes them to heart.

Let us parse this process. First, this is not simply a passive reception. Preparation is required, for as Emerson observes elsewhere, "books are good only as far as a boy is ready for them." After all, to read well, one must be literate, have time, be willing and able to concentrate, be open to having one's mind changed, what is, all in all, as much a matter of mood as it is of opportunity and ability, as Emerson himself notes in "Experience." "We animate what we can, and we see only what we animate. It depends on the mood of the man whether he shall see the sunset or a fine poem. There are always sunsets, and there is always genius; but only a few hours so serene that we can relish nature or criticism." Second, one needs to acquire a sense for that to which the work is a response, matters at times quite evident (for instance, throughout his life, Emerson rejects the leveling authority of commerce), and at other times barely perceptible (in championing intuition and conversation, Emerson both instantiates the philosophy of the subject—which regards every thought as a presentation of self-consciousness—and pushes past that paradigm into a more intersubjective one that regards every thought as also presented to an interlocutor). Third, we must also imagine the prospects that await us should our own active power be claimed by thoughts like these, for Emerson is insistent that "[e]very act of intellection is mainly prospective." For example, if it is the case that, for the attentive, sublimity lurks in every thing, event, even moment, then we must begin to imagine what it would mean to live in the sublimity of a conversation, a meal, a quick trip to the store, a morning shower, and so forth.

I should stress that prospecting is a risky business, for one might find forecast in a given claim a future at odds with the manner in which the claim first announced itself. For example, Emerson's trust in self-trust, in self-reliance, is empowered by the purportedly divine ground of our involuntary perceptions. But once so empowered, involuntary perceptions may turn against that ground, even venture futures without it, as Emerson seems to do when he says, somewhat peevishly, "but if I am the Devil's child, I will live then from the Devil." Mining prospects thus may broach changes that not only follow from certain claims, but double back upon them, exposing a tenuous force field where, at least initially, there had been a simplicity—that behind which analysis cannot go, to recall Emerson's own description of involuntary perceptions. In other words, prospecting may chance upon futures almost unthinkable at the outset.

These three efforts—preparation, ascertaining that to which the text is a response, and prospecting—amount to a conspiracy with our teachers within an apprehensive and sympathetic hour. Not that our assent is required, as if sympathy necessitated agreement. Rather, the task is to take the claim to heart and apprehend it such that it *might* also claim us for its own, perhaps even in a new manner, one more Bacon than Bacon. In other words, one who conspires with a text may at some point realize, as Emerson did, "Our best thoughts came from others. We heard in their words a deeper sense than the speakers put into them, and could express ourselves in other people's phrases to finer purpose than they knew."

In taking Emerson personally, in receiving his responsive address on the shorelines of my heart, in conspiring with him, I am driven to eschew a strictly historicist regard for textuality. Such readings limit a text's illocutionary reach to its peers. But if I am to receive that address on the shoreline of my heart, then I must also be implicated in what Emerson essays. And if I am implicated in those experiments, then I too am called to attend to that to which they bear witness. Now, it may be the case that I can only share in that witness if I bind the intension of Emerson's claims to concepts extant at the time of their articulation or to then current situations to which a thought or phrase would be a response. I doubt it. Such a position underplays what we might term a text's "prospective force," the ways in which its dynamics, even while employing extant forms, bring new meanings to worn tropes. (Consider the fate of "experience" in Dewey's *Experience and Nature* or "asceticism" in Nietzsche's *Genealogy of Morals.*) Moreover, such emergences may only come to light given the altered presumptions of future readers, of unknown friends. Emerson records in his journal that "it was not possible to write the history of Shakspear until now. For it was on the translation of Shakspear into German by Lessing that 'the succeeding rapid burst of German literature was most intimately concerned.' Here certainly is an important particular in the story of that great mind yet how recent! And is this the last fact?" In short, historicism seems to preclude the ways in which a text may prove untimely, or rather, timely for a later set of readers, as Plutarch proved to Emerson. "Plutarch fits me better than Southey or Scott, therefore, I say, there is no age to good writing."

I should stress that by embracing Emerson's address as a living provocation and challenge, I am not receiving it ahistorically. If anything, I am receiving it with a finer feel for historical occurrence than historicism provides. In "History," Emerson writes: "The student is to read history actively and not passively; to esteem his own life the text, and books the commentary. Thus compelled, the muse of history will utter oracles, as never to those who do not respect themselves." This insistence is well grounded for at least three reasons. First, insofar as histories are not only told but also received, discursively or otherwise, some activity on the part of the recipient is required. To deny this, to skulk about one's own receptions, to conceal oneself within the repetitions that propel our lives, is tantamount to a kind of self-denial that estranges us from the historical dimensions of our being. Moreover, such denials are hermeneutically suspect. Not only are they naively positivistic, as if historical events were ascertainable without interpretation, but they conceal the purposes prompting and orienting their interpretations, the kind of *teloi* that accompany all practices. This kind of concealment troubles me less for the biases it might introduce than for the way in which it obscures the commitments and contributions that orient and follow from a reckoning with history that is itself the unfolding of history. In receiving Emerson's claims, therefore, we need to bring those commitments and effects within the folds of self-culture, both to better apprehend who it is we are becoming and to consider whether those ends and results square with our deepest wishes.

In refusing the limits of historicism, in treating Emerson as if he were in some sense my contemporary, my reading enters into a perplexing time signature. Let me again make my way with the help of Celan. "For the poem is not timeless. Certainly, it raises a claim to the infinite, it seeks to grasp it through time—but through, not over and above it." In receiving Emerson outside the hermeneutic sensibility of historicism, I am not setting these texts or their reception outside of time: neither event is timeless, *Zeitlos*, literally, "without time." The texts, full of quotations, explicit and implicit, are repetitions, the paper of the centenary edition at least one hundred years old. And my readings are no less repetitions, responses to previous readings such as Cavell's, dialogues with other addresses, some named (Heidegger) some not (Habermas). But in receiving the texts of Emerson, I am receiving an address that lays claim to the infinite, and in the following sense: it lays claim to a perpetual now in which it speaks. This is not the infinite of indefinite duration nor the omnipresence of what is at once alpha and omega, beginning and end. Rather, it is a perpetually living present, one that arrives with every reception of the work.

I am not suggesting that Emerson's texts are about infinity, although some are. Rather, they grasp the infinite in the performativity of their address, in the hand they extend to their secret addressees, in the bottle to which they have entrusted their fate. As he writes in a journal of 1839: "A lecture is a new literature, which leaves aside all tradition, time, place, circumstance, & addresses an assembly as (pure) mere human beings,—no more." And a bit later, again reflecting on lecturing: "I am to invite men drenched in time to recover themselves and come out of time, & taste their native immortal air."

Readers of the essay "History" may find my line of thinking oblique given Emerson's assertion therein, "When a thought of Plato becomes a thought to me, when a truth that fired the soul of Pindar fires mine, time is no more. When I feel that we two meet in a perception, that our two souls are tinged with the same hue, and do, as it were, run into one, why should I measure degrees of latitude, why should I count Egyptian years?" But one must not receive this claim concerning the cessation of time too passively. In the same essay, some pages later, Emerson states: "No man can antedate his experience, or guess what faculty or feeling a new object shall unlock, any more than he can draw to-day the face of the person whom he shall see to-morrow for the first time." Read back into the earlier remark, this dependence upon the temporality of experience draws the reception of Pindar's fire into a present moment, one that is always potentially novel, even shocking. Emerson's position is thus closer to Celan's then one might have thought. His move to the point beyond Egyptian years is one that moves through the time of experience, and thus, strictly speaking, is not *Zeitlos*. It arrives in time, perhaps just in time, and not like a mummy, preserved but lifeless—if I have heard the qualifier *Egyptian* well. Rather, it arrives still living, still speaking, still seeking a secret addressee, and doing so now, as I address you.

In accepting the infinite offer of Emerson's texts, one enters, perhaps, what Walter Benjamin regards as the *Jetztzeit*, the "now-time" in which a past might be citable in all its moments, in which nothing is lost and everyone has their say. But what does this mean for reading? Benjamin takes the *Jetztzeit* to interrupt the histories of the victor, histories that are told in order to vindicate the privileges and choices of those with the power to tell (and/or publish), histories that murder victims a second time. In our context (to the degree we know it), to receive the provocative offer of an Emersonian claim within the *Jetztzeit* of its address is to resist the reckoning of the victor who claims figures as his or her own, like spoils of war, or consigns them to the graves of the defeated. More concretely, this entails not insisting that Emerson is principally one kind of thinker to the exclusion of another—a proto-pragmatist, a neo-Hegelian, a Vedantist, or an American original. Likewise, it requires that we struggle against ourselves to receive all that claims our attention in his texts, everything to which his texts bear witness, all the moments marked on the list just given, as well as others left off it.

Let me be clear about the task this Benjaminian turn initiates. Taking Emerson personally involves inheriting him, actively. And where we find thoughts, images, and omissions that we would not inherit, we must disinherit them in an equally active manner, rather than read as if they were not there. Are you thrilled, as I am, by the strands of neo-Platonism that run throughout Emerson's texts? Or are you frustrated by what you regard as premodern lapses? Do you accept his attempt in *English Traits* to come to terms with the conception of race, relying upon it "for convenience, and not as exact and final"? Or do you, like me, find even a nominalist-inflected racialism untenable? However one answers, the point is that such queries must be answered, that is, they must be essayed in the course of a reading, regardless of whether we would perpetuate them or set them aside.

In setting Emerson's essays and lectures within the context of Benjamin's and Celan's remarks, I am intensifying the stakes erected in William Gass's "Emerson and the Essay." Gass regards an Emersonian essay as a convocation of writers quoted and invoked for the purpose of pleasure, praise, and a confirmation of the "continuity, the contemporaneity, the reality of writing." A convocation of pleasure and praise, while it may evince the enduring value of writing, lacks the responsive pathos of the Emersonian essay. For Emerson, the reality of writing (and of reading, for that matter) is a reality of witness and provocation, and thus a reality unwilling to celebrate itself on its own behalf. Emerson's writing clamors for our attention so that we might also essay the matter at hand, whether friendship, gifts, or worship. For readers of Emerson, this means that we should care less that Emerson is citing the Koran, Goethe, or himself, and attend instead to the prospects that await one should she or he take a remark to heart. As Emerson says at the outset of *Representative Men*: "But I find him greater, when he can abolish himself and all heroes, by letting in this element of reason, irrespective of persons, this subtilizer, and irresistible upward force, into our thought, destroying individualism;—the power so great, that the potentate is nothing."

If one receives Emerson's texts within the now of their address, his corpus undergoes an amazing transformation: it assembles into one long, multifaceted collection of essays, lectures, journals, letters, and sermons. Or, said otherwise, reading Emerson in the now of his address is a matter of moving among one massive conversation, each remark a message in a bottle signed "RWE." This is not to presume that the whole presents a unified view. Contemporaneity in no way insures congruence. In fact, the artificial unity sometimes imposed upon a corpus by the author function fractures when every claim is admitted. In the now of their address it may prove easier, therefore, to critically engage Emerson's claims, for instance his occasional racial determinism, because we will receive them alongside others, such as his denial in "Experience" that temperament is in any why final or fixed. But more important, by essaying Emerson's corpus as a contemporaneous phenomenon its manifold witness and challenge can be shared, taken up, and possibly deepened. As Emerson says: "The Past is for us; but the sole terms on which it can become ours are its subordination to the Present."

The view I am offering is not as crazy as it sounds. The address of an Emersonian text is ever present, always asking to be taken to heart, to be taken personally, and in the fullness of its responsive provocations. His efforts are thus no exception to a rule he so rightly recounts. "A good sentence, a noble verse which I meet in my reading are an epoch in my life. From month to month from year to year they remain fresh & memorable."

I first read "Self-Reliance" when I was fifteen, with Mary Capello, a first-year teacher from Dickinson College, if my memory serves. Now, more than twenty years later, its address persists, that is, it awaits me, perpetually arriving, even though I am no longer that boy, and it is no longer that text for me or anyone else, except perhaps with regard to that time signature I have been calling "Emerson." I say this because I am still its secret addressee, and I will be whenever I read: "I read the other day some verses written by an eminent painter which were original and not conventional."

I am not claiming that Emerson's texts offer secure, timeless truths. What is eternally now is not some propositional content but the now of the event of our reading, the meeting of speaker and addressee, the now in which we might find ourselves upon a stair, upon a series of steps of which we do not know the extremes. This is the now in which self-culture unfolds, conspiring with teachers, one in which we might meet ourselves and change our lives or, more likely, the now in which we prove afraid of ourselves, of one another, of fortune and death. This is the now of agitation, of an inspiration that convicts us of being something less than inspired and inspiring. In short, this is the now of crisis, a turning point, an unstable moment that no one can resolve for us. As Emerson says in a lecture from 1837, "There are heights of character to which a man must ascend alone—not to be foreshown,—that can only exist by the arrival of the man and the crisis." To take Emerson personally is to risk that arrival, to read as if one's life were at stake, here and now.

Bibliography

Adorno, T. W. *Notes to Literature: Volume I*. New York: Columbia University Press, 1991.

Atkins, G. Douglas. *Estranging the Familiar*. Athens: University of Georgia Press 1992.

Benjamin, Walter. *Selected Writings: Volume 4, 1938–1940*. Cambridge: Harvard University Press, 2003.

Blackie, John Stuart. *Self-Culture*. New York: Scribner, Armstrong, 1874.

Butrym, Alexander J. *Essays on the Essay*. Athens: University of Georgia Press, 1989.

Cavell, Stanley. *Emerson's Transcendental Etudes*. Edited by David Hodge. Stanford: Stanford University Press, 2003.

Celan, Paul. *Gesammelte Werke: Dritter Band*. Frankfurt am Main: Suhrkamp, 1983.

Channing, W. E. *The Works of William E. Channing: I–II*. New York: Franklin, 1882.

Clarke, James Freeman. *Self-Culture*. Boston: Houghton Mifflin, 1880.

De Obaldia, Claire. *The Essaying Spirit*. Oxford: Clarendon, 1995.

Emerson, Ralph Waldo. *Centenary Edition: Volume 8*. Boston: Houghton, Mifflin, 1904.

———. *Collected Works: Volume I*. Cambridge: Harvard University Press, 1971.

———. *Collected Works: Volume II*. Cambridge: Harvard University Press, 1979.

———. *Collected Works: Volume III*. Cambridge: Harvard University Press, 1983.

———. *Collected Works: Volume IV*. Cambridge: Harvard University Press, 1987.

———. *Collected Works: Volume V*. Cambridge: Harvard University Press, 1994.

———. *Collected Works: Volume VI*. Cambridge: Harvard University Press, 2003.

———. *The Early Lectures: Volume I*. Cambridge: Harvard University Press, 1966.

———. *The Early Lectures: Volume II*. Cambridge: Harvard University Press, 1964.

———. *Journals and Miscelaneous Notebooks: Volume V*. Cambridge: Harvard University Press, 1965.

———. *Journals and Miscelaneous Notebooks: Volume VII*. Cambridge: Harvard University Press, 1969.

————. *Journals and Miscelaneous Notebooks: Volume X.* Cambridge: Harvard University Press, 1973.

————. *Journals and Miscelaneous Notebooks: Volume XII.* Cambridge: Harvard University Press, 1976.

Gass, William H. "Emerson and the Essay." *The Yale Review* 71, no. 3 (1982).

Heidegger, Martin. *Gesamtausgabe: Band 39: Hölderlins Hymnen >>Germanien<< und >>Der Rhein<<.* Frankfurt am Main: Vittorio Klostermann, 1980.

Kirklighter, Cristina. *Traversing the Democratic Borders of the Essay.* Albany: State University of New York Press, 2002.

Mandelstam, Osip. *The Complete and Critical Prose and Letters.* Ann Arbor: Ardis, 1979.

McDermott, John Joseph. *Streams of Experience: Reflections on the History and Philosophy of American Culture.* Amherst: University of Massachusetts Press, 1986.

O'Leary, R. D. *The Essay.* New York: Crowell, 1928.

Speare, M. Edmund. *The Essay.* New York: Oxford University Press, American Branch, 1927.

West, Cornel. *The American Evasion of Philosophy.* Madison: University of Wisconsin Press, 1989.

Local Knowledge

Paul Hoover

They float; they
mean. Ripping their
there. What reaches

them, what smother?
Expected . . . seems to
lean as every

other voice soaking
in its moan,
its name and

evening pronounced as
words, vocables flashing
back—here, where

she's expected—like
refinement & forgiveness.
Throughout her head,

petroglyphs of sand
are crazed with
faults. Recent evidence,

local knowledge, like
light on faces
(gone again, due)

her first glance
takes. Not ripe
things seen. Thimble

in heaven. Van
Gogh's thousands of
grey-greens competing

for the landscape
because the mind
moves over it

like a hand.
Insistent sound of
keys turning in

locks, ice easing
down rivers, collard
green squeak. These

are memory's freaks,
the past breathing
back. Overadorned

and catastrophic, nature
takes serial journeys
past historic sites.

Hatched in water,
pinched life stirs.
As Emerson writes,

"Under every deep
a lower deep
opens." Not now,

but soon enough
and in language
one succumbs to

the cold mind's
warmth, immune to
praise, pitiless as

blame, having arrived
on different trains
and leaving each

by each. There's
no "new meaning."
Old worlds circle

beyond our contriving
yet with such
flavor the living

gods are flattered
back into their
graves. Balance means

cancel. They float,
they mean. Apparent
in their fervor.

Chapter 7

Face to Face with Emerson

David Marr

*I*f only Emerson had not flaunted his illogicality, had not wavered in his observance of the difference between meaning and naming, had not dismissed the homonymy principle, and had been less in touch with his American audience's craving for cultural independence, he might, in *Nature*, have left us a duller treatise. The three aforementioned philosophical indiscretions, wrapped as they are in a rousing appeal to the audience for his first book, occur in the sweeping introduction, a four-paragraph masterpiece of Emersonian sleight-of-hand. The errors, if that is what they are, unfold as follows. Emerson flaunts his illogicality when he uses the term he would define, *nature*, in the definition—and then declares himself immune to logical criticism. Readers will recall the first sense of 'nature' announced in the axiomatic opening sentence of the fourth paragraph: "Philosophically considered, the universe is composed of Nature and the Soul."[1] This sense of 'nature,' he explains, also is covered by the synonym "Not-Me": "all that is separate from us, . . . both nature and art, all other men and my own body."[2] We have, as he suggests, Philosophy to thank for this first meaning of 'nature' as the not-Soul. We have common sense, by contrast, to thank for the second meaning, according to which nature picks out "essences unchanged by man." *Its* opposite is *art*, Emerson's synoptic term in the introduction for the made, built world. Cheerily, Emerson assures us that this fundamental equivocation, which he dubs an "inaccuracy," is nothing to worry about; because when it comes to grand projects like his own, the project of "find[ing] a theory of nature" that can account for "an impression so grand as that of the world on the human mind," the mixing of man's will with unchanged essences does not alter the outcome.[3] In short, Emerson offers two conflicting definitions of 'nature' and uses the definiens of the one in the definiendum of the other.

Are Emerson's two uses of 'nature' a case like Quine's illustrating the gulf that must be observed between *naming* and *meaning*, as in Evening Star and

141

Morning Star naming the same physical object, Venus, but carrying different meanings, the point being that only the name of the physical object belongs to the enterprise of what there is, whereas the dual meanings belong to an altogether different enterprise, and that Quine's (and before him Frege's) cautionary tale teaches us to beware of trying to derive an X in the enterprise of what there is from a Y in that other enterprise?[4] Yes—insofar as Emerson appears to recognize just this difference between 'nature' used in what he calls the "philosophical" and the "common" senses respectively, the philosophical sense giving rise to multiple meanings and the common sense serving the class of physical objects, each with its own name. The term is the same (Venus, 'nature'), but the meanings vary, and it is the meanings Emerson seeks. Or, as he says in chapter 4 of *Nature*, "words are signs of natural facts."[5] Into the *existence* of natural facts, Emerson does not purport to inquire; he takes them as they are. But also no—insofar as Emerson not only dismisses as inconsequential this distinction and the cautionary tale but does so with a boast. So, now what? Perhaps our return to nature$_1$ and nature$_2$ and the simultaneous presence and absence of difference signified by the distinction takes us to a rough inversion of Quine's case, namely, Aristotle's homonymy principle.[6] We have moved, that is, from the question of what Emerson is doing with the same name for two things considered in two different contexts with the contextual difference turning out to be beside the point to what he is doing with the same name for two things, again considered in different contexts, this time with the relevant contexts impossible to ignore. Consider Fred and his portrait. Aristotle says that Fred's *eyes* with which he looks at the portrait of himself are to be distinguished from Fred's *eyes* depicted in the portrait on the ground that a different account of *eyes* is required in each case. Emerson would, of course, agree. The two accounts of nature$_1$ and nature$_2$, like the two accounts of eyes, obviously are different accounts. The difference, moreover, is profound. However, once again Emerson acknowledges the point and promptly declares it irrelevant to his purpose: "to find a theory of nature."[7]

Emerson tries to win over the literate public in his day, if not as fellow participants in this arcane project, then as interested readers, by challenging Americans to throw off their second-hand existence and cultivate "an original relation to the universe." To this day, however, the latter expression remains opaque, even if it also can be counted on to fetch a standing ovation. No matter. Emerson's much-remarked rhetoric of celebration and uplift both serves up tenets central to his philosophy of experience in *Nature*—such as the pure naturalism of "Undoubtedly we have no questions to ask which are unanswerable"—and cloaks their meaning, producing a kind of open secret in the text. The identity of this secret agent, like the spy Polonius', is known to all save the tragic soul bent on discovering the truth. The first three sentences of the magnificent opening paragraph of the introduction, I argue, tell all and veil all: "Our age is retrospective. It builds the sepulchers of the fathers. It writes biographies, histories, and criticism. The foregoing generations beheld God and nature face to face; we, through their eyes."[8] What to make of this little jeremiad? The two possibilities I see are the following. The first and probably more common reading seems to depend on a temporal sequence in which God and nature are anterior to the foregoing generations who in turn are anterior to the present generation. The classical principle of anteriority, which locates humanity's finest hour in a prelapsarian existence, is the cornerstone of this reading. The originality of the foregoing generations' relation to the universe derived from their face-to-face proximity to both God and nature. We in the present, by contrast, lead derivative, spectatorial lives. We see through the eyes of the foregoing generations and suppose that we have God and nature in view. But such seeing, the jeremiad warns, is mere voyeurism, a deformation of Newton's standing on the shoulders of giants to see far. At our most fortunate, if not worthiest, we are but prosperous parasites. Our spot in this chain of being is minute, a barely visible speck. This dwarfing of the present generation through comparison with the foregoing generations is finally extended by Emerson to all of humanity, "whose operations taken together are so insignificant," at the close of the introduction.[9]

The second and probably less common reading retains the polemical tone of the first but otherwise differs in three ways. Taken together, these differences run the spy through, and chapter 1 of *Nature* can begin. First, temporal sequence is out, beside the point. In its place in the second account is a spatial arrangement of the three principles: God, Nature, and the generations. Second, the object of the generations' beholding is now altogether different. Third, so, too, is the act of beholding. For in this picture of Emerson's meaning man is not face to face with God, for such an unmediated relation finds no support in Emerson's thought. Nor is man face to face with nature, if by this is meant a pantheistic relation; "Nature is thoroughly mediate," he writes in chapter 5.[10] Rather, it is God and nature that are beheld face to face with each other, a relation brought into being by the beholder in the generative act of beholding. To behold is what Emerson would have us do. In place of two distinct objects (God and nature) with no relation between them specified, as in the first reading, in the second there is one object with two faces, obverse and reverse. The foregoing generations' "original relation to the universe" consists precisely in their act of beholding God and Nature so conceived and interrelated. Indeed, God and Nature are not available each for direct apprehension without the other, not even by the foregoing generations. For, if God, then Nature; and if Nature, then God. As for the present (literary) generation of biographers, historians, and critics, Emerson plays the witness who reminds us that were it not for our predecessors' splendid achievements in the art of life, which we dutifully record, and by whose brilliant reflection we feeble ones are nearly blinded, we would have nothing to our credit at all. But one day, we, too, will be the foregoing generation. Will we be venerated? By virtue of *what* ought we to be? Emerson's answer is that, like our forebears, we will be venerated, if at all, *as a generation*, that is, for our generative power or capacity for renewal: not because *we came before* but because *we played our part* in the soul-nature-God relation.[11] In "Experience" Emerson calls this achievement "the true romance which the world exists to realize, . . . the trans-formation of genius into practical power."[12]

Emerson's philosophy of experience, set forth in the eight chapters of *Nature*, is a consistent brief for mediated, functional relationships between nature and the soul as proper objects of study for the pupil man: commod-ity, beauty, language, discipline, idealism, and spirit. To be a pupil, more-over, just is to be attuned to the triad of God, Nature, and Soul. Unraveled, the ambiguity caught in the imagery of "face to face" describes, or in-scribes, a triad whose members designate not discrete entities or discrim-inable beings (as the first reading suggests) but relational possibilities open to man the analogist who "studies relations in all objects."[13] It is life's work, the study of the interrelatedness of all beings and things: (1) the relation of Soul to Nature that resembles seal and print,[14] (2) the relation of sensation to morals in the constitution of every fact,[15] and (3) the relation of morals to matter in the constitution of physical laws ("The laws of moral nature answer to those of matter as face to face in a glass."[16]

A concluding word about the Emersonian act of beholding. It is tempt-ing to construe Emerson's verb *behold* as synonymous with *see*. I think this substitution would be, if not a mistake, at least an incongruous interpretive move. On either reading, it would tend to import into the introduction the transparent eyeball of chapter 1 of *Nature*, along with, doubtless, the nu-merous other ocular images and usages prominent in Emerson's writings. To reduce *behold* to *see* threatens to erase the world-shaping function of which Emerson wishes us to be mindful when he would have us behold God and nature face to face at the very start of his project. The famous transparent eyeball, removed to the introduction, would be ahead of its time, so to speak. Emersonian seeing subserves Emersonian beholding. *Be-hold* is to *see* as *look* is to *see*, as when Fry remarks that "biologically speak-ing, art is a blasphemy. We were given eyes to see things, not to look at them."[17] Beholding, so understood, takes God and nature as such, and tak-ing them as such authorizes the crescive functionality of Emerson's natu-ralism. The "author" of this act of beholding is, of course, the soul; but the soul can act at all only within the triadic relation which it founds and in which it (literally) finds itself. Moreover, as his exposé of the present gen-eration's (present) second-hand existence makes plain, Emerson does not believe that the act of taking God and nature as facing each other was a singular act carried out, once and for all, by our forebears. To believe that it was would, arguably, be Emerson's definition of cynicism. On the contrary, the act of taking God and nature as facing each other is at once an ethical decision and the first move in the elaboration of Emerson's naturalistic ontology.

Emerson's injunction presupposes that such a choice is *assuredly* also ours to make. Every act of taking God and nature as facing each other renews our lives, and conversely every renewal proceeds from such an act. Renewal is not moral uplift in new garb but experience *formed*. A century after the publication of *Nature* John Dewey sharpened this point when he distinguished between experience and *an* experience, the primary distinction ruling his *Art as Experience*. "Experience occurs continuously" in the life of any living thing, Dewey wrote, but only in "*an* experience" is the indifferent flow "composed" and "so rounded out that its close is a consummation and not a cessation. Such an experience is a whole and carries with it its own individualizing quality and self-sufficiency."[18] On the first reading we have moral indignation, the rhetoric of uplift, and for our trouble, mere continuously occurring experience: a merely derivative existence. On the second reading we lose none of the moral polemic while gaining a meaningful world—meaningful because marked not by experience only but by experiences. Emerson's amusing dismissal of all previous human achievement, presumably even including that of the esteemed foregoing generations, as "a little chipping, baking, patching, and washing," turns out, when recast in Deweyan terms, not to be self-serving mockery of forebears. It may be only ostensive pointing, with nature$_2$ functioning as the name of that which may yet become *an* experience. The bitter rapture with which hitherto they have been acknowledged shall be heard no more; and good riddance, he seems to imply, to this tired complaint. The second reading links God, Nature, and *all* generations; it is the first reading which, by making the foregoing generations larger than life, cuts us off from the past.

"All science has one aim," Emerson writes in the introduction, "namely, to find a theory of nature," a unified, comprehensive theory, one that will "explain all phenomena." The abstractions that constitute such a theory, deeply grounded in phenomenal evidence, would be altogether "practical."[19] In a word, a philosophy of experience in the vein of scientists and philosophers since Bacon and Galileo. That there is no royal road to such a theory is a lesson that Charles Sanders Peirce, Emerson's brilliant successor, regarded as the profoundest revelation of his life as a scientist, logician, and philosopher. A brief look at Peirce's discovery reveals a naturalism that had lain hidden from view in his own work of a lifetime, just as Emerson's triad of Nature, God, and Soul lies hidden in plain sight in the introduction to *Nature*. That the two secrets resemble each other closely, in form and content, links Emerson and Peirce in American philosophical history.

From his anti-Cartesian papers of the 1860s on, in which he demolished the stance of feigned doubt and sought to replace it with his doubt-
belief theory, Peirce was a vigorous opponent of formalism.[20] All the greater
his chagrin, then, late in his life to realize he himself had been caught up, in
an odd way, in this signal occupational hazard of the professional thinker. At
issue was not simply what he took to be fundamental errors in method. Nor
had he slipped into the Cartesianism he had earlier criticized. Rather, he
learned that all his philosophical life he had not really understood what he
was doing. It was not enough to refute armchair doubt and extol the real
thing. The more fundamental mistake was to turn away from, to denatural-
ize, the human. To avoid this trap and fulfill the aim of science, Peirce realized, the investigator must strive for the simplest, most facile hypothesis
each time out. Here is Peirce's critical story in full:

> Modern science has been builded after the model of Galileo, who founded
> it, on *il lume naturale*. That truly inspired prophet has said that, of two hy-
> potheses, the *simpler* is to be preferred; but I was formerly one of those who,
> in our dull self-conceit fancying ourselves more sly than he, twisted the
> maxim to mean the *logically* simpler, the one that adds the least to what has
> been observed, in spite of three obvious objections: first, that so there was
> no support for any hypothesis; secondly, that by the same token we ought
> to content ourselves with simply formulating the special observations actu-
> ally made; and thirdly, that every advance of science that further opens the
> truth to our view discloses a world of unexpected complications. It was not
> until long experience forced me to realize that subsequent discoveries were
> every time showing I had been wrong, while those who understood the
> maxim as Galileo had done, early unlocked the secret, that the scales fell
> from my eyes and my mind awoke to the broad and flaming daylight that it
> is the simpler Hypothesis in the sense of the more facile and natural, the
> one that instinct suggests, that must be preferred; for the reason that, unless
> man have a natural bent in accordance with nature's, he has no chance of
> understanding nature at all.[21]

It was only after careful reflection on his own long experience as an investigator that Peirce at last realized he had not understood Galileo's
maxim urging the simpler hypothesis. One imagines that there came a moment when the reflective Peirce was at last bothered by the strange clash
between his scientific practice and his scientific theory: his scientific practice enacted, as it were, a correct understanding of Galileo's maxim, but
Peirce did not know that it did. The scales fell from his eyes when his theory was finally corrected by his practice—by what specific experience, however, he does not specify. He now saw that Galileo was urging a kind of
hypothesis, not a kind of *simplicity*. Galileo was urging the simpler *Hypothesis*,

by which he meant the "more facile and natural." The simpler hypothesis is to be preferred because the simpler is the more instinctive. This seems to mean that the simpler hypothesis is, or is grounded in, proceeds from, a hunch, a conjecture, a guess, an aperçu as to how it is in the world.

The "instinct," the hunch, the conjecture, the guess, the aperçu signifies the natural in man. This, I would add, is one of our Emersonian inheritances. Only man can understand nature, and man can understand nature only because he can make, use, and learn from the guesses he makes as to how it is in nature. This is not trial and error. Rather, it is the belief, imbedded in the introduction to *Nature*, that the categories of thought and the categories of things are conterminous. The constructions of the mind somehow get us to the constructions of nature. Emerson, after him Peirce, envisioned existence as an open-ended affair, above all as the home of man the analogist, who is naturally equipped with the *simpler* hypothesis at every turn. Hence Emerson's extravagant expression of faith in the introduction to *Nature*: "Undoubtedly we have no questions to ask which are unanswerable."[22] Or urging a return of Man Thinking in his address to his Harvard audience seventy-odd years before Peirce disclosed his life's principal discovery: "The astronomer discovers that geometry, a pure abstraction of the human mind, is the measure of planetary motion. The chemist finds proportions and intelligible method throughout matter; and science is nothing but the finding of analogy, identity, in the most remote parts. The ambitious soul sits down before each refractory fact; one after another reduces all strange constitutions, all new powers, to their class and their law, and goes on forever to animate the last fiber of organization, the outskirts of nature, by insight."[23]

I said above that there is a strong family resemblance between Emerson's hidden-in-plain-sight ambiguity which rules the introduction to *Nature* and Peirce's discovery of the true meaning of Galileo's insistence on the simpler hypothesis. The resemblance might be described like this: In Emersonian terms, Peirce's discovery comes down to an algorithm for beholding. In Peircean terms, Emerson's ambiguity dissolves and Man Thinking returns once the triad of God-Nature-Soul is conceived as a triad of meanings. For Emerson, everything depends on how the soul takes God and Nature, on whether the first or the second reading best introduces his theory of nature. If the soul takes God and nature as specified in the second reading, then the triad becomes a triad of meanings. On this account, God and Nature have what Aquinas would call the "passive power" to be taken *as* facing each other, but to be taken as such actively requires that the soul harbor within it the idea of that relationship. Beholding the face-to-faceness of God and Nature is Emerson's compact way of describing this continuous action. For Peirce, essentially the same thought process takes the following form: "*A REPRESENTAMEN [i.e. a sign] is a subject of a triadic relation TO a second, called its OBJECT, FOR a third, called its INTER-PRETANT, this triadic relation being such that the REPRESENTAMEN determines its interpretant to stand in the same triadic relation to the same object for some interpretant.*"[24] In Peirce's semiotic, outlined thus, there can be no triad, and therefore no cognition, unless the sign called "Interpretant" *takes* the sign called "the Representamen" *as* the sign of the Object. So, too, Emerson holds that "[w]ords are signs of natural facts," yes, but unless and until the pupil man studies the texts before him closely enough to earn the next two conclusions in turn—"Particular natural facts are symbols of particular spiritual facts" and "Nature is the symbol of spirit"[25]—natural facts will remain devoid of meaning. He also holds that "[t]he sun shines today also"[26] is a necessary but not sufficient condition of the possibility of the God-Nature-Soul triad—and of Man Thinking's return.

Stanley Cavell marks Emerson's emergence as a philosopher with the great writings that came immediately after *Nature: The American Scholar* (1837), *An Address* ("The Divinity School Address," 1838), and "Self-Reliance" (1841). On his reading, *Nature* is rather prephilosophical because, he argues, it is less concerned than the others with the problem of skepticism.[27] I am not as convinced as Cavell appears to be of Emerson's struggle to avoid falling into skepticism. To Emerson skepticism is more tool than problem, and as with the "Ideal theory" he would caution us not to make ourselves "merry with it"[28] but instead to use it, perhaps in the spirit that recognizes the priority of wonder over doubt. There is, I have tried to suggest, something of keener philosophical importance to Emerson than the perils of skepticism, beginning with *Nature*, which might be thought of as a metaphysical and ethical test of the soul's mettle, reserves of phronēsis, and capacity to overcome stupidity. The punishment Emerson reserves for the undisciplined soul which fails to constitute the triadic relation with God and nature is not to push him off the cliff into skepticism but to plague him and the rest of us with monstrosity: the grotesque transfiguration of the fabled One Man into society's "so many walking monsters" in *The American Scholar*[29] and the stultifying absence of individuality abetted by society's conspiratorial "joint-stock company" in "Self-Reliance."[30] Man generates his own Lusus Naturae, as the freaks on the loose in these two essays show. Nature in Emerson's philosophy, unlike that which goes by the same name in the thought of medieval naturalists, plays no tricks on man. On the contrary, nature underwrites eudaimonia but does so severely, as an altogether forfeitable birthright. "The wheels and springs of man are all set to the hypothesis of the permanence of nature," he writes in chapter 6 of *Nature*.[31] It is with this hypothesis that Emerson begins his philosophical career in the introduction to *Nature*.

Notes

1. *Ralph Waldo Emerson: Essays and Lectures*, ed. Joel Porte (New York: Library of America, 1983), 7.

2. Ibid., 8.

3. Ibid.

4. Willard Van Orman Quine, *From a Logical Point of View: Nine Logico-Philosophical Essays*, 2nd ed., rev. (Cambridge: Harvard University Press, 1980), 9.

5. *Ralph Waldo Emerson: Essays and Lectures*, ed. Joel Porte (New York: Library of America, 1983), 20.

6. Aristotle, *Nicomachaen Ethics*, tr. Terence Irwin (Indianapolis: Hackett, 1985), 1096b27. On homonymy, see Jonathan Barnes, *Aristotle* (New York: Oxford University Press, 1982), 41–42.

7. *Ralph Waldo Emerson: Essays and Lectures*, ed. Joel Porte (New York: Library of America, 1983), 7.

8. Ibid.

9. Ibid., 8.

10. Ibid., 28.

11. On renewal, of language and therefore of our culture, see Richard Poirier, *The Renewal of Literature: Emersonian Reflections* (New York: Random House, 1987), and *Poetry and Pragmatism* (Cambridge: Harvard University Press, 1992).

12. *Ralph Waldo Emerson: Essays and Lectures*, ed. Joel Porte (New York: Library of America, 1983), 492.

13. Ibid., 13.

14. Ibid., 56.

15. Ibid., 690.

16. Ibid., 24.

17. Roger Fry, *Vision and Design* (New York: Meridian Books, 1957 [1925]), 47. I first came upon this remark in Susanne K. Langer, *Philosophy in a New Key: A Study in the Symbolism of Reason, Rite, and Art*, 3rd ed. (Cambridge: Harvard University Press, 1957), 266–67 n1.

18. John Dewey, *Art as Experience* (New York: Capricorn Books, 1958 [1934]), 35.

19. *Ralph Waldo Emerson: Essays and Lectures*, ed. Joel Porte (New York: Library of America, 1983), 7.

20. Peirce's best-known paper in this series is probably "The Fixation of Belief" (1877). See *The Essential Peirce*, ed. Nathan Houser and Christian Kloesel (Bloomington: Indiana University Press, 1992). An excellent introduction to Peirce is Christopher Hookway, *Peirce* (London: Routledge, 1985); ch. 1 examines Peirce's attack on Cartesian universal doubt.

21. This passage is from "A Neglected Argument for the Reality of God," *Hibbert Journal* (1908), in *The Essential Peirce*, ed. Peirce Edition Project (Bloomington: Indiana University Press, 1998), vol. 2, p. 444. Cf. Alfred North Whitehead: "It is a well-founded historical generalization, that the last thing to be discovered in any science is what the science is really about. Men go on groping for centuries, guided merely by a dim instinct and a puzzled curiosity, till at last 'some

great truth is loosened.'" *An Introduction to Mathematics* (London: Oxford University Press, 1948 [1911]), 166–67. The latter line is from Shelley's *Prometheus Unbound*, II.iii.40–41.

22. *Ralph Waldo Emerson: Essays and Lectures*, ed. Joel Porte (New York: Library of America, 1983), 7

23. Ibid., 55.

24. Charles Sanders Peirce, *The Collected Papers of Charles Sanders Peirce*, ed. Charles Hartshorne and Paul Weiss, vol. 1 (Cambridge: Harvard University Press, 1933–38), 285. For a brief account of Peirce's theory of signs, cognition, and synechism, see David Marr, "Signs of C. S. Peirce," *American Literary History* 7, no. 4 (Winter 1995): 681–99.

25. *Ralph Waldo Emerson: Essays and Lectures*, ed. Joel Porte (New York: Library of America, 1983), 20.

26. Ibid., 9.

27. Stanley Cavell, *This New yet Unapproachable America: Lectures after Emerson after Wittgenstein* (Albuquerque: Living Batch, 1989), 79.

28. *Ralph Waldo Emerson: Essays and Lectures*, ed. Joel Porte (New York: Library of America, 1983), 32.

29. Ibid., 54.

30. Ibid., 261.

31. Ibid., 32.

Chapter 8

Emerson's Natures

Origins of and Possibilities for
American Environmental Thought

Douglas R. Anderson

I often find myself frustrated with contemporary debates on what has come to be called "the environment" because parties of thinkers contend for my affection and drive me constantly to outmoded puzzles of either/or. Either I am "green" or I am "not-green." I am either a conservationist or a preservationist, and so on. These puzzles strike me first and foremost as lingering effects of the analytic tradition of the twentieth century; indeed, even Richard Rorty, who challenged that tradition from within, is fond of leading his readers into these sorts of box canyons by way of his own *sic et non* method. This habit, I think, overlooks the insights of several other philosophical traditions that seek to see continuities as well as disjunctions in both experience and nature. In what follows, then, I want to turn to one such tradition—New England transcendentalism—and explore what it might have to offer us regarding the complexities of our relationship to nature. To accomplish this, I offer a commentary on Ralph Waldo Emerson's essay "Nature," and along the way I suggest avenues that might be further explored were we to take Emerson's insights into the twentieth and twenty-first centuries' conversations regarding "environmental issues."

Emerson was not a close reader of the history of German idealism, yet his work is pervasively influenced by this idealism. Charles Peirce often argued that ideas have their own lives and that the best thinkers see coincidentally what is next implied in a historical trajectory. This seems an apt way to think of the relationship between Emerson and Schelling. In some ways, Emerson is quite directly influenced by Schelling's writings, especially those writings to which he was exposed by Frederic Henry Hedge. In other ways,

151

Emerson simply moved into the spirit of Schelling's transcendental idealism. Some of the specific Emersonian ideas attributable to Schelling's influence are the "Over-Soul," natural divinity, fate, and nature as a living organism. In his two essays on nature, then, Emerson reveals traces of Schelling's thought and puts these traces to work in an American setting. My specific goal is to show what some of the consequences of Emerson's Schellingeanism might be for later American conceptions of the natural environment and to suggest that we still might have something to learn from Emerson's Schellinglike conception of nature.

For some folks, the New England transcendentalists seem like the original environmentalists. They wrote extensively about nature, and they seemed to take seriously the notion that European Americans were on some sort of "errand in the wilderness." Some of them tried, though most unsuccessfully, to live simplified lives and lived, as it were, off the land. Most notably Ripley's Brook Farm and Alcott's Fruitlands were aborted attempts at living communally and more simply with the land. In his essay "Walking," Thoreau went so far as to speak a word for nature and wilderness. Indeed, at one point in the text Thoreau addresses our tendency to over-civilize ourselves and sounds quite contemporary: "Nowadays almost all man's improvements, so called, as the building of houses and the cutting down of the forest and of all large trees, simply deform the landscape, and make it more and more tame and cheap."[1] Despite the suggestiveness of such readings of the transcendentalists, they bear a trace of anachronism: their eyes were not always on the same mark as those of contemporary environmentalists however much they say things along the way that agree with our contemporary sensibilities. On this score, Emerson is an even more challenging figure than Thoreau. Emerson wrote no platform on environmental issues, but he did write two essays bearing the title "Nature." In commenting on the latter of these, which appeared in *Essays: Second Series*, I hope to distill a few Emersonian ideals, albeit vaguely constituted, concerning our relationship to what we have now come to call "the environment."

Most readers are more familiar with the earlier of Emerson's two essays, the 1836 *Nature* that established his reputation as a thinker and writer. This essay sets up Emerson's basic orientation concerning the relationship between persons and nature. The later essay develops this relationship in significantly more detail, attending to its nuances. Emerson, true to his own insights on philosophical writing, never presents a straightforward argument concerning our obligations to nature or the environment; instead he gives the reader sufficient material to discern an outlook revealing a complex understanding of these obligations. Concerning nature, then, I have found at least four Emersonian conceptions working together. Nature in its most common meaning is the apparently fixed environment of things in which we find ourselves: *natura naturata*. This nature, however, reveals a secondary feature: dynamic or living beauty. At another level, insofar as we humans are natural, we constitute another, and an active, mode of nature: *natura naturans*. The transaction between these two modes constitutes yet another Emersonian Nature: the place and the process of the dialectical development of *natura naturans* and *natura naturata*. This environing Nature is occasionally identified as Being or Soul. "In his original *Nature*, Emerson identifies nature with whatever is "not-me": Strictly speaking, therefore, all that is separate from us, all which Philosophy distinguishes as the NOT ME, that is, both nature and art, all other men, my own body, must be ranked under this name, Nature."[2] Drawing on the dialectical distinction that Schelling, following Fichte, used to bring epistemology and ontology together, Emerson gives to nature the role of one's environment: what is outside and other than oneself. Taken in itself, this not-me is "objective," a presentation for the agency of the ego; it is thus *naturata* or "natured." Emerson, in down to earth fashion, proceeds to characterize the "natural" side of this nature in its "common" and "philosophical import": "*Nature*, in the common sense, refers to essences unchanged by man; space, the air, the river, the leaf."[3] This description puts us in mind of wildness and wilderness. Unqualified, this nature is simply an aggregate of things or commodities. But Emerson pushes further, locating in this nature an aesthetic power of an independent, objective sort that can stand on its own in judgment of us. This dual "not-me," environmental account of nature makes us see it as one's "other" and therefore as crucial to any understanding of oneself. Thus, as we will see, Emerson later adds two more conceptions of nature: *natura naturans*, or the agency of the "I," and the all environing Nature that is the source of and context for transactions between the active agent (the ego) and the not-me. In "Self Reliance" we are offered a foreshadowing of our place in this larger Nature. Without personifying Nature, Emerson describes our dual status: "We lie in the lap of immense intelligence, which makes us receivers of its truth and organs of its activity."[4]

The first half of Emerson's later "Nature" essay trades on the uses of the not-me presentation of nature in its objective form. Emerson begins at home: "There are days which occur in this climate, at almost any season of the year, wherein the world reaches its perfection, when the air, the heavenly bodies, and the earth, make a harmony, as if nature would indulge her offspring."[5] Calling on New England's natural beauty, Emerson begins by examining his own home environment. Later, he invites readers to begin to consider their own local, natural perfections. As we will see, *any* place can reveal nature's perfections.

This not-me environment of perfection satisfies us in our finitude and invites us to explore: "At the gates of the forest, the surprised man of the world is forced to leave his city estimates of great and small, wise and foolish."[6] Emerson forces us to hear "man of the world" ironically, since "world" in this phrase aligns with civilization, which is now to be trumped and judged by the natural "world." Nature, as we enter, compels us to reorient—it judges us, our actions, our beliefs, our habits of living. "Here," says Emerson, "is sanctity which shames our religions, and reality which discredits our heroes."[7] Nature's perfection, as we enter its surroundings, shows us possibilities beyond our habits, practices, and conventions, and "judges like a god all men that come to her."[8] Two necessities of import appear here. There must *be* such a nature to which we have access, *and* we must choose to enter into it and to suffer its judgment.

Nature as it judges us by way of its perfections may shame us, but its work is not fulfilled unless it also inspires us and propels us toward new possibilities. It must be "stimulating and heroic." For Emerson, there is at least the possibility that Nature—in the widest sense—is self-ameliorating. In his initial essay, Emerson marked this edifying dimension as the "Beauty" of nature through which "the sky, the mountain, the tree, the animal, give us a delight *in and for themselves.*"[9] Nature, as perfecting wilderness, has a decivilizing effect so that we can refresh ourselves and come to our senses. It is one condition of our recivilizing. "I am," says Emerson, "taught the poorness of our invention, the ugliness of towns and palaces."[10] Thus, as we enter this not-me, this environing Nature, we feel its healing and inspiring powers. Our pretensions are stripped away, we are made to feel our own finitude, and, ironically, out of this proportioning of ourselves we learn of our empowerment: "We nestle in nature, and draw our living as parasites from roots and grains, and we receive glances from the heavenly bodies, which call us to solitude, and foretell the remotest future."[11]

Emerson develops the aesthetic powers of nature in one example after another, illustrating how human life is raised in every corner by nature's objective and awesome presence as *natura naturata.* Here we find the Emerson that so enthralled John Muir and Walt Whitman, whose experiences seemed documented by Emerson's mental journey. But just as we are about to be tempted into a full-blown romance with nature *or* to be put off by the poet's euphuism, Emerson makes a turn in the text—a dialectical return from the not-me to the active "I." "It is easy," says Emerson, "to outrun the sympathy of readers on this topic, which schoolmen call *natura naturata*, or nature passive."[12]

This dialectical turn is foreshadowed in the essay "Experience" when Emerson reminds us that "Nature, as we know her, is no saint." Rather, "She comes eating and drinking and sinning."[13] Moreover, the turn brings *us*—persons—back on the scene; until now, we had been silent observers and the objects of Nature's judgment. Nature—now in its fullness—is not consummated until the agency of the "I" appears on the scene; nature's agency in part runs *through* us, through human endeavor. "The sunset is unlike anything that is underneath it: it wants men. And the beauty of nature must always seem unreal and mocking, until the landscape has human figures, that are as good as itself."[14] We hear in this the foreshadowings of Lamarckian evolution and Bergson's vital force. *Natura naturans* is nature in action—doing, creating, making, moving. Here we humans are thoroughly implicated. Nature is now not an objective environment but a creative environing. We *are* this aspect of nature, and we become "not ourselves" if we slip into the state of mere witnesses of nature's judging perfection.

The deep sense of democracy that John Dewey noted in Emerson's thinking manifests itself in the last half of "Nature" and foreshadows the focus in "Nominalist and Realist" on our representative natures. Each of us represents an angle of vision through our particular excess and talent, and we must each rely on others for any sense of wholeness or community. For Emerson we give nature a character; we constitute Nature's natures. Emerson sees possibility in each of us though he admits, "Man is fallen" and "nature is erect." We *are* living, natural possibility however debilitated: "[I]f our own life flowed with the right energy, we should shame the brook."[15] *Natura naturans* begins in nature's motions—its heat, pressure, transformations—and moves with a hard fatality toward, and perhaps beyond, *us*: "It is a long way from granite to the oyster; farther yet to Plato." Emerson sees nature's habits of action wherever he looks: "The whirling bubble on the surface of a brook, admits us to the secret of the mechanics of the sky."[16] Nature as action and verb is not the still life beauty of *natura naturata* but exceeds the still life in its ability to transcend itself or, in the words of the pragmatists, to ameliorate. We, as conscious creators, *are* nature in its active form. The idealists' dialectic of the ego and the not-me shows us that nature has two codependent aspects; it is here we must find and accept our own importance as *natura naturans* without abandoning the importance of the judgments of *natura naturata*. We must embrace our freedom but without hubris. With John Muir we must be receptive to nature's beauties and her aesthetic judgment of our lives; and with Gifford Pinchot, we must accept the responsibilities of making and remaking our world. In short, we must be both Muir and Pinchot if we are to fare well in our world and bring some divinity to bear on finite experience. "Let us be men instead of woodchucks," Emerson chided.[17]

Emerson reflects on the order of nature—its consistency and its organization. He reflects on the originary "push" that set the world in motion—his version of the Big Bang. But like William James and Charles Peirce some years later, Emerson recognizes imbalance in the order: the atom swerves and things run to excess. Nature naturing—human action—is a risk: "without a spice of bigot and fanatic, no excitement, no efficiency."[18] It is just this imbalance that gives us the life to be creative, to generate our own beauties and energies. But this same imbalance puts us at risk for failure:

"No man is quite sane; each has a vein of folly in his composition, a slight determination of blood to the head, to make sure of holding hard to one point which nature had taken to heart."[19] This is both the adventure and the danger of how humans are natured; we represent both nature's risks and its possibilities. This is an experiential truth that resists the probing critiques of determinists and fatalists. As Emerson later wrote, "nature usually in the instances where a marked man is sent into the world, overloads him with bias, sacrificing his symmetry to his power."[20]

This slight insanity leads to our exemplary human endeavors but it invariably comes with a price to pay. This is our representative nature, and it arises even in our own ordinary experiences, in our youthful diaries: "Days and nights of fervid life, of communion with angels of darkness and of light, have engraved their shadowy characters on that tear-stained book."[21] The upshot of our representativeness and imbalance is that while we realize many human possibilities, we always fall short in some respect; we remain in need of the judgment of *natura naturata*. "All promise," Emerson says, "outruns performance. Our music, our poetry, our language itself are not satisfactions, but suggestions."[22]

For Emerson, the extreme danger of this imbalance and slight insanity is systematic egoism. We have a tendency to overrate our thoughts and abilities, and we then try to set ourselves outside of and above nature. "The man runs round a ring formed by his own talents," warns Emerson, "falls into admiration of it, and loses relation to the world. It is a tendency in all minds."[23] We build a New York or a Chicago, and we come to believe that merely exercising our powers is enough; we become mad, excessive, and blind versions of Pinchot. Thoreau later warned of such blindness: "I saw the fences half consumed, their ends lost in the middle of the prairie, and some worldly miser with a surveyor looking after his bounds, while heaven had taken place all around him, and he did not see the angels going to and fro, but was looking for an old post-hole in the midst of paradise."[24] The issue here is not any specific environmental issue; the issue is about ontological attitude. To be stubbornly blind to nature precludes our ability to fulfill well our own natural role as *naturans*.

Emerson's cure—or at least his treatment—for this poverty of attitude was to keep humans alert to what's around them: "The antidote against this organic egotism are the range and variety of attractions, as gained by acquaintance with the world, with men of merit, with classes of society, with travel, with eminent persons, and with the high resources of philosophy, art, and religion."[25] "Acquaintance" is the key. No thin, academic knowing of nature and environment will suffice. One must engage nature directly to know by acquaintance; this is the enduring relevance of wilderness to human beings. We need only think of those who write and politicize about the poor and the marginalized, never having shared their experiences. Even when such talk is useful, it remains blind and unacquainted to that particular angle of experience suffered by the impoverished. One exemplar of those acquainted with nature as natured was, for Emerson, the farmer, who "times himself to Nature, and acquires that livelong patience which belongs to her."[26] If we move outside western culture, we find many whose sense of time is governed not by clocks and calendars but by the moods of the local environment. In spite of this, we in the "west" still often seek to dominate nature while remaining unacquainted with it. Then, Emerson says, "We are as much strangers in nature as we are aliens from God."[27]

As the second "Nature" essay concludes, Emerson returns to *natura naturata*, now not as a judge of our creativity but as a reflection of our limitation. "There is in woods and waters a certain enticement and flattery, together with a failure to yield a present satisfaction. This disappointment is felt in every landscape."[28] The mood has shifted, and the moment of perfection has passed. Emerson reminds us of the complexity of nature natured: "But Nature is as subtle as she is strong . . .all things are flowing, even those that seem immovable."[29] Nature reminds us in yet another way of the dangers of hubris, of getting "above our raising." But it also provides a temptation to cynicism: "Are we tickled trout, and fools of nature?" Are we, then, puppets in the hands of nature, living an illusion of freedom and empowerment? Emerson rejects cynicism while admitting limitation. He returns to the central thought of the poem that opens the essay: "Throb thine with Nature's throbbing breast, And all is clear from east to west."[30] This is the final dialectical turn of the text.

The opposition of—or the tension between—the ego and the not-me is finally overcome when they work together. Instead of reducing the active ego to another deadened aspect of the not-me, the active ego must learn to work in league with the not-me. There it will find its empowerment: "But if, instead of identifying ourselves with the work, we feel that the soul of the workman streams through us, and the fathomless, powers of gravity and chemistry, and, over them, of life, preexisting within us in their highest form."[31] The attitudinal orientation is crucial to our dealings with nature; we must abandon "hostility to nature" and seek a "child's love to it . . . to expand and live in the warm day like corn and melons."[32] The work of Frank Lloyd Wright and Andy Goldsworthy comes to mind in this context: how can we produce in such a way as not to deracinate nature's own aesthetic powers? The power of the artist and the poet is not merely human; they act in and through nature so that their "power consists in the multitude of [their] affinities, in the fact that [their] life is intertwined with the whole chain of organic and inorganic being."[33] Insofar as we live in this nature of approximations, change, and possibilities, we must avoid dogmatic stances that entrench us in outmoded environmental themes. The natural attitude, as it were, is the one that moves with nature. Again, the wild side of nature is exemplary for the wild side of experience, and it reveals to us both limitation and possibility if we are attentive. "In the wilderness," Emerson says, "I find something more dear and connate than in streets or villages." The lover of nature and of the wild becomes one "whose inward and outward senses are still truly adjusted to each other."[34]

Emerson is no deep ecologist, nor is he a user and taker of nature. The normative story woven into the fabric of "Nature" is more subtle and more complex. Emerson is at once a romantic naturalist and a practical Yankee, but in such a way as to bring these characters/natures into a working harmony. We cannot get on without civilizing, without making, building, learning, creating, and enjoying; indeed, civilizing is always recivilizing. But Emerson looks for the tempering constraints on our agency. We must learn from nature how to build well, how to live erectly, and how to create beauty. This requires a preservation of a wilderness into which we might enter—places where nature may continue to shame us and keep us attentive. It requires also that we recognize in ourselves the very limitations on perfection that nature shows us. We must maintain some humor and humility as we civilize ourselves and nature. We must preserve and conserve, even as we find new ways to make ourselves better. "Environmentalism" in Emerson's hands cannot be a story of opposition. On the contrary, it is a story of reciprocity, of transaction, and of integration. If I kill off nature, I will lose myself not just physically but personally. If I am too natural or wild, I will lose myself in yet another way; I will become the berry-eating woodchuck.

What is the practical upshot? Certainly no recipe for maintaining the environment. One of Emerson's points would be that we should not look for recipes. We find ourselves in nature, and we find our own acts to be natural ones. The trick of moving to higher platforms, to ameliorating any present transactions we conduct with nature, is to attend to the perfections nature presents us. We know these special "days" of nature because of their experiential impact on us: we need not seek abstract criteria to identify them. But to learn from them, wherever we are, we must attend to them. "The difference between landscape and landscape," Emerson says, "is small, but there is great difference in the beholders."[35] At the same time, we must embrace our agency and develop our worlds of art and science under the influence of these days of perfection. Again, no recipe, no narrow set of criteria; we must enspirit our actions with nature's divinity. Then, finally, we must beware hubris and egotism in our successes; we must remain attentive to our own madnesses and fragilities. There is always more to be done, farther to go. The circles of growth move ever outward: "There are no fixtures in nature. The universe is fluid and volatile."[36]

Drawing the lessons of Emerson's "Nature" into twentieth- and twenty-first century conversations of environmentalism is too much to hope to accomplish here. But we can begin a sketch by noting that both John Muir and Gifford Pinchot with their relative emphases on beauty and utility capture a side of Emerson's thinking about our relationship to nature as not-me. But to find a twentieth-century thinker who more carefully balances and integrates these features, we might turn to Aldo Leopold as one who captures the spirit of Emersonian environmentalism. Leopold clearly understood that humans are agents in this world. He was a practical man who enjoyed working in nature; he enjoyed what Emerson called "the plain pleasures, kindly and native to us."[37] But some of his actions he found to be judged by nature, by the earth's own ways of being, and these judgments persuaded him to alter his own ways of being in the world. He experienced an awakening at the hands of nature. His "land ethic," he said, "changes the role of *Homo sapiens* from conqueror of the land-community to plain member and citizen of it."[38] Whatever rules we employ, whatever "land ethic" we might develop, we need to be guided by this sort of dialectical movement wherever and whenever. Even if Leopold takes us a step in an Emersonian direction, there is more to be found in the workings of the transcendentalist vision. The contemporary environmentalist is in step with Emerson when claiming that we all have a stake in nature and that it is "up to us" to act. "Nature," says Emerson, "sends no creature, no man into the world, without adding a small excess to his proper quality."[39] Because of our excesses, we *will* make a difference in our and in nature's features. The question is not *will* we "affect the day," as Thoreau put it, but *how* will we affect the day? This is the point of a Schellingian beginning in a dialectic of the I, the ego, and the not-me. We find ourselves, then, right where Emerson found us. We are in nature, and nature is in us, and the task is to keep our balance and bring some beauty to bear on our future. This requires most fundamentally an attitude that is at once receptive to nature's language and open to human possibility. The only fatal excesses are a runaway cynicism and an unconstrained hubris. In those cases, we lose our senses and with them our sensitivity to our precarious but important place in Nature's natures.

Notes

1. Henry David Thoreau, *The Portable Thoreau*, ed. Carl Bode (New York: Penguin Books, 1968), 598.

2. Ralph Waldo Emerson, *The Complete Essays and Other Writings of Ralph Waldo Emerson*, ed. Brooks Atkinson (New York: Modern Library, 1940), 4. Emerson makes a clear distinction here between the "natural" and "artifactual" dimensions of *natura naturata*. Though the distinction is an important one and raises

interesting questions, I will focus for the purposes of this paper on the "natural" side of the divide.

3. Ibid., 4.

4. Ibid., 156.

5. Ibid., 406.

6. Ibid.

7. Ibid.

8. Ibid.

9. Ibid., 9.

10. Ibid., 408.

11. Ibid., 407.

12. Ibid., 410.

13. Ibid., 352.

14. Ibid., 411.

15. Ibid.

16. Ibid., 412.

17. Ibid., 414.

18. Ibid., 415.

19. Ibid., 416.

20. Ibid., 717.

21. Ibid., 417.

22. Ibid.

23. Ibid., 718.

24. Henry David Thoreau, *The Portable Thoreau*, ed. Carl Bode (New York: Penguin Books, 1982), 598.

25. Ralph Waldo Emerson, *The Complete Essays and Other Writings of Ralph Waldo Emerson*, ed. Brooks Atkinson (New York: Modern Library, 1940), 721.

26. Ibid., 750.

27. Ibid., 36.

28. Ibid., 418.

29. Ibid., 753.

30. Ibid., 406.

31. Ibid., 420.

32. Ibid., 33.

33. Ibid., 141.

34. Ibid., 6.

35. Ibid., 410.

36. Ibid., 279.

37. Ibid., 407.

38. Aldo Leopold, *A Sand County Almanac* (New York: Oxford University Press, 1968), 204.

39. Ralph Waldo Emerson, *The Complete Essays and Other Writings of Ralph Waldo Emerson*, ed. Brooks Atkinson (New York: Modern Library, 1940), 414–15.

Shudder

Dorene Evans

The last of undulant summer, late August,
afoot on the meadowtrail trod wide and rutted,
I feel the eye of the universe open within me to set
things to rights. Matter's conserved:—nerves spark,
the bones' phosphor flares, lustering to archetypal light
like the flash of a short-lived star whose
furnace burns out.

In that instant I am everything at once, and
also all things' opposite—the dense, dark changeling
born twin to time. This happens so quickly that the fox
and vixen who happen by seconds after do not
even sense it. Switchgrass unsinged. Air
uncamphored. But the world and my
place in it: changed.

Chapter 9

Emerson and the Reinvention of Democracy

A Lesson for the Twenty-first Century

Len Gougeon

[E]ven if Emerson has no system, none the less he is the prophet and
herald of any system which democracy may henceforth construct and
hold by, and . . . when democracy has articulated itself, it will have no
difficulty in finding itself already proposed in Emerson.[1]
—*Dewey, "Ralph Waldo Emerson"*

$\mathcal{T}$he Civil War was a defining moment in the history of American
democracy. It precipitated the passage to the Thirteenth, Fourteenth, and Fifteenth Amendments to the Constitution, which destroyed
slavery, guaranteed equal protection under the law to all citizens, and en-
franchised all adult males, regardless of race. These amendments, collec-
tively, constituted the greatest expansion of freedom in America since the
Revolution. Additionally, because it is inevitable, as Emerson once observed, that "one truth leads in another by the hand, [and] one right is an
accession of strength to take more,"[2] these Amendments provided the
groundwork for another radical expansion of freedom in the twentieth century, this time in the form of Woman's Suffrage, the Civil Rights Act of
1964, and the Voting Rights Act of 1965. Emerson had a hand in all of this.

As America's foremost public intellectual, Emerson emerged in the
1850s and 1860s as the spokesperson for liberal democracy in America. His
notion of democracy was a direct outgrowth of his transcendental philosophy. The core of transcendentalism is a belief in the divinity, unity, and
equality of mankind. This unity derives from the fact that all human beings

162

participate in a universal, spiritual dynamic that Emerson often called "the Over-Soul." In a classic essay by that name, he defines this entity as "that great nature in which we rest, as the earth lies in the soft arms of the atmosphere; that Unity, that Over-Soul, within which every man's particular being is contained and made one with all other."[3] Alternative names for the Over-Soul include "the Reason," the "eternal One," or simply "God." Emerson believed that *all* people share in this divinity. In his seminal essay "Circles," he appropriates St. Augustine's description of God as "a circle whose centre was everywhere, and its circumference nowhere."[4] By this measure, all of humanity is necessarily included in the circle that is God and therefore shares in the divine nature that is the ultimate source of human dignity and self-worth. This fundamental belief informs Emerson's concept of 'democratic equality,' as well as his opposition to slavery. As he notes in an early journal entry, "Democracy/Freedom has its root in the Sacred truth that every man hath in him the divine Reason." This is "the equality & the only equality of all men, [and] because every man hath in him somewhat really divine therefore is slavery the unpardonable outrage it is."[5] Emerson reached this conclusion through a process of intuition and insight wherein such truths appear as "self-evident." These truths, in turn, provided the basis for his life-long campaign to liberalize and reform America. Emerson believed that these intuited truths were available to all, but few had the self-confidence to act on them. Among those who did, however, were America's own Founding Fathers. In the July issue of the *Dial* Emerson included an article on the "Chardon Street and Bible Conventions," recently held in Boston. Following his short essay on the gathering, he appended the entire address of one "Mr. Nathaniel H. Whiting," whom he describes as "a plain unlettered man." Emerson clearly admired the sentiments expressed in the address, as well as the speaker's "very considerable power of statement." The essence of the presentation is captured in the following excerpt, which emphasizes the authority of what Emerson often called "moral sentiment." "Few there are who dare appeal to the God within their bosoms, and decode all questions according to their own understanding and conscience. Even in the case of Slavery, that most flagrant of all wrongs, seldom do we see one who ventures to rest the case of human freedom on the axiom that 'life, liberty, and the pursuit of happiness' are the common birth-right of the human race; most men pour over the '*Book*' to see if that will not sustain a truth which is as self-evident as their own existence." Emerson's goal as a reformer was to remind others of their ability as well as their obligation to make such judgments. As Gregory Garvey has argued, "Emerson sought to promote a mode of reform that was premised on the possibility of infusing all of society with the same kind of insight that the individual gains at moments of inspiration." Garvey calls this, appropriately, Emerson's "political spirit."[6] For Emerson, the values of the Declaration, or any other ethical principles, are only valid if they resonate in accord with the ultimate source from whence they are derived. This feeling or resonance, in turn, provides the self-confidence that is the necessary prelude to any effort at social reform, especially those that might require personal sacrifice. Thus, in an 1854 antislavery address he insists that "the teachings of the spirit can be apprehended only by the same spirit that gave them forth. To make good the cause of Freedom you must draw off all these foolish trusts on others. You must be citadels and warriors, yourselves Declarations of Independence, the charter, the battle, the victory."[7] Greg Crane rightly identifies this inner divinity as the source of Emerson's concept of an intuitively perceived 'Higher Law' that overrides the authority of such vicious human enactments as the Fugitive Slave Law of 1850, which required the citizens of the free states to cooperate in the capture and return of runaway slaves. As Crane points out, "This indwelling and universal faculty of moral perception enables even an untutored child to intuit the wrongness of slavery."[8] Emerson's validation of individual moral intuition both inspired and authorized those who wished to oppose the evil of slavery but felt intimidated because they had no apparent legal leg on which to stand, that is, no authority other than their own feeling that slavery is a moral and social abomination. Emerson's concept of Higher Law provided a convenient counterpoint to Constitutional law and served to authorize civil disobedience that is undertaken in the name of justice. Thus, in his first public address on the Fugitive Slave Law, delivered to the citizens of Concord in the spring of 1851, Emerson urged outright civil disobedience by encouraging his fellow citizens to break this heinous law "on the earliest occasion." He defended such apparent lawlessness on the grounds that this "filthy enactment" of Congress is "contrary to the primal sentiment of duty." To require free citizens to detain a person who is fleeing for his or her freedom from the oppression of slavery is contrary to the self-evident truth articulated in the Declaration of Independence, a truth that is inscribed in the soul of every virtuous person. As Emerson reminded his fellow citizens, "A man's right to liberty is as inalienable as his right to life."[9]

Emerson's philosophy of transcendental reform was very appealing to the liberal reformers of his day. It provided the sanction of America's foremost intellectual to their cause, and thus offered a powerful validation to a movement that was seen by many as dominated by uneducated fanatics and women. It is not surprising, therefore, that Emerson was also able to stimulate others, especially younger transcendentalists such as Thomas Wentworth Higginson and Moncure Conway, to take an active stand on the great moral issue of the day. As Albert von Frank has observed, "What these men show themselves as responding to, in statement and in action, is the liberating progressive quality of Emerson's thought," which authorized "a bolder, more lively engagement with the world, opening up for them a further range of novel and authentic action."[10] This influence would continue to grow throughout the 1850s.

By the time of the Civil War, and in part because of it, Emerson's reputation reached its zenith. Robert Richardson notes that "Emerson had become by 1863 an inescapable part—a fixture—of American public life."[11] And Lawrence Buell points out, "For moderates as well as for progressives, [Emerson] seemed to personify the union's highest ideals."[12] His status as an American icon was international. He was considered, almost literally, a feature of the American landscape. At the International Exposition in Paris in 1863, a portrait of Emerson was put on prominent display as a part of the American exhibit, along with Bierdstadt's picture of the Rocky Mountains and Church's Niagara.[13] He would use this prominence throughout the war to promote the values of liberal democracy.

When the war erupted on April 12, 1861, only the abolitionists saw it as a war of emancipation, and their views were not popular. The vast majority in the North saw the conflict as a war to preserve the Union as it was, with slavery unmolested in those areas where it already existed. Gradually, this would change. Emerson was convinced that the war would inevitably become a crusade for universal freedom. Following Lincoln's announcement of his Preliminary Emancipation Proclamation in September 1862, Emerson was elated. Not everyone in the North felt the same. When Lincoln subsequently used the occasion of his speech at Gettysburg in November 1863 to redefine the character and purpose of the war as a struggle to ratify the notion that "all men are created equal," he was criticized for it. Garry Wills maintains that in his famous address Lincoln vindicated the importance of "abstract truths" and, in effect, displaced the Constitution with the Declaration as America's premier foundational document, something that Emerson and the abolitionists had done years before. In doing so, says Wills, "Lincoln had revolutionized the Revolution, giving people a new past to live with that would change their future indefinitely."[14] This redefinition, Wills maintains, was influenced in part by the transcendental idealism that was very much in the air at the time. Lincoln (whom Wills describes as a "Transcendentalist without the fuzziness"[15]) was undoubtedly familiar with transcendentalism through frequent conversations with his one-time law partner, William Herndon. Herndon had a deep interest in transcendentalism and personally corresponded with radical transcendental reformer Theodore Parker. This was at a time (mid-1850s) when, according to von Frank, Lincoln and Herndon were "engaged . . . in a lengthy study of the slavery question; trying to see their way through the collapse of old parties and the rise of new ones." In a letter to a friend,

Herndon reported that "he was spreading the gospel of Parker's works and Emerson's works to everyone he met."[16] By this time, both Parker and Emerson were immersed in their own antislavery campaigns.

Early in the war, Emerson had established a de facto alliance with the Radical Republicans in Congress, and he offered strong support for their political agenda. When he visited Washington in January 1862 to speak at the Smithsonian, Emerson urged immediate emancipation both as a moral imperative and as a war measure. It was clear to him that slavery was the ultimate cause of the war and, hence, "it can never go well with us whilst this mischief of slavery remains in our politics and that by concert or by might we must put an end to it." For Emerson, "The end of all political struggle is to establish morality as the basis of all legislation," and morality demands freedom, equality, and justice for all.[17] Slavery is an anachronism and has no place in what promised to be the world's most liberal and progressive society.

During his stay in Washington, Emerson was taken about by his friend Senator Charles Sumner of Massachusetts, one of the foremost of the Radical Republicans in Congress. Sumner arranged for Emerson to meet with Lincoln twice during this trip, and Emerson came away from these meetings with a very favorable impression of America's wartime leader. It is not unreasonable to assume that Emerson used these occasions to promote his ideas on universal emancipation with the president.[18] Conservatives, however, objected to Lincoln's liberal redefinition of the war as a struggle for equality. In responding to the Gettysburg Address, they defended the Constitution as it stood and claimed that Lincoln was "betraying this instrument he was on oath to defend [and] traducing the men who *died* for the letter of that fundamental law."[19] The Chicago *Times* was explicit in the matter and insisted, "It was to uphold this constitution, and the Union created by it, that our officers and soldiers gave their lives at Gettysburg. How dare he, then, standing on their graves, misstate the cause for which they died, and libel the statesmen who founded the government? They were men possessing too much self-respect to declare that negroes were their equals, or were entitled to equal privileges."[20] Emerson, on the other hand, was delighted with the address. He had long believed that the Declaration, with its strong affirmation of the "self-evident" truth that "all men are created equal," was a far superior statement of values than the Constitution, which was marred by the moral compromise that the Southerners demanded in order to accommodate slavery. In a lecture in 1864, Emerson celebrated the Declaration as "the matin song of the universe" and "the greatest achievement of American literature."[21] While conservatives grumbled that emancipation was a violation of the Constitution, Emerson applauded the measure, violation or not, since it was undertaken in order to establish freedom, equality, and social justice. It is these universal principles, the products of an intuitive "moral sentiment," that matter most.

As he noted in his journal at the time, "If the theory is right, it is not so much matter about the facts. . . . All our action now is new & unconstitutional, & necessarily so."[22] For Emerson, emancipation was just the first step in the reinvention of American democracy. African Americans, he felt, must have the same rights as other Americans. As a means toward this end, in the early months of 1863 he joined Frederick Douglass and others in publicly encouraging enlistments and providing financial support for the newly formed Massachusetts Fifty-Fourth, the first official Negro regiment in the regular Union Army. The formation of this regiment was opposed by conservatives, but Emerson recognized that it was yet another important step toward social equality for black Americans. As he declared in 1864, American character is improving because of the war. "We have grown internally—have begun to feel the strength of our strength. This strength is emerging as oppression is lifted from the shoulders of the oppressed. They are now, gradually but steadily, making their contribution to the Union cause and to the future greatness of the nation." Thus, as Emerson told a Boston audience at the time, "American genius finds its true type—if I dare tell you—in the poor Negro soldier lying in the trenches by the Potomac, with his spelling book in one hand and his musket in the other."[23]

Emerson's influence in liberalizing American democracy was also felt firsthand by New England's intellectual elites. One of the many advantages that the Union held over the Confederacy is the fact that the most estimable American authors in the midnineteenth century were New Englanders. Boston was the center of America's literary universe in 1860. Most of these elites were friends of Emerson, all were acquainted with him. The central gathering place for these individuals during the war years was the exclusive Saturday Club. This informal organization, established in 1855, was designed to provide a social meeting place where the members might regularly gather to discuss America's literature, history, and sometimes politics. Many of the members in 1860 were social conservatives who held themselves at arm's length from radical abolitionists such as William Lloyd Garrison, Wendell Phillips, and others who had been agitating for an end to slavery since the 1830s. Some, like James Russell Lowell and Henry Wadsworth Longfellow had used their pens in the 1840s to promote the cause of antislavery, but the increasing radicalism of the movement in the tumultuous and often violent 1850s caused them to virtually abandon the cause. Others, like Oliver Wendell Holmes, had never been sympathetic toward the abolitionists or their cause. Indeed, as one scholar notes, "Many Northerners as well as Southerners perceived prewar abolitionism as a threat to the established order."[24] It is safe to say that, until the attack on Fort Sumter, Emerson was the only prominent intellectual figure in New England who actively supported the radical abolition cause.

With the outbreak of hostilities, however, members of the Saturday Club ran to the defense of the Union. As an early history of the organization indicates, "The scholars, writers, poets of the Club loyally did their various parts with pen, or such personal service as they could do for the soldiers, or in stimulating public opinion."[25] Nevertheless, their hostility to the South did not immediately lead them to the support of emancipation and civil rights for all. Gradually, however, and one might fairly assume with the guiding example of Emerson, most members of the Club came to embrace a liberal agenda. In 1862 the Club accepted only one new member, Emerson's friend and fellow crusader for human rights Charles Sumner, by now the leading voice of the Radical Republicans in the US Senate. The *Atlantic Monthly*, very much the child of this group when it was established in 1857, now became the voice of liberalism, often publishing Emerson's various speeches and patriotic poems, including "The President's Proclamation Address" (November 1862), where Emerson celebrated Lincoln's Preliminary Emancipation Proclamation, issued in September, as a huge moral victory that clearly sounded the death knell for slavery in America. He describes it as a statement that

> commits the country to this justice; [and] compels the innumerable officers, civil, military, naval of the Republic, to range themselves on the line of this equity.... It is not a measure that admits of being taken back. Done, it cannot be undone by a new administration. For slavery overpowers the disgust of the moral sentiment only through immemorial usage. It cannot be introduced as an improvement in the nineteenth century. This act makes that the lives of our heroes have not been sacrificed in vain. It makes a victory of our defeats. Our hurts have been healed; the health of the nation is repaired. With a victory like this, we can stand many disasters. It does not promise the redemption of the black race: that lies not with us: but it relieves it of our opposition.[26]

The *Atlantic* also published Emerson's moving poetic tribute to the heroism of the Massachusetts Fifty-Fourth and its leader, Col. Robert Gould Shaw, following the heroic yet failed attack by the regiment on Fort Wagner in July 1863. "Voluntaries" appeared in the October 1863 issue. Eventually, the once conservative and always venerable *North American Review*, one of New England's oldest and most prestigious journals, was pressed into service for the liberal cause. While the journal was objecting to immediate Negro emancipation as late as 1861, by 1863, when Lowell and Norton took over editorship, the journal was defending the "extra-constitutional methods" of Lincoln's government (April) and publishing positive reviews of James E. Cairnes' searing indictment of American slavery, *The Slave Power* (April), as well as John Stuart Mill's democratic manifesto, *On Liberty* (July).

In a lecture titled "Perpetual Forces" (November 1862), Emerson shared his vision of the new America that he believed would eventually emerge from this crisis. It was a decidedly liberal one. When the Constitution was rewritten, Emerson felt, it would be necessary to "[l]eave slavery out. Nothing satisfies all men but justice, let us have that, and let us stifle our prejudices against commonsense and humanity, and agree that every man shall have what he honestly earns, and, if he is a sane and innocent man, have an equal vote in the state, and a fair chance in society."[27] The notion of universal emancipation that Emerson articulated in this speech was a radical concept. Even Lincoln in his Preliminary Emancipation Proclamation in September had restricted emancipation to those states that remained in rebellion after January 1, 1863. As it turns out, Emerson's concept of 'equal rights,' including universal male suffrage, was more than even some liberals could bear. Following his lecture, a newspaper reported that Emerson's presentation was "a re-hash of his Abolition sophistry" and noted specifically, "When he argued in favor of forcible emancipation, a few old ladies and gentlemen applauded; but when he insisted that the negro should have 'an equal chance with the white man,' even they were indignantly silent."[28] Emerson, however, was not deterred. As the war dragged on, and war weariness threatened to undermine Union resolve in the crisis winter of 1863–64, he came forth with what is arguably the most important lecture of his career. "Fortune of the Republic" was delivered no fewer than fourteen times in the relatively brief period from December 1, 1863, to February 9, 1864. Never in his lengthy career as a lecturer had Emerson repeated a single address so often or consecutively. Clearly, he was responding to the crisis at hand. In the address, he offers unqualified support for Lincoln, whose reelection was then in doubt. He also articulates in compelling terms his vision of liberal democracy, which he believed represented the ultimate fulfillment of America's destiny.

At the outset of his address Emerson indicates the need for abstract values or principles to provide guidance in life. "A man for success must not be *pure* idealist," he notes, for "then he will practically fail: but he must have ideas, or he might as well be the horse he rides on." The particular ideas or ideals that Emerson had in mind were simple and straightforward. At this time of crisis, Emerson declares, "It is the young men of the land, who must save it; it is they to whom this wonderful hour, after so many weary ages, dawns, the Second Declaration of Independence, the proclaiming of liberty, land, justice, and a career for all men; and honest dealings with other nations."[29] For Emerson, the progressive evolution of American democracy, so long held hostage to Southern conservatism, can now go forward once again. "We [are] in the midst of a great revolution" he states, "still enacting the sentiment of the Puritans, and the dreams of young people of thirty years ago,—we, [are] passing out of old remainders of barbarism . . . into freedom of thought, of religion, of speech, of the press, of trade, of suffrage, or political right." He believed it was possible for American society to progress morally as well as materially. In his 1855 lecture "Slavery" he had complained bitterly that the dominant political parties at that time had "failed to inspire us with any exalted hope." Democracy did not "stand for the good of the many . . . of the poor . . . [and] for the elevation of entire humanity" even though it should have. The reason for this stagnation was that historically "The Party of Property, of education, has resisted every progressive step" since "[t]hey wish their age should be absolutely like the last. There is no confession of destitution like this fierce conservatism."[30] Now that this intolerable incubus has been cast off, the nation has a real opportunity to go forward. Indeed, as Emerson points out, it had already taken substantial steps in that direction. Through the Homestead Act of 1862, the government had become proactive in promoting the welfare of all citizens. This groundbreaking piece of legislation offered "a patch of land in the wilderness to every son of Adam who [would] till it," and thus began "to strike off the chains which sniffling hypocrites have bound on the weaker race."[31] (The act allowed property ownership to every head of household, regardless of race or gender.) Also, in 1862, the Morrill Act granted to each state substantial Federal lands for the purpose of endowing agricultural colleges. Emerson applauded this government effort to provide for and support higher education, and he looked forward (presciently) to the evolution of these institutions into first-class universities. "It looks as if vast extension was given to . . . popular culture, and, as the appetite grows by feeding, the next generation will vote for their children,—not a dame-school, nor a Latin school, but a university, complete training in all the arts of peace and war, letters, science; all the useful and all the fine arts. And thus the voters of the Republic will at last be educated to that public duty."[32] None of this was possible when the government was dominated by the conservative, aristocratic values of the slave-holding South where opportunities for advancement were already decided at the time of birth.

In his speech, Emerson consistently envisions an expanding role for the government in protecting the rights of all citizens and providing care for the poor and needy. "Humanity asks that . . . democratic institutions shall be more thoughtful for the interests of women,—for the training of children, for care of sick and unable persons and serious care of criminals than was ever any the best government of the old world."[33] This view was not entirely new for Emerson. As early as 1844 he had declared that "government exists to defend the weak and the poor and the injured party; the rich and the strong can better take care of themselves."[34] Such concern for the weak and oppressed had immediate application to the plight of the Freedmen. At the present hour, Emerson notes, "it is possible that . . . we shall have the happiness of lifting the low." However, this will require a long-term commitment, and "the steps already taken to teach the freedman his letters, and the decencies of life, are not worth much if they stop there."[35]

If America stays the course in this time of crisis, Emerson insists, this new vision of democracy can at last become a reality. "Here let there be what the earth waits for,—exalted manhood, the new man, whom plainly this country must furnish."[36] Victory in this great struggle would be worthy of any sacrifice. Already, "slavery is broken," Emerson asserts, "and, if we use our advantage, irretrievably. For such a gain,—to end once for all that pest of all free institutions,—one generation might well be sacrificed,—perhaps it will be,—that this continent be purged, and a new era of equal rights dawn on the universe."[37]

Emerson viewed the eventual Union victory in the war as an affirmation of the principles of liberal democracy, the idea that the government has an obligation to protect the weak from the strong and insure freedom, justice, and equality for all citizens, regardless of race or gender. Emerson also envisioned a proactive government that would provide opportunities for education and thus promote the social and material advancement of all citizens. In the years immediately following the war, he was pleased to see his vision of America enacted into law. The passage of the Thirteenth Amendment (1865) ended slavery forever; the Fourteenth Amendment (1866) guaranteed equal protection to all citizens, and the Fifteenth Amendment (1870) guaranteed suffrage to all adult males "without regard to race, color, or previous conditions of servitude." Reflecting on all of this in 1871, Emerson took comfort that a truly great victory had been won. Slavery had been defeated and "the Constitution not only amended, but construed in a new spirit."[38] As Crane notes, these amendments, which came about as a result of a persistent emphasis on the importance of abstract principles by reformers such as Emerson, Frederick Douglass, and others, "succeeded in revising fundamental conceptions of citizenship and justice."[39] Emerson realized that the struggle to maintain these tremendous gains would be a long one because old attitudes are difficult to change. Thus, he wrote to his friend Thomas Carlyle in January of 1866 that the nation now has to deal those "thieves that are stealing not only the public gold, but the newly won rights of the slave, & the new measures we had contrived to keep the planter from sucking his blood."[40] Nevertheless, he remained confident that the principles that were affirmed by the war would endure.

In the postwar years, Emerson continued to lend his authority to liberal causes. In his address at Harvard in July 1867, appropriately titled "Progress of Culture," he celebrated the "fusion of races and religions" in

America and the freedom of movement that allowed "every wanderer to choose his climate and government." He also applauded "the new claim of woman to a political status." He saw this development as "an honorable testimony to the civilization which has given her a civil status new in history."[41] Of course, woman's suffrage at this time was almost as controversial as emancipation had been earlier. Not surprisingly, the women of America looked to Emerson for support for their cause. While in the 1850s he had some reservations regarding the possibly pernicious effects of full enfranchisement on women's refined sensibilities, the call of principle, at last, was too strong to resist. He threw his support unambiguously behind the women's effort. In a speech delivered in Boston at a gathering of the New England Woman's Suffrage Association, in May 1869, and later reported in detail in the *Boston Post* (May 27, 1869), he declared, "The claim now pressed by woman is a claim for nothing less than all, than her share in all. She asks for her property; she asks for her rights, for her vote; she asks for her share in education, for her share in all the institutions of society, for her half of the whole world; and to this she is entitled." At the same meeting, America's most estimable public intellectual accepted the vice-presidency of the New England Woman's Suffrage Association. It is clear that the events of the war had an influence in liberalizing Emerson on the woman question and removing any doubts that he might have had about the propriety of introducing universal adult suffrage. In his handwritten notes for the address, he observes, "Civilization is progressive. One truth leads another by the hand, & her activity in putting an end to Slavery & in serving in the Hospitals of the Sanitary Commission in the war & in the labors of the Freedman's bureau have opened her eyes to larger rights & duties."[42] Following his 1869 address, and to the end of his life in 1882, Emerson was consistently seen as a friend to the cause of women's rights. As Julia Ward Howe would later recall, "At more than one suffrage meeting, he ha[d] entered his protest against the political inequality which still demoralizes society. Some of us remember the sweet *naif* manner in which he did this, the sincerity and the measure with which he spoke, as if urged and restrained by a weight of conviction which called for simple and solemn utterance. He was for us, knowing well enough our limitations and short-comings, and his golden words have done much both to fit us for the larger freedom, and to know that it belongs to us."[43]

In 1878, Emerson returned once again to the topic of "The Fortune of the Republic" in what would be one of his last public lectures. In this presentation, he summarized his vision of America's new liberal democracy. "The genius of this country has marked out our true policy," he notes, "opportunity. Opportunity of civil rights, of education, of personal power, and not less of wealth; doors wide open. If I could have it,—free trade with all the world without toll or custom-houses, invitation as we now make every nation, to every race and skin, white men, red men, yellow men, black men; hospitality of fair field and equal laws to all."[44]

Following this, Emerson's mental powers waned, and he slowly withdrew from the public stage. During this time he continued to be revered as a national treasure. The post–Civil War period witnessed a tremendous expansion of the American economy, as industry and trade grew exponentially. Unfortunately, it was also during this time that Emerson's concept of 'self-reliance,' which he defined as reliance on "God . . . here within,"[45] was warped into the notion of "rugged individualism" and used to justify the predatory practices of the captains of industry, something that would have appalled him. Daniel Aaron points out that for some, Emerson appeared as the "seer of laissez-faire capitalism and the rampant individual." Even though "Emerson . . . never intended his exhortations to justify the practices of the 'Robber Barons,'" his political philosophy, in the eyes of some at least, seemed to "len[d] support to the belief in *laissez-faire* and the necessity of the minimized state."[46] Obviously, this construct of Emerson's political philosophy disregarded most of what he had stood for throughout his entire public life.

Unfortunately, this pernicious misreading of Emerson continues today in some quarters. Thus, as recently as 1981 a president of Yale University (A. Bartlett Giamatti) could assert that "with extraordinary literary skills at a crucial moment in our nation's life, it is Emerson who freed our politics and our politicians from any sense of restraint by extolling self-generated, unaffiliated power as the best foot to place in the small of the back of the man in front of you." According to Mr. Giamatti, "Emerson is as sweet as barbed wire, and his sentimentality as accommodating as a brick."[47] A later, less toxic misreading of Emerson holds that, "Emersonian transcendentalism and Emerson's political commitments from 1844 to 1863 are fundamentally at odds with each other" and that "Emersonianism is ill-suited to social and political reform."[48]

Despite such occasional misreadings, Emerson's message of liberation remained a potent force in American culture well into the twentieth century, and beyond. His writings were a source of inspiration to those involved in the pursuit of social justice from the women's movement, to the modern civil rights movement. Moorfield Storey, a Boston reformer who was destined to become the first president of the NAACP (1920–1929), was an Emersonian idealist who often quoted from Emerson's antislavery addresses in his own campaign for social justice. In a memorial address on Emerson in 1903, delivered as part of a major celebration in Concord on the one-hundredth anniversary of Emerson's birth, Storey, who was also a leader in the anti-imperialism movement, paid tribute to the lessons in liberal democracy that he had learned from America's most revered prophet. Among these was the following. "That every man, able or dull, superior or inferior, white, brown, or black, had his right to his chance of success, and it followed that no other man had a right to take that chance away or to insist that his fellow should be remade according to his ideas."[49] This Emersonian ideal would inform Storey's long reform career.

At the time Storey was elected to the presidency of the NAACP, W. E. B. Du Bois was named a full-time staff director of publicity and research. Emerson would be an important resource for Du Bois also in his pursuit of social justice in America. His biographer indicates that Emerson was one of Du Bois' favorite writers. This is not surprising given his long association with Storey and also the fact that he is described as "an idealist by temperament, always believing that it was possible, somehow, to get from the world's welter . . . to the bedrock of principles—upper case Truth."[50] Possibly because of this, as Anita Patterson observes, "Emerson's writings represent a considerable resource for the development of Du Bois's political philosophy." The same scholar points out that "Du Bois himself was regarded by many of his contemporaries as a literary successor to Emerson."[51] The next generation of Civil Rights activists would also find inspiration and support in Emerson's words. As Patterson reports, "Martin Luther King, Jr. repeatedly and explicitly referred to Emerson in his speeches, lectures, and sermons."[52]

It was Emerson's dedication to the principles of liberal democracy and his irrepressible faith in the ability of mankind to remake the world in the image of the ideal that led one scholar to describe him as an "anticipator of a thoroughgoing democratic pluralism."[53] Through his activism in the cause of social justice in the nineteenth century, Emerson helped to set the stage for inclusiveness, freedom, and equality in the twentieth century. I am convinced that influence will carry over into the twenty-first century. Those who might find Emerson's transcendental writings to be oblique or obscure, with little relationship to the world as we know it, should simply read his philosophical essays in conjunction with his antislavery and reform writings. The latter demonstrate clearly how Emerson "put his creed into his deed." Throughout his long career as America's foremost public intellectual, he recognized that philosophical insight means nothing if it does not lead to moral conduct. As early as 1837, he advised the young men of Harvard, "Action is with the scholar subordinate, but it is essential. Without it, he is not yet man. . . . Inaction is cowardice."[54] When faced with the moral abomination of slavery, the denial of civil rights to women, and the general devaluation of life in a material society where it often seemed that "Things are in the saddle, / And ride mankind," Emerson took action. His life offers eloquent testimony to his enduring commitment to freedom, social justice, and equality, as well as his irrepressible belief in the infinite preciousness of all humanity. As we consider the growing conservatism of the present time, when states are passing laws and amending their constitutions in order to deny the benefits of marriage to those who are regarded as having the wrong gender mix, as stem cell research and Darwin's genius are threatened by the narrow religious concerns of one segment of the population, when the future of a woman's reproductive rights may be determined by one or two political appointments to the US Supreme Court, when the USA Patriot Act threatens the right to privacy as well as the principle of free inquiry in the name of defense, when the US Constitution is once again construed as an instrument to limit rather than guarantee rights, when the president of the United States declares the torture of prisoners of war to be acceptable in defiance of the Geneva Conventions and specific legislation forbidding such brutal and inhumane conduct, when accused enemy combatants are held for years without trial or access to attorneys in off shore gulags maintained by the United States government in defiance of international law and an international outcry, American citizens might do well to remember Emerson's notion of universal human rights, symbolized by the all inclusive circle of humanity. He believed deeply that in a free society, "[n]o citizen will go wrong who on every question leans to the side of general liberty."[55]

The violation of this principle strikes at the very heart of democracy. By tolerating slavery, the Founding Fathers had attempted to allow an exception to the "self-evident" truth of human equality because it seemed convenient at the time. Their attempt at compromise on this sacred principle nearly brought about the nation's ruination. When Emerson gave his Civil War address "American Civilization" in Washington in 1862, he sought to point out where the nation had gone wrong and how we might re-create ourselves in a fashion that would prevent future catastrophe. "Civilization," he said, "depends on morality. Everything good in man leans on what is higher."[56] The compromise with slavery was patently immoral, and America was teetering on the edge of destruction as a result. The nation, he felt, could only rectify this wrong by destroying slavery. With the end of this heinous institution, America could rightfully assume the moral leadership of the world as the only nation proclaiming *universal* liberty and equality. He saw it as our destiny. "Our whole history appears like a last effort of the Divine Providence in behalf of the human race,"[57] Emerson declared. Indeed, the issue was one that transcended national boundaries. The future of democracy itself was at stake. "It looks as if we hold the fate of the fairest possession of mankind in our hands," Emerson observed, "to be saved by our firmness or to be lost by hesitation."[58] Lincoln, who might have been present at Emerson's address, issued his Preliminary Emancipation Proclamation just months later, in September 1862, thus turning the Civil War into

America's second revolution. In justifying that historic act in his address to Congress in December, Lincoln echoed Emerson when he said, "In *giving* freedom to the slave, we *assure* freedom to the *free*—honorable alike in what we give, and what we preserve." And he added that America was now at a crossroad of its history. At this moment, he warned, "We shall nobly save, or meanly lose, the last best hope of earth."[59] Thankfully, America made the right decision and went on to assume the position of moral leadership that both Lincoln and Emerson anticipated, a position that it has held until now. With their political and moral insight, Americans came to understand that there could be no exceptions to the principle of universal human rights. Either they were truly universal, or they were nothing. Subsequent documents, such as the "Universal Declaration of Human Rights," proclaimed by the United Nations in 1948, would hardly be possible without the American example. That declaration begins with the statement that "recognition of the inherent dignity and of the equal and inalienable rights of *all* members of the human family is the foundation of freedom, justice and peace in the world" [emphasis added].

These are the rights that Emerson stood for throughout his long career, and this is why, on the threshold of the twenty-first century, he is more relevant and necessary than ever.

Notes

1. John Dewey, "Ralph Waldo Emerson," *Emerson: A Collection of Critical Essays*, ed. Milton Konvitz and Stephen E. Whicher (New York: Prentice Hall, 1962).

2. Ralph Waldo Emerson, *The Later Lectures of Ralph Waldo Emerson*, ed. Ronald Bosco and Joel Myerson, vol. 2 (Athens: University of Georgia Press, 2001), 25.

3. Ralph Waldo Emerson, *The Collected Works of Ralph Waldo Emerson*, ed. Alfred R. Ferguson, Joseph Slater, and Douglas Emory Wilson, vol. 2 (Cambridge: Harvard University Press, 1971), 160.

4. Ibid., 179.

5. Ralph Waldo Emerson, *The Journals and Miscellaneous Notebooks of Ralph Waldo Emerson*, ed. William H. Gilman and Ralph Orth, vol. 4 (Cambridge: Harvard University Press, 1960–82), 357.

6. T. Gregory Garvey, "Emerson's Political Spirit and the Problem of Language," *The Emerson Dilemma: Essays on Emerson and Social Reform*, ed. T. Gregory Garvey (Athens: University of Georgia Press, 2001), 15.

7. Ralph Waldo Emerson, *Emerson's Antislavery Writings*, ed. Len Gougeon and Joel Myerson (New Haven: Yale University Press, 1995), 83.

8. Gregg Crane, *Race, Citizenship, and Law in American Literature* (Cambridge: Cambridge University Press, 2002), 113.

9. Emerson, *Emerson's Antislavery Writings*, 60, 57.

10. Albert von Frank, *The Trials of Anthony Burns: Freedom and Slavery in Emerson's Boston* (Cambridge: Harvard University Press, 1998), 101.

11. Robert Richardson, *Emerson: The Mind on Fire* (Berkeley: University of California Press, 1995), 551.

12. Lawrence Buell, *Emerson* (Cambridge: Harvard University Press, 2003), 34.

13. Barbara Packer, "Ralph Waldo Emerson," *Columbia Literary History of the United States*, ed. Emory Elliott (New York: Columbia University Press, 1988), 381.

14. Garry Wills, *Lincoln at Gettysburg: The Words that Remade America* (New York: Simon and Schuster, 1992), 37–38.

15. Ibid., 174.

16. Von Frank, *Trials of Anthony Burns*, 265–66.

17. *Atlantic Monthly*, "American Civilization," (April 1862), 510–11.

18. Len Gougeon, *Virtue's Hero: Emerson, Antislavery, and Reform* (Athens: University of Georgia Press, 1990), 276–77.

19. Wills, *Lincoln at Gettysburg*, 38.

20. Quoted in ibid.

21. Ralph Waldo Emerson, *Uncollected Lectures by Ralph Waldo Emerson*, ed. Clarence Gohdes, Jr. (New York: Rudge, 1932), 40.

22. Ralph Waldo Emerson, *The Journals and Miscellaneous Notebooks of Ralph Waldo Emerson*, ed. William H. Gilman and Ralph Orth, vol. 15 (Cambridge: Harvard University Press, 1960–82), 301–02.

23. Emerson, *Uncollected Lectures by Ralph Waldo Emerson*, 41–42.

24. Earl J. Hess, *Liberty, Virtue, and Progress: Northerners and Their War for the Union* (New York: Fordham University Press, 1997), 98.

25. Edward Waldo Emerson, *The Early Years of the Saturday Club, 1855–1870* (Boston: Houghton Mifflin, 1918), 254.

26. Emerson, *Emerson's Antislavery Writings*, 131–32.

27. Emerson, *The Later Lectures*, 30.

28. Ibid., 288.

29. Emerson, *Emerson's Antislavery Writings*, 140.

30. Ibid., 95–96.

31. Ibid., 146–47.

32. Ibid., 144.

33. Ibid., 147.

34. Ibid., 26.

35. Ibid., 149.

36. Ibid., 151.

37. Ibid., 153.

38. Emerson, *The Later Lectures*, 344.

39. Gregg Crane, *Race, Citizenship, and Law in American Literature* (Cambridge: Cambridge University Press, 2002), 129.

40. Ralph Waldo Emerson, *The Correspondence of Emerson and Carlyle*, ed. Joseph Slater (New York: Columbia University Press, 1964), 548.

41. Ralph Waldo Emerson, *The Complete Works of Ralph Waldo Emerson*, ed. Edward Waldo Emerson, vol. 8 (Boston: Houghton Mifflin, 1903–04), 207–08.

42. Quoted in Len Gougeon, "Emerson and the Woman Question: The Evolution of His Thought," *The New England Quarterly*, vol. 71 (December 1998), 570–92.

43. *Woman's Journal* (May 6, 1882).

44. Emerson, *Complete Works*, 11:541.

45. Ralph Waldo Emerson, *Collected Works*, p. 41.

46. Daniel Aaron, "Emerson and the Progressive Tradition," *Emerson: A Collection of Critical Essays*, ed. Milton Konvitz and Stephen E. Whicher (New York: Prentice Hall, 1962), 89, 94.

47. A. Bartlett Giamatti, *The University and the Public Interest* (New York: Atheneum, 1981), 27.

48. John Carlos Rowe, *At Emerson's Tomb: The Politics of Classic American Literature* (New York: Columbia University Press, 1997), 25.

49. Moorfield Storey, "Speech of Moorfield Storey," *The Centenary of the Birth of Ralph Waldo Emerson, as Observed in Concord May 25 1903 under the Direction of the Social Circle in Concord* (Cambridge: Riverside, 1903), 105–06.

50. David Levering Lewis, *W. E. B. Du Bois: Biography of a Race, 1868–1919* (New York: Holt, 1993), 282, 89.

51. Ibid., 162–63.

52. Anita Patterson, *From Emerson to King: Democracy, Race, and the Politics of Protest* (New York: Columbia University Press, 1997), 177.

53. Buell, *Emerson*, 287.

54. Emerson, *The Collected Works*, 1:59.

55. Emerson, *Emerson's Antislavery Writings*, 105.

56. *Atlantic Monthly* (April 1862), 504.

57. Ibid., 508.

58. Ibid., 509.

59. Abraham Lincoln, *The Collected Works of Abraham Lincoln*, vol. 5 (New Brunswick, NJ: Rutgers University Press, 1953), 537.

Chapter 10

Individualism,
Natural Law, Human Rights

Emerson on "The Scholar" vis-à-vis
Emerson on Reform

Lawrence Buell

*E*merson's single best-known essay, "The American Scholar," unfolds for the first time what became his single favorite lecture theme: to provide "a theory of the Scholar's office," as he stated it telegraphically just before the event.[1] Throughout his long-year career as public lecturer, he loved nothing better than discoursing at college commencements and other academic occasions on the traits and duties of the paradigmatic figure he calls the "scholar," which was also his favorite *self*-descriptor. Given at Harvard in 1837, "The American Scholar" was the first of a dozen or so orations of this kind he delivered during his long career. The last (and unfortunately least potent) speech in this vein came almost forty years later at the University of Virginia, after Emerson had fallen into his dotage but nonetheless felt compelled to accept the invitation against the advice of his handlers as a gesture of cross-sectional good will. These discourses are remarkably little discussed as a series. "The American Scholar" has preempted virtually all the attention. The voluminous exegetical literature on it, its place in Emerson's unfolding career, and its broader significance as a barometric indicator and influence upon American literary and cultural history tends to take its successors for granted and thereby understate the gravity of Emerson's commitment to this long series of ceremonial performances and the evolution of his prevailing script along the way according to local contexts, changing convictions, and current events.[2]

Emerson's series of disquisitions on the scholar was by no means the only instance of oratorical self-repetition during his long career. Both as

179

minister and as lyceum lecturer he frequently delivered the "same" text over and over, with minor revisions and improvisational variations each time around. Sometimes he might even be said to have "rewritten" the same essay, as with the reprises of *Nature* (1836) in "Nature" (1844) and the first portion of "Fate" (1860), not to mention countless instances of microlevel self-quotation-with-a-difference. But Emerson's various "scholar" performances offer a unique case of multiple discrete texts on the "same" theme spanning almost the entire span of his intellectual maturity. As such they stand as his single most characteristic essayistic subgenre.

"Scholar" was not for Emerson a specialist category like "college student" or "bookman" or "professor" or "compiler of scholarly books." It meant rather something like "independent-minded, alive-at-the-top thinking person." "Man Thinking" is his short-form encapsulation in "The American Scholar." "College gowns do not make scholars any more than uniform[s] make heroes," insists a later definitional oration.[3] But always Emerson's defining image and primary target audience was the mentally alert young collegian or recent graduate.

This scholar idea has both an elitist face and a populist face. Emerson believed both that "every man is a scholar potentially" and that as a practical matter few measure up, though he never ceased to hope to inspire more recruits.[4]

The dozen or so surviving texts of Emerson's inspirational scholar lectures show strong family resemblances: the emphasis on transformation of individual selves as the key to transforming society; the call to resist trendiness or groupthink; and the call to read books critically rather than slavishly. But such constants also make the shifts that do occur seem all the more notable.

I
Defining "The Scholar" in Career-Long Context: "Nature," "Books," "Action" Revisited

In "The American Scholar" Emerson itemizes what he calls the scholar's "resources": *nature*, *books*, and *action*. Nature comes first because it is the most perennial: the resource literally for all seasons. Emerson sees nature as a mystic mirror and counterpart of the human spirit. "Its laws are the laws of [one's] own mind." Therefore, he declares "the ancient precept, 'Know thyself,' and the modern precept, 'Study nature,' become at last one maxim."[5] Whether you go to nature as an object of study or as a place of invigoration, your mind will be enlarged.

In a move he presumably knew would sound counterintuitive for a talk in academia about the proper work of scholars, Emerson puts books second rather than first. Books are mighty monuments to the intellectual accomplishments of the past but by the same token potential stumbling blocks to original genius. Therefore books, as he mischievously asserts, are for "the scholar's idle times"[6] rather than for times of peak experience when the creative juices are flowing.

Action comes third because it is subordinate to thought, yet crucial if the thinking person is not to remain a cloistered mandarin. Thinking in and of itself is only "a partial act." Emerson emphatically refuses to "shut myself out of this globe of action, and transplant an oak into a flower pot, there to hunger and pine."[7]

In later disquisitions on the scholar figure, Emerson never again invokes this identical trinity of resources, though all three regularly reappear. Broadly speaking, Emerson's in-principle valuation of books remains much the same; but his assessment of nature changes markedly, and his theory of action pursues an irregular and troubled course as he struggles to confront the contradictions in his own thinking.

The saga of Emerson on nature is the simpler of these two stories to tell, though easy to misrepresent. From youth to age, Emerson loved the outdoors, though he was hardly an outdoorsman. He far preferred life in the exurbs to city dwelling, and he liked to depict that life in a Wordsworthian vocabulary of enthused romantic seclusion. He loved rural walks. He bought the Walden lot on which Henry Thoreau later built his hut largely because of a combination of being charmed by the spot and wanting to save it from commercial development. All this together with Emerson's evocations of the mystique of nature in his early essays and poems doubtless helped set Thoreau on the path to his own much more determined and intensive exploration of the natural world. On the one hand, and thinking of such touchstone parts of the early Emerson canon as the disquisition on nature in "American Scholar" and especially his first book *Nature*, we can see him as a prophet and formative influence on modern American nature poetry and nature writing, on the emergence of nature protection, and on the more scientistic thinking and more biocentric ways of conceiving environmental ethics we find in figures such as Thoreau and Muir.[8] On the other hand, Emerson was also, from the start, committed to thinking of nature as a human resource: for its use-value (in all the various senses of the word *use*) in unlocking human powers—most especially powers of *mind*, but also utilitarian powers of technology, environmental design, and so on. Hence the rough justice behind the oft-made claim that Emerson's first book *Nature* (1836) should rather have been titled *Man* instead, and behind environmental historian Richard White's claim, in his book *The Organic Machine*, of straight-line descent from *Nature* to the harness-the-wild mentality behind the aggressive engineering of the flowage of the Columbia River.[9] Indeed, *Nature* explicitly ends with the biblical-sounding prophecy of the coming "kingdom of man over nature."[10] Emerson surely did not mean to license unregulated clear-cutting of forests and paving over wetlands. But no less patently does he mean to insist that nature's ultimate value is anthropocentric—to steady, sustain, guide, and uplift humankind.

The later Emerson, however, less often invokes nature as humankind's instructive book, resource, and soulmate and more often envisions nature in protoevolutionary terms as a power that produces and shapes all life forms, including humankind itself, which he sees as willy-nilly subject to that power and shaped by it. The result is (at least up to a point) a more postprovidentialist, biocentric cast of mind than before, but the long-range result is to make him less affirmative and more queasy about the humankind-nature relation than he was before.[11]

At first we find, in middle Emerson, some quite rhapsodic passages in this vein, as in the commencement speech he gave at Colby (then "Water-ville") College in 1841: "The method of nature: who could ever analyze it? That rushing stream will not stop to be observed. We can never surprise nature in a corner; never find the end of a thread; never tell where to set the first stone. The bird hastens to lay her egg: the egg hastens to be a bird."[12] This bubbly mood does not last long without severe qualification, however. Along with the sense of nature as increasingly elusive and ungraspable slowly dawns the intimation of natural law itself as far more morally prob-lematic than he once thought. Emerson would dearly love to continue to believe that "the axioms of physics translate the laws of ethics" (to quote one of his favorite recycled quotations, used in *Nature*).[13] But increasingly he is forced to wonder whether natural law is not rather incongruent with, if not positively opposed to, moral law: to wonder whether in fact so-called law of nature might—morally speaking—be nothing more than a law of force.

These doubts surface most famously in the late essay "Fate," which opens—in stark contrast to his earlier self—with an extended portrait of the state of nature as a state of disease, disaster, and mutual predation, "race liv-ing at the expense of race."[14] But all the way through his middle and late work Emerson is recurringly at odds with his earlier, less troubled self in strange and intriguing ways over the morality of natural process, as in this passage from his "Politics" (1844) on the subject of human versus natural law. Human law "is only a memorandum." Nature is its foundation. Nature itself, however, "is not democratic, nor limited-monarchical, but despotic, and will not be fooled or abated by any jot of her authority. . . . and as fast as the pub-lic mind is opened to more intelligence, the code is seen to be brute and stammering."[15] Emerson here invokes natural law as the origin and standard for measuring the inadequacy of human law but in the same breath imagines that natural standard most unappetizingly and the defects of human law as "brute"-like. Small wonder, then, that Emerson's later definitional pieces on the scholar, starting with a lecture given at Middlebury College in 1845, the year after "Politics" was published, tone down the tributes to nature as the scholar's resource into perfunctory and standardized asides—as for example an 1861 address that declares, "I would have you rely on Nature ever,—wise, omnific, thousand-headed Nature, equal to each emergency, which can do very well without colleges."[16] Here "Nature" does not mean much more than something like "good old unpedantic common sense."[17]

So even as middle and late Emerson's sense of *Homo sapiens* as controlled by natural law increases, his prescriptions of physical nature as intellectual resource, spiritual energizer, and moral authority become more perfunctory and equivocal.

So much for the saga of nature's diminishing place in Emerson's accounts of the paradigmatic scholar—always, again, to be understood as oblique autobiographical self-portraiture as well. The saga of Emerson's theory of "action" is more tricky to follow and unpack. This is a story of repeated attempts to revisit the impasse "The American Scholar" creates for itself around this idea.

Here Emerson wants to assert both that thinking in and of itself counts for nothing without being translated into lived experience—without thought being put into practice—and yet also that scholars must not rush promiscuously into the public arena.

> Some great decorum, some fetish of a government, some ephemeral trade, or war, or man, is cried up by half mankind and cried down by the other half, as if all depended on this particular up or down. The odds are that the whole question is not worth the poorest thought which the scholar has lost in listening to the controversy. Let him not quit his belief that a popgun is a popgun, though the ancient and honorable of the earth affirm it to be the crack of doom. In silence, in steadiness, in severe abstraction, let him hold by himself, etc.[18]

The preeminent importance Emerson attaches to intellectual self-reliance ("self-trust") drives him back to the image of the scholar as a solitary astronomer "in his private observatory, cataloguing obscure and nebulous stars of the human mind,"[19] which in turn keeps him from being able to imagine scholars as social beings even though he himself at this very moment is of course being social: performing the central part in a social ritual at the heart of the region's intellectual nerve center: a social ritual, what is more, that he clearly hopes will have a social impact.

Emerson's emphasis on the need for the scholar or thinking person to stay free-lance runs strong throughout his career. In his Middlebury speech, for instance, Emerson defines the scholar as the "speculative" or "spiritual" person, warns that "inaction" is preferable to "misaction," and declares that true scholars reject all popular isms.[20] Indeed, of all Emerson's scholar speeches, this one is the most insistent—almost to the point of obsessiveness—about picturing the scholar as a kind of detached ascetic standing austerely aloof from society. But all Emerson's scholar speeches show some such disjuncture, more or less, between performance and argument. Performatively, Emerson the lecturer was always, and increasingly, thrusting his bodily self into public arenas—in academia or elsewhere—in order to ignite his hearers in transformative ways, and with quite stunning results. In time, Emerson became the nation's first and leading public intellectual. But doctrinally, he always preached the principle of solitary independent thinking first.

The key to this disjuncture between antisocial theory and socially engaged behavior is of course that Emerson truly believed in the power of independent thinking to have not just a private result but also a social consequence. This conviction would have been fortified by the trust he shared with many other intellectuals of his era—in this respect following in the footsteps of his early national and Puritan precursors—in the power of oratorical eloquence not only to carry conviction but also to move audiences, not only to think and feel but also to act, and thereby achieve a social result.[21] "Power of thought makes us men . . . distributes society; distributes the work of the world; is the prolific source of all arts, of all wealth, of all delight, of all grandeur. Men are as they believe. Men are as they think. . . . And the man who knows any truth not yet discerned by other men, is master of all other men, so far as that truth and its wide relations are concerned."[22] This particular passage occurs, significantly, in the first of several college commencement speeches during the Civil War—at Tufts, in the summer of 1861. Here and on such occasions during the war, Emerson always makes a point of emphasizing that the work of the intellect must be allowed to go on even in a time of national emergency. "When Medford is invaded," he exclaims, "I hope the Faculty will release you from Euclid and Plato just so long as the enemy dares to threaten Tufts College. But only so long: you must use your better weapon and rally to invisible power."[23] He then cites the precedent of the poet Milton campaigning on behalf of religious liberty at the height of the English Civil War.

Remarks like these show clearly that Emerson was not framing his views about the life of the mind in a social vacuum. Such indeed had been the case from the start. "The American Scholar" makes reference (for example) to the macrocurrents of Euro-American social thought and to the microdisturbance of the so called panic of 1837. But most especially is this true of the wartime commencement addresses. Throughout them runs a skein of allusions to the war context and to the intellectual life itself in terms the rhetoric of war: as battle, as victory or defeat, and so on. Though scholars may seem irrelevant in wartime, actually they are "Nature's Home-Guard" (317). Indeed it was scholars (that is, creative, far-sighted thinking people) who invented gunpowder and the arts of war in the first place.

In this way Emerson transmits a potentially confusing double message: the life of the mind demands both a kind of critical detachment and a kind of social engagement. As for instance in this one-two thrust: "Does anyone doubt between the strength of a thought and that of an institution? Does anyone doubt that a good general is better than a park of artillery?"[24] The first statement draws a stark contrast between the realms of thought and public affairs that the second sentence largely takes back—though by no means completely. Yes, the scholar must not defer "to the men of this world" but "stand by his order," as Emerson elsewhere in this same talk puts it, using an intriguing religiomilitary turn of phrase repeated over and over again during the war years. (The idea of an "order" of scholars conjures up—quite intentionally, I suspect—at once a cohort of monks and a military regiment.) But by the same token this order is not to be thought of only as a hermitic monasticism, operating without reference to the social. On the contrary, Emerson will also blame scholars for standing *too* aloof, such that their intellectual wealth turns to poverty. Indeed, scholars rightly conceived are the army's potential brains, its "generals."

Emerson's most striking statement of this point actually comes in the runup to the war years rather than during, in the parting shot to a commencement speech given first at Williams, then at Amherst. "Why do the minority have no influence?" he asks rhetorically. "Because there is not a pure minority, because there is not a minority of one that is grand in design." Note how Emerson echoes his former disciple Henry Thoreau's famous proclamation about the power of a minority of one in "Resistance to Civil Government."[25] "Things have been done in America within late years that will make this age dark in history. Our scholars were reading Demosthenes, our priests were reading in the Talmud, and whilst they wondered that the Romans should make a consul of Caligula's horse, the foremost freemen of mankind suffered themselves to be saddled, and bridled, and made to run and carry the offal of the dark ages into opening [the] West of America."[26] Small wonder this speech inspired a future US president, James A. Garfield, to say in later years that he dated his own intellectual life from that hour.[27] For Emerson is talking about the interrelated aggressions of rampant slavery and rampant expansionism, and especially the push by Southern interests to promote expansion in the interest of extending slave territory. Emerson, for his part, might have cited Garfield in his speech at Tufts as an embodiment of the scholar general; for Garfield did in fact become a Union general that same year, at the age of thirty-one, after having been a college professor and president.

In passages like the one just quoted, Emerson's longstanding commitment to defining the role of scholar or thinking person within a republic preeminently in terms of his resistance to what Alexis DeTocqueville famously called "the tyranny of the majority" gets fused and transfused by a newer social-justice-driven commitment, especially to emancipation, in which Emerson also always believed but to which he did not lend consistently active support until the decade before the Civil War.[28] The subject of abolition provoked Emerson to a series of discourses no less eloquent and searching than those on the scholar, even if slightly fewer and more compressed in time (1844–63).

Emerson studies have been a thriving industry for almost a century; but, rather amazingly, it has only been within the last dozen years that both sequences of Emerson discourses have been published in their entirety, insofar as they can be reconstructed from manuscripts and reports: the scholar lectures and the antislavery lectures.[29] Emersonians today are still trying to figure out what to make of these two bodies of writing and the relation between them. To date, by far the greater attention has been paid to the antislavery discourses as a group, even though "The American Scholar" has been far more minutely and repeatedly scrutinized than any other single work in either set. The two groups deserve closer comparison, especially for what they suggest about Emerson's views of social justice more generally. That not only helps us better focus our attention on a number of vital points about Emerson's life, thought, and career but also, beyond that, insofar as Emerson can be taken as a barometer or nodal point or transfer station for premodern American thinking generally about the claims of private conscience versus of public obligation, comparative analysis opens up the broader subject of the overall American legacy of reflection on the relative claims of individual liberty versus social equity.

Concerning Emerson's views specifically, here in summary is the gist as I see it:

1. The place in his mind where he thought about "the scholar" was not clearly quite the same place where he thought about "antislavery."
2. But from the start, as we have seen, the "scholar" idea implied a greater degree of public action and social accountability than it seems at first sight.
3. Over the years this aspect of his thought became more overt.
4. The reasons for this shift were multiple, starting it would seem with Emerson's awareness of his own growing influence as an opinion-maker, but certainly including his mid and late career as antislavery activist.
5. In his antislavery speeches as well as in his scholar addresses, Emerson placed great emphasis on the value of the self-sufficiency ethic, on individual liberty and resistance to mass opinion as vital to one's integral personhood—whether he was praising slave insurgents, imagining the happy state of emancipation, castigating white southerners or northern fellow travelers for kowtowing to slave interests, or deploring the spectacle of a society holding people in bondage.

6. Yet because of Emerson's continuing attachment to individual liberty as core value, his practical commitment to social justice always outran his ability and/or willingness to theorize it. And this, in turn, is in large part why

7. overall, Emerson's disquisitions on the scholar—from start to finish, even the later, wartime ones—continued overtly to stress the value of untrammeled thought in the face of public pressure more greatly than they stress the scholar's public accountability.

Only once, toward the end of a commencement speech the summer after Lincoln's Emancipation Proclamation, and a mere few weeks after the Battle of Gettysburg, did Emerson let himself say anything like this: "slavery is broken, and, [if] we use our advantage,—irretrievably. For such a gain,—to end once for all that pest of all free institutions, one generation might well be sacrificed—perhaps it will,—that this continent be purged and a new era of equal rights dawn on the universe. Who would not?—If it could be made certain that the new morning of universal liberty should rise on our race,[30] by the perishing of one generation,—who would not consent to die?"[31] These same words get repeated in Emerson's next major address on public affairs with special reference to the war and the slavery issue, "Fortune of the Republic." The persona of the scholar as public intellectual and the persona of the scholar as activist man of affairs here montage. But only for a moment. Emerson ends that commencement talk, for instance, by switching abruptly back to the scene at hand, "the precinct of the College," as he puts it. For now, he exhorts, "let us indulge ourselves with defying for this day the political and military interest and indulge ourselves with topics proper to the place at the risk of disgusting the popular ear."[32] In other words, for better and for worse, Emerson the critic of the canons of propriety nonetheless observes them to the extent that in his speeches and writing, even if to a lesser degree in his thinking and overall life practice, he never quite coordinates his commitment to the principle of independent thought's need for critical detachment from the public arena with his increasing commitment to the thinking person's social accountability.

II
Individuality versus Accountability: Some Further Implications

Although it obviously oversimplifies to take Emerson's thinking about human individuality as representing American thought in general, it is at least a halfway pardonable reduction given his stature and percolation effect as a public figure; and I shall succumb unabashedly to that temptation now as I extend my time line in this next section down into the twentieth century.

I begin with the thought experiment of imagining Emersonian individualism in relation to the United Nation's 1948 "Universal Declaration of Human Rights"—the now-canonical document on the subject, whatever its loopholes and howevermuch it has been evaded and ignored.[33]

I have found no evidence that Emerson influenced in any direct way the handful of figures most responsible for putting this document together—including even Eleanor Roosevelt, who periodically likes to quote Emerson for window dressing, and the foreign diplomats with American PhD's in philosophy, P. C. Chang of the Republic of China and Lebanon's Charles Habib Malik.[34] It seems telling, though, to find Malik affirming after the fact that "the American spirit of freedom . . . and profound respect for individual human beings permeated and suffused our atmosphere all around. . . . I cannot imagine the Declaration coming to birth under the aegis of any other culture emerging dominant after the Second World War, not excluding that of England and France."[35] To be sure, this somewhat overstates the case, since the "Declaration" represents an attempted compromise between and attempted fusion of Western Enlightenment individual-centered rights-of-man thinking and socialist thinking about collective rights. It is also true, as Malik hints but is too polite or politic to state baldly, that since 1948 US administrations have often cynically used appeals to "human rights" of the individualistic sort as a cover for advancing economic and political self-interest abroad. Yet it also makes historical sense that "human rights" should have a mantra status in US policy talk and public opinion even when its agenda is pursued in a Machiavellian way.

Despite being a codification that defines minimal rather than maximal guarantees for others having to do more with matters of basic protection than with intellectual emancipation, human rights resonates with Emersonianism insofar as it makes, as Michael Ignatieff puts it, "a radical demand of all human groups, that they serve the interests of the individuals who compose them," including respect for "an individual's right to exit when the constraints of the group become unbearable."[36] Emerson was the most prominent spokesperson in the nineteenth-century Anglo-American world for the proposition that core individual personhood should not be held in bondage to the claims of the social self.[37] The "Universal Declaration" does also certainly make a point of recognizing individual emplacement within family, communal, and national contexts. But the charter's central thrust is to honor the rights of the individual person "without distinction of any kind, such as race, colour, sex, language, religion, political or other opinion, national or social origin" (Article 2). A similar post-Enlightenment universalist way of conceiving individual human beings as constituting a world community of individual agents whose commonality cuts across whatever sort of national or cultural or somatic particularity stands behind both Emerson and the 1948 "Declaration." Emerson articulated this ethos in his first major antislavery address when he asserted as "a doctrine alike of the oldest, and of the newest philosophy, that, man is one, and that you cannot injure any member, without a sympathetic injury to all the members."[38]

Whether or not Emerson's memory has been more than fleetingly invoked by human rights advocates, for at least two reasons it is illuminating to reflect on how assertions like these place his thought in the context of universal human rights as an emerging doctrine, from the American and French declarations to the Anglo-American abolition campaigns then and later, to the "Universal Declaration's" formulation of a global ethic. First is as a corrective to the impression I have doubtless given up to this point of a thinker focused chiefly on the national scene. That Emerson was not. As a statement like the one just quoted shows, even at those points in his career when he was most intensely focused on national issues, Emerson's ultimate concern was not tribal or national but universal ("man is one"). The same goes for the scholar idea. None of Emerson's dozen or so definitional think pieces except the first refers to nationness in its original title, even the first. "The American Scholar," the title by which we know that 1837 address, was added a dozen years later upon its publication as part of *Nature, Addresses, and Lectures* (1849). Emerson's vision of man thinking was designed, in other words, more as a universal template for intellectuals than as the manifesto of cultural nationalism it is commonly read as being after the fact.

Second and conversely, however, thinking about Emerson in a broader human rights history context—particularly with the disparities between his antislavery speeches and his scholar think pieces in mind—points us toward an image of unfulfilled potential that is notoriously symptomatic of an imbalance in mainstream American thought generally. That the "equal rights" side of Emerson's thinking visible in his reform writings never quite catches up to and synchronizes with the libertarian element in his model for man thinking is roughly speaking the story in miniature of the history of mainstream US thinking, down to the present, on the subject of individual rights versus social accountability.[39]

In his antislavery speeches of the 1850s and 1860s, Emerson develops a touchstone encapsulation of his theory of liberty that he repeats many times: "to each man the largest liberty compatible with the liberty of every other man."[40] Or (in an alternative phrasing: the same principle stated negatively): the "limitation of my liberty by yours,—allowing the largest liberty to each compatible with the liberty of all."[41] When Emerson allowed himself to think along these lines, he was capable of some strikingly progressive thoughts, such as endorsement of miscegenation and the idea that free blacks should be exempt from taxation so long as racism denied them their full rights as citizens. But in the long run, for better and for worse, his most longstanding and deeply embedded concern, lest free thought be jeopardized by social conformity and slothful torpor, kept him coming back again and again to celebration of the freestanding individual mind.

Let it also be said to Emerson's credit that he applied this principle outside his own ethnic tribe as well as within. His very last scholar talk before his mind failed was an extemporized speech at Howard University in 1872, even as the force of Reconstruction was beginning to dissipate. In it Emerson prescribes, just as he had been prescribing to groups of students at white colleges for decades, a gospel of intellectual self-reliance: to find "what it is that you yourself really want," and do it, "freeing yourself from all importunities of your friends . . . and insisting upon that thing which you like and can do"[42]—advice that was greeted with enthusiasm.

In conclusion, I want to return to Emerson on nature. Though nature tends to drop out of Emerson's vision statements about the scholar, in at least one unobtrusive but telling sense his early thoughts about the resources of nature for the intellectual person do persist, and in a way that constitutes another significant bridge between his individualism and his social thought. Here I refer to Emerson's fondness for imagining scholars against the background of naturescapes. In part such images were doubtless simple projections of his own stylized self-image as a rural sage surveying the world from his Concord retreat. Beyond this, however, they can often be seen as attempts to register the actual settings at hand; for most of the campuses where he spoke were in outbacky or at least cloistrally pastoral locales. Sometimes this taste for naturizing the scene of scholarly intellection seems deployed simply in order to underscore the habits of solitude that Emerson persistently associates with the lifestyle of the independent thinker. But it can also take the argument in a populist direction by prompting him to conjure up, for example, the scholar's putatively agrarian roots or (as he puts it in one commencement address) the instructive value of making a person's "hands acquainted with the soil by which he is fed, and the sweat that goes before comfort and luxury."[43] This framing of the scholar as a figure presumed to have arisen from the nonprivileged populace helps offset equally typical declarations to the effect that the scholar "belongs to a superior society and is born one or two centuries too early for the rough and sensual population into which he is thrown."[44]

It is notable that Emerson consistently declines to identify the paradigmatic scholar as an academic brat or a metropolitan product. To the extent that he makes reference to a pedigree or autobiographical background of any sort he seems rather to take for granted that the scholar will be a first-generation collegian. This in spite of Emerson's being very much the elitist himself on the question of the percentage of individuals he thinks will actually desire and/or manage to live up to the scholar ideal as he defines it, notwithstanding his conviction that in principle everyone might. In short, among its various other functions in Emerson's thought, "nature"—not simply in the abstract senses of "human nature" or "universal quasi-pantheistic spirit" but in the more concrete sense of exurban context or background—is enlisted as a leveler of social inequalities; and this in turn helps define the Emersonian scholar identity as a model or path more open and accessible than might be suggested by the imagery he deploys elsewhere of the lonely high plateau on which the life of the mind is most intensely lived.

This tendency to imagine Man Thinking as intellectually privileged without necessarily being from a privileged background is of course very much in keeping with Emerson's conception of the true scholar as a nonpedantic generalist. Indeed, he goes so far as to claim that the scholar is "unfurnished who has only literary weapons"—using "literary" here, I presume, as a synecdoche for high cultural sophistication in general. On the contrary, Emerson continues, the scholar "ought to have as many talents as he can;—memory, arithmetic, practical power, manners, temper, lion-heart"—but these too, he immediately adds, "are superficial." The one *sine qua non* is something "for which no tutor, no book, no lectures, and almost no preparation can be of the least avail." It is the ability to face and deal with the great life-questions, such as "Who are you?" "Is there method in your consciousness? Can you see tendency in your life? Can you help any soul?"[45]

In a sense, this account of what scholars should do, what education should do, is hopelessly archaic, out of tune with what the modern university effectively defines as its central mission: the mastery of disciplinary methods, the pursuit of knowledge at the cutting edge. Emerson's prescriptions might have been suited well enough to the one-horse institution Middlebury College then was—and Harvard too for that matter—but surely they type him as an obsolescent premodern. Considered more generously and thoughtfully, however, what else after all is education about? What is all that specialized knowledge worth without the underlying centeredness and alertness and commitment to which these questions point? No matter how much we seem to outgrow him, so long as first principles of education and human rights are thought to matter, so too will Emerson's work.

Notes

My thanks to Jared Hickman for research assistance, and to my hosts and audiences at Middlebury College and Harvard's John F. Kennedy School of Government for the opportunity to venture some of these thoughts in lecture form.

1. *The Journals and Miscellaneous Notebooks of Ralph Waldo Emerson*, ed. William H. Gilman, Alfred R. Ferguson, Morrell R. Davis, Merton M. Sealts, and Harrison Hayford (Cambridge, MA: Harvard University Press, 1960–86), 5: 347. Hereafter abbreviated as *JMN*.

2. Excellent previous critical treatments of "The American Scholar" and Emerson's idea of "the scholar" include Merton M. Sealts, *Emerson on the Scholar* (Columbia: University of Missouri Press, 1992); Robert Milder, "The American Scholar as Cultural Event," *Prospects* (1991): 99–147; and Kenneth Sacks, *Understanding Emerson: "The American Scholar" and His Struggle for Self-Reliance* (Princeton: Princeton University Press, 2003).

3. *The Later Lectures of Ralph Waldo Emerson, 1843–1871*, ed. Ronald A. Bosco and Joel Myerson (Athens: University of Georgia Press, 2001), 1:364. Hereafter abbreviated *LL*.

4. *LL* 2:309.

5. *The Collected Works of Ralph Waldo Emerson*, ed. Robert E. Spiller, Joseph Slater, et al. (Cambridge MA: Harvard University Press, 1971–), 1:55. Hereafter abbreviated *CW*.

6. *CW* 1:57.

7. Whether by influence or serendipity, Emily Brontë puts this same image in the mouth of her Byronic hero Heathcliff a decade later in chapter 14 of *Wuthering Heights*.

8. On these points, see for example Robert D. Richardson, Jr., "Emerson and Nature," *The Cambridge Companion to Ralph Waldo Emerson*, ed. Joel Porte and Saundra Morris (Cambridge: Cambridge University Press, 1999), 97–105.

9. Richard White, *The Organic Machine: The Remaking of the Columbia River* (New York: Hill and Wang, 1995), 34-37 and passim.

10. *CW* 1:45.

11. On Emerson's (increasing) scientistic literacy, see especially Laura Dassow Walls, *Emerson's Life in Science: The Culture of Truth* (Ithaca: Cornell University Press, 2003).

12. *CW* 1:124.

13. *CW* 1:121. Emerson's source was de Staël's *Germany* (*cf. JMN* 3:255).

14. *CW* 6:4.

15. *CW* 3:118.

16. *LL* 2:250.

17. John McWilliams, "Emerson's Challenge to the Middlebury Scholar," in *Emerson at Middlebury College: Including the Commencement Address of Ralph Waldo Emerson . . .* (Middlebury: Friends of the Library, Middlebury College, 1999), provides a valuable account of the argument and significance of this address.

18. *CW* 1:63.

19. Ibid., 62.

20. *LL* 1:91–92, 88, 98.

21. See for example Buell, *New England Literary Culture: From Revolution through Renaissance* (Cambridge: Cambridge University Press, 1986), 137–65; James Perrin Warren, *Culture of Eloquence: Oratory and Reform in Antebellum America* (University

Park: Pennsylvania State University Press, 1999); Sandra Gustafson, *Eloquence Is Power: Oratory and Performance in Early America* (Chapel Hill: University of North Carolina Press, 2000); and Michael T. Gilmore, "The Plot against America," *Raritan* 26 (Fall 2006): 90–113.

22. *LL* 2:245.

23. Ibid., 241.

24. Ibid., 312.

25. Henry David Thoreau, "Resistance to Civil Government," *Reform Papers*, ed. Wendell Glick (Princeton: Princeton University Press, 1973), 74.

26. *LL* 1:366.

27. Ralph Leslie Rusk, *The Life of Ralph Waldo Emerson* (New York: Columbia University Press, 1949), 385.

28. The most thorough treatment of Emerson's emergence as an antislavery thinker and activist is Len Gougeon, *Virtue's Hero: Emerson, Antislavery, and Reform* (Athens: University of Georgia Press, 1990), and numerous subsequent articles; for somewhat more astringent appraisals, see for example Anita Haya Patterson, *From Emerson to King: Democracy, Race, and the Politics of Protest* (New York: Oxford University Press, 1997); and Peter S. Field, *Ralph Waldo Emerson: The Making of a Democratic Intellectual* (Lanham, MD: Rowman and Littlefield, 2002). For an excellent case study attesting to Emerson's influence in abolitionist circles, see Albert J. Von Frank, *The Trials of Anthony Burns: Freedom and Slavery in Emerson's Boston* (Cambridge, MA: Harvard University Press, 1998).

29. For the antislavery lectures, see *Ralph Waldo Emerson's Antislavery Writings*, ed. Len Gougeon and Joel Myerson (New Haven: Yale University Press, 1995). (Hereafter abbreviated as *EAW*.) The scholar lectures have not (yet) been published in a single volume; but *LL* (2001), together with *CW* (volume 1) and volumes 8 and 10 of *The Complete Works of Ralph Waldo Emerson*, ed. Edward Waldo Emerson (Boston: Houghton Mifflin, 1903–04), provide the full roster, even though the texts of the latter edition are unreliable.

30. "Race" is used lumpingly here—a common nineteenth-century practice—for "national populace," rather than in the sense of this or that particular ethno-racial group.

31. *LL* 2:317.

32. Ibid., 318.

33. For text, see http://www.un.org/Overview/right.html.

34. Mary Ann Glendon, *A World Made New: Eleanor Roosevelt and the Universal Declaration of Human Rights* (New York: Random House, 2001); Johannes Morsink, *The Universal Declaration of Human Rights: Origins, Drafting, and Intent* (Philadelphia: University of Pennsylvania Press, 1999); *The Autobiography of Eleanor Roosevelt* (New York: Harper, 1958).

35. Charles Habib Malik, "The Universal Declaration of Human Rights," *Free and Equal: Human Rights in Ecumenical Perspective*, ed. O. Frederick Noble (Geneva: World Council of Churches, 1968), 9–10.

36. Michael Ignatieff, "Human Rights as Idolatry," *Human Rights as Politics and Idolatry*, ed. Amy Gutmann (Princeton: Princeton University Press, 2001), 68–69.

37. Thoreau's "Resistance to Civil Government" of course became more famous and directly influential than any individual Emerson text for the twentieth century, and for the nineteenth some would argue that John Stuart Mill's *On Liberty* (1859), admittedly far more influential within political philosophy than Emerson's writings, better fits my description. I should argue, however, that Emersonian self-reliance reveals by contrast the guardedness of Mill's defense of free-standing individuality (versus my *Emerson* [Cambridge MA: Harvard University Press, 2003], 99–101).

38. *EAW*, 32.

39. Since "new historicist" revisionism of the 1980s, many scholars have diagnosed Emersonian individualism as captive and/or abettor of hegemonic American ideologies. Impressive exemplars of the two most prevalent (also rather divergent) lines of argument are Myra Jehlen, *American Incarnation: The Individual, the Nation, and the Continent* (Cambridge: Harvard University Press, 1986), 76–122, and Christopher Newfield, *The Emerson Effect: Individualism and Submission in America* (Chicago: University of Chicago Press, 1996). For Jehlen, Emersonianism underwrites westward expansionism and Manifest Destiny; for Newfield, the subsequent "incorporation of America" (Alan Trachtenberg's phrase), specifically individual accommodation to corporate culture. If one were to be forced to choose between the two alternatives of aggressive/dominationist versus submissive/conformist interpretations, as I intimate here the former strikes me as by and large more persuasive, insofar as it gives greater weight to Emerson's emphasis on the worth and the potentially catalytic social force of the efforts of the free-standing individual. But both, I believe, overshoot the mark. Certainly the Emerson who delivered the sardonic putdown of westward expansion that Garfield heard at Williams College (see above) was no naive manifest destinarian. My forthcoming "Transcendentalism, Nonresistance, and Manifest Destiny" will address these matters more fully.

40. *EAW*, 105.

41. *EAW*, 104.

42. Reported in "What Books to Read," *New York Tribune*, January 11, 1872. For brief discussion, see Buell, *Emerson*, 360–61.

43. *CW* 1:113.

44. *LL* 2:305.

45. *LL* 1:95–96.

For the Children

Gary Snyder

The rising hills, the slopes,
of statistics
lie before us,
the steep climb
of everything, going up,
up, as we all
go down.

In the next century
or the one beyond that,
they say,
are valleys, pastures,
we can meet there in peace
if we make it.

To climb these coming crests
one word to you, to
you and your children:

stay together
learn the flowers
go light

Chapter 11

After Emerson

Of General Knowledge and the Common Good

Ann Lauterbach

*W*hen I asked Dean Tamny[1] what people talk about when they talk to the Phi Beta Kappa Society he said, "Well, no one talks about the life of the mind or anything like that." He was probably trying to put me at ease, letting me know that I could talk about snow in spring if I so chose. It is snowing now and it is almost spring. Today's snow seems more ferocious than any this winter, the flakes are as big as dimes and they are falling rapidly, as if from a casino jackpot. There is a stiff wind coming from the north. I am sitting at my desk, facing west, and just beyond the small hemlocks in the foreground there is a graveyard that dates from 1710. Many of the stones in it have been rubbed smooth, so you can no longer read the name of the person buried there.

Just now I can hear the train as it moves along the Hudson River, heading either to Canada or to New York City, I cannot tell in which direction. In the graveyard I can see two small American flags blowing in the wind. I saw a PBS special the other night, well it wasn't a special, it was a promotion, as they were in their fundraising mode, and the special guest was Peter from the folk music group Peter, Paul, and Mary. During the show, there were many film clips of Peter, Paul, and Mary in their heyday, when they sang, for example, in Washington during the great march at which Dr. King gave his seminal address. Watching these tapes, it was difficult not to feel, once again, a sense of loss for the unanimity of a crowd brought together by the power of an idea, and a belief in the possibilities of change. I thought, watching the flags wave in the graveyard, of Bob Dylan's melancholy refrain: "The answer my friend is blowing in the wind, the answer is blowing in the wind."

Not long ago, I was at a small dinner after a poetry reading at Bard College, where I teach. There was a lively and articulate young Jamaican American student there. She had protested the imminent war in Iraq last year, and she had joined in the enthusiasm for Howard Dean. The fact that these efforts had failed left her thinking there wasn't any point in voting next fall; she was thinking of becoming an anarchist. Her short-sighted impatience alarmed me; it seemed symptomatic of a general cultural habit, a curtailed investment in process, a desire for quick-fix answers before difficult questions are asked, for goals met almost before quests are undertaken.

I have chosen as my guiding spirit today the nineteenth-century American philosopher/poet Ralph Waldo Emerson. When I was an undergraduate in the 1960s at the University of Wisconsin, I took a year-long course called "American Intellectual History," taught by William Appleman Williams, who had, in turn, studied with the great Harvard historian, Perry Miller. In the decades since then, this course has stood in my mind as crucial to my understanding of the relation between American ideas, social behavior, and political will; that is, the ways in which language mediates, imagines, and reflects these unstable but essential dynamics. The materials for the course were almost all primary; we read contemporaneous speeches and journals, essays, letters, sermons, narratives, autobiography. This exposure to original texts, unusual at the time, animated history, rendering it less a matter of factual event, narratives of linear cause and effect, than a matrix of oppositional and irresolute forces, where those that were dominant were often shadowed by those that were recessive. The notion that America was itself an idea, an experiment, formulated largely in two written documents, gave me a sense of its frailty as well as its peculiar optimism. It was in this course that I first read Emerson.

Why Emerson? He was born in Boston in 1803, into the millennial cusp of the nineteenth century, as we are at the millennial cusp of the twenty-first. His father, pastor at Boston's First Church, died when Emerson was eight, leaving eight children to be raised by his mother, Ruth, and his eccentric aunt Mary. He went to Harvard College, where he, like so many other undergraduates since, waited on table and taught school to help defray costs. He kept a journal. After graduation, he continued to teach, but often felt dejected and at a loss. He had eye troubles, and other physical symptoms of distress. He fell in love and married Ellen Tucker, but she died, age nineteen, in 1832. By then Emerson had become junior pastor at Boston's Second Church.

By the time he was thirty, Emerson had rejected a profession in the church, calling it "antiquated" and, in poor health and already a widower, he traveled to Europe, to Rome and Paris and London, where he met the philosopher John Stuart Mill as well as the great Romantic writers Coleridge and Wordsworth and Thomas Carlyle. Returning to America to settle in

Concord, he wrote in his journal, "I wish I knew where & how I ought to live." From this moment on, he undertook to answer these questions. By 1837, he had begun to lecture, on nature and history and the lives of great men. In that same year, he gave a celebrated address, later titled "The American Scholar" to the Phi Beta Kappa Society at Cambridge.

But why Emerson?

Emerson was committed to the idea of human life as a deep reciprocity between a given self and the world. "The eye is the first circle; the horizon it forms is the second" he wrote. "The world—this shadow of the soul, or *other me*—lies wide around. Its attractions are the keys which unlock my thoughts and make me acquainted with myself."[2] At the heart of Emersonian thought, for me, is an almost constant desire to reconcile what he called "polarities," into manifestations of flow, circuits and cycles, relation and concordance. I think this urge came from his wish to bring his spiritual faith into alignment with his equally strong belief in reason. Within this typology of reconciliation comes an immense intellectual permission to explore the moody and mercurial shapes of life, to be digressive and uncertain. He writes, "There are no fixtures in nature. The universe is fluid and volatile. Permanence is but a word of degrees."[3] This perception of the instability of things leads him to distrust what he called "the false good" of immediate rewards: "[M]en, such as they are, very naturally seek money or power; and power because it is as good as money. . . . And why not? For they aspire to the highest, and this, in their sleepwalking, they dream is highest. Wake them, and they shall quit the false good." Writing, for Emerson, is a constant exploration of relations, fueled by a conviction that knowledge itself is both the means and the end of the true good. "Fear" he comments, "always springs from ignorance."

One feels in Emerson the pressure of affective thought finding its way to a practical outcome; his writing is less a display of erudition than an exploration of how knowledge might infuse and influence ordinary, daily action. He continually stresses his desire for a uniquely American culture, one that rises from the low, the common, and the near. A person of some social and economic privilege, he situates himself within his own writing as much student as teacher, as much lay person as preacher. One feels that his convictions are at risk, his conclusions not foregone. He writes to find out what he knows about what he knows. He was, along with William James, one of our first "public intellectuals," giving talks and addresses to large crowds. He was one of our first celebrities, an intellectual rock star.

But, as Philip Fisher has pointed out in his book *Still the New World*, this template of speaker and audience is not in essence democratic. Fisher writes, "Performer and audience define the world of both entertainment and professionalism, along with the larger worlds of mass politics and religious revival, and even the world of radical politics, from the time of the abolitionists, through the temperance movement, the civil rights and anti-Vietnam movements of the 1960s. This antidemocratic space of speaker and audience has been, as the example of Martin Luther King, Jr., would show, decisive even where the goal has been a more democratic social life. Even American philosophy was invented in public by Emerson and William James as lectures given to crowds."

What is missing, of course, is conversation, dialogue, the expressing and sharing of thoughts and ideas across the social space, so that the mute acquiescence of the many is not relinquished to the authority of the one. American social space is not a fluid transparency; it is ruptured, in Fisher's word, "damaged," by institutionalized inequities that begin with slavery and continue as endemic racism, economic disparity, uneven distribution of social services, medical care, education.

Emerson was not unaware of these disparities; the fact that he was able to construct an optimism from personal griefs and public dismay is one of the reasons I continue to consult him. "This time, like all times, is a very good one," he comments wryly, "if we but know what to do with it." It is difficult for me, as I am sure it is for you, to accept such an optimistic dictum. Our time seems saturated with both fear and ignorance. The daily rhetoric seems contaminated with words pulled loose from their moorings. There is a kind of indiscriminate evocation of such potent abstractions as "freedom" and "evil" that move through our public discourse with promiscuous abandon. A confusion between the true and the real percolates up from the core; dissimulation is stitched into the fabric of our sense of events so that correction, if it comes, is often too late, too hidden from public view, to alter our perceptions.

I often find myself thinking about the fact that we seem to know the world through a system of contraries; the English language itself embraces one of the most fundamental, the one between subject and object, and its extension into subjectivity and objectivity. For writers, the conversion of subject into object is perhaps our most basic and perplexing task: how to conceive of words as not locked within the self awaiting liberty, but as freely circulating outside of the self, waiting to be taken in, transformed, and sent back out. Emerson says, "The scholar of the first age received into him the world around; brooded thereon; gave it the new arrangement of his own mind, and uttered it again. It came in to him, life; it went out from him, truth." Wallace Stevens understood that imaginative work is the work of truth; that fiction aspires, in the form of "a new arrangement" to tell a truth which is not necessarily fixed on fact, but on the interpretative motions of a perceiving mind. In "Notes Toward a Supreme Fiction" Stevens makes of duality a kind of hymn to change:

Two things of opposite natures seem to depend
One on another, as a man depends
On a woman, day on night, the imagined

On the real. This is the origin of change.
Winter and spring, cold copulars, embrace
And forth the particulars of rapture come.

Music falls on the silence like a sense,
A passion that we feel, not understand.
Morning and afternoon are clasped together

And North and South are an intrinsic couple
And sun and rain a plural, like two lovers
That walk away as one in the greenest body.

In solitude the triumphs of solitude
Are not of another solitude responding;
A little string speaks for a crowd of voices.

The partaker partakes of that which changes him.
The child that touches takes character from the thing,
The body, it touches. The captain and his men

Are one and the sailor and the sea are one.
Follow after, O my companion, my fellow, my self,
Sister and solace, brother and delight.

Recently, I heard a talk by the marvelous environmentalist and jour-
nalist Bill McKibben. He was talking about issues of global significance,
about the destruction of the ecosystem, and about the possibilities of
human cloning. He wasn't interested in talking about the sacred space of
human individuality as such, but rather the way cloning might make of
human life yet another commodity. He said, in answer to a student's question about what makes humans human, that we are the only animals for
whom there is a decision to make when faced with desire; we know the
word *no*. No, not as an order from another, but from the inner self, the part
of the self that says "you have had enough" or "don't do that."

The narrator of the great South African Nobel Laureate J. M. Coetzee's
novel *Waiting for the Barbarians* speaks about a certain Colonel.

Since his second day here I have been too disturbed by his presence to be
more than correct in my bearing towards him. I suppose that, like the roving

headsman, he is used to being shunned. (Or is it only in the provinces that headsmen and torturers are still thought of as unclean?) Looking at him I wonder how he felt the very first time: did he, invited as an apprentice to twist the pincers or turn the screw or whatever it is they do, shudder even a little to know that at that instant he was trespassing into the forbidden? I find myself wondering too whether he has a private ritual of purification, carried out behind closed doors, to enable him to return and break bread with other men. Does he wash his hands very carefully, perhaps, or change all his clothes; or has the Bureau created new men who can pass without disquiet between the unclean and the clean?

In detailing atrocities at the Abu Ghraib prison, an American soldier repeatedly refers to one of the Iraqi detainees as "it." This use of a tiny two-letter word, in which a person is turned into an object, a thing, is as revealingly abhorrent as any of the horrific images that have surfaced. Like Emerson, I believe that words are a form of action; their use, and abuse, can travel with stupendous speed into our hearts and minds. This is why the words that are uttered by persons in power are of such critical significance. I want to say that the ubiquitous application of universals, such as freedom, terror, and evil, unmoored from both context and concrete example, move with weedy rapaciousness to contaminate both their meanings, and acts committed in their name.

Aristotle writes, in book 3 of the *Ethics*, "For an irrational being the appetite for what gives it pleasure is insatiable and indiscriminate, and the exercise of the desire increases its innate tendency; and if these appetites are strong and violent, they actually drive out reason."

Emerson says: "the ancient precept, 'Know thyself,' and the modern precept, 'Study nature,' become at last one maxim."[4]

The radical American modernist Gertrude Stein commented, "I am I because my little dog knows me." Stein makes a charming elastic shape out of the ingredients of self-knowledge, different, for example, from the Cartesian formulation which makes thinking, or consciousness, the necessary construction of the I AM. Stein's writing is permeated with what we might call a deliberate strangeness or alienation, one that does not allow the reader an immediate access to a normal real. Her self rarely appears in the guise of the first-person pronoun. Her amusing comment "I am I because my little dog knows me" suggests that we are constituted by the ways in which we are known by others, and that this recognition is based on our behaviors toward them. She anticipates recent theories of personality that suggest we are not static and stable entities, but fluid and varied, that we change somewhat according to whom and with whom we are communicating, which in turn influences and affects how we measure our self-knowledge. I am not quite the same when I am teaching a class as when I am holding my friend Terry's daughter in my arms or paying for my groceries at the local market. We change depending on what we are doing in our lives. "Where do we find ourselves?" Emerson asks at the opening of his essay "Experience."

For many people, poems are understood to be tidy linguistic utterances that emit from a given self, as if poets were like those pretty Italian pots that fizz and spurt tiny cups of thick, bitter truths about life. On this model, poets are curiously exempt from accusations of narcissism, since the poet's self, his or her "I," is somehow meant to give to the mute and inarticulate reader linguistic counters for the inexpressible. On this reading, the subjectivity of the writer is rendered objective through a sort of threshold of mutual, perhaps cathartic, identifications. But in our age of rampant information and exploited privacies, such self-examinations, however dressed up in pretty language, are insufficient. We want our life lessons in the form of scandal and expose; we want our happy endings, our sweet closures, as a kiss at the end of a film, a victorious lawyer in *The Practice*.

I want to return here to how Emerson sought to find common ground between religious faith and secular reason. He did not, in his writings, forfeit his use of the word *God*, and he speaks frequently of spirit, and of souls. But at each turn, God exists not as an authority, not as supreme being, but as an initiating animation or energy from which nature, and ourselves, evolve. Responsibility is in the minds and hands of persons: "[I]n proportion as a man has any thing in him divine," he writes, "the firmament flows before him and takes his signet and form. Nor he is great who can alter matter, but he who can alter my state of mind."[5]

In the "Divinity School Address," he says, "The time is coming when all men will see, that the gift of God to the soul is not a vaunting, overpowering, excluding sanctity, but a sweet, natural goodness, a goodness like thine and mine to be and to grow."

Emerson's notion of "natural goodness" which connects humans to their environment, to be and to grow, rests at least in part on a concept of the local, the near, the particulars and peculiarities that form immediate experience. His rhetorical strategies move quickly between flares of roiling heightened eloquence to simple pronouncements and memorable epithets, as if he were always wanting to return to the vitality of the actual, to touch the immediate, acknowledge the proximity of his audience. He writes, "It is a great stride. It is a sign,—is it not? Of new vigor, when the extremities are made active, when currents or warm life run into the hands and the feet. I ask not for the great, the remote, the romantic, what is doing in Italy or Arabia; what is Greek art, or Provencal minstrelsy; I embrace the common, I explore and sit at the feet of the familiar, the low. Give me insight into today and you may have the antique and future worlds."[6]

This turn toward the local, the near, is one of the dominant traits of nineteenth-century American aesthetic and cultural vision, as it comes to replace European classical, often hierarchical orders, and begins to find in the proliferation of local incident a way to articulate and map the complex ratios between the One and the Many. The still new country would come to embrace a new paradigm where the coordinates of time and space were marked by the here and now of an individual presentness and presence. Thoreau's Walden becomes the template for this universe of particulars, what Ezra Pound would later call "radiant details." By the midtwentieth century, this idea would express itself in a unique abstraction, built up by single gestures, as in much abstract expressionist painting, where each mark is absorbed into the panoply of a diverse but unifying field.

There was, not so long ago, a categorical noncategory, "of general interest." I am not sure now where it appeared—in bookstores, on newspaper lists. It assumed something about the public, about the needs of the public to be generally informed about things that did not necessarily apply to a particular person's interests, his or her stuff. The noncategory of the category "of general interest" suggested that there were things about the world, in the world, of the world, which persons without specific expertise might find useful or stimulating or even necessary. This category has vanished, to be replaced by the generic "nonfiction," which covers everything from super-string theory to, say, *The Unconquerable World*, Jonathan Schell's study of strategies of war and peace.

In a recent issue of the *New York Review of Books*, there is an essay about the Marxist literary critic Terry Eagleton's new book, entitled *After Theory*. The reviewer gives it scant, provisional praise: "*After Theory*," he writes, "is an ambitious and thought provoking book as well as an exasperating one, but it overestimates the importance of Theory outside the academy." He then adds, "But to anyone outside the arena (of the academy), "the educated general reader," for instance—the excruciating effort of construing this jargon-heavy discourse far exceeded the illumination likely to be gleaned from it, so they stopped reading it, and nonspecialist publications stopped reviewing it, which was bad for both academia and culture in general."

This decision on the part of nonspecialist publications, general circulation magazines, and daily newspapers, to stop writing about theory is also true for poetry, and the result is also, in my view, bad for both academia and for "culture in general." A certain disdain prevails, a sense that poetry, like theory, takes too much effort to be worth the time. But poetry, unlike theory, has never been, until recently, confined to the academy. For Emerson, the poet represented the epitome of articulated hope and vision. He called poets "liberating gods," whose work was the "ravishment of the intellect by coming nearer to the fact."

But American culture has moved quickly from such heralds and avatars; poems, neither pure information (nonfiction) nor pure entertainment (fiction) are seen as remnant vestiges of a dying literary culture. Poems rub against the prevailing need for pragmatic expertise, for sharp focus, single study, the idea that we should all find our subject and stick to it: the writings of Prince Machiavelli; the life cycle of the roundworm. This bias toward the expert, the professional, has been in the works for a long time, and has slowly erased such quaint notions "of general interest" "the general educated reader." General interest now finds itself erupting in the degraded form of Reality TV, such strangely disorienting, fake news shows as *Dateline*, or bogus, delirious fantasies like *Extreme Makeover* and *The Bachelor*. These shows parody "of general interest."

In perhaps his best known essay, "Self-Reliance," Emerson writes: "Whoso would be a man must be a nonconformist. He who would gather immortal palms must not be hindered by the name of goodness, but must explore if it be goodness." This insistence on the necessity for each person to undertake his or her own moral exploration is a key to the radical nature of Emersonian ethics. From the standpoint of our present moment, it is almost beyond what we can imagine: that the public, one by one, can and will think outside of the proscriptions and prescriptions of political and social commerce and commentary; that each of us is both willing and able to find our way out of received ideas that govern so much of our discourse. Emerson writes:

> If I know your sect, I anticipate your argument. I hear a preacher announce for his text and topic the expediency of one of the institutions of his church. Do I not know beforehand that not possibly can he say a new and spontaneous word? Do I not know that, with all this ostentation of examining the grounds of the institution, he will do no such thing? Do I not know that he is pledged to himself not to look but at one side,—the permitted side, not as a man, but as a parish minister? He is a retained attorney, and these airs of the bench are the emptiest affectation. Well, most men have bound their eyes with one or another handkerchief, and attached themselves to some one of these communities of opinion. This conformity makes them not false in a few particulars, author of a few lies, but false in all particulars. Their every truth is not quite true. Their two is not the real two, their four is not the real four; so that every word they say chagrins us, and we know not where to begin to set them right.[7]

This is not the voice of a true believer, but of someone who has agreed to move through his world with the open demeanor of doubt. I want to suggest that for Emerson, doubt was a prerequisite of reason, of knowledge as well as of faith. He had inherited the Enlightenment, where skepticism was part of what it meant to be human. I think what most deeply frightened him was a burgeoning sense of American entitlement, God-given, invincible, irrefutable, where freedom would be conceived as unfettered self-interest, opportunity as unlimited choice, and success as one or another form of acquisition and victory. Doubt, for Emerson, was the engine of curiosity; curiosity the path to knowledge, and knowledge, itself unsteady and plural, both agent and receptor of experience.

Emersonian knowledge rarely steadies itself into certitude. He says, "But lest I should mislead any when I have my own head and obey my whims, let me remind the reader that I am only an experimenter. Do not set the least value on what I do, or the least discredit on what I do not, as if I pretended to settle any thing as true or false. I unsettle all things. No facts are to me sacred; none are profane; I simply experiment, an endless seeker. . . . People wish to be settled; only as far as they are unsettled is there any hope for them."[8]

This idea of being unsettled resonates now, as it must have when Emerson first wrote it. America, we say, was settled by the early pioneers. On the West Bank and Gaza, there are "settlements." We tell our children to "settle down" and we, in turn, wish to settle into the safety of our homes, to come to rest in a secure setting. To remain unsettled, then, goes against the ways in which our hope for happiness is pictured to us. To be unsettled is to join the great diaspora of the world as we move toward the global village.

I took this contrary, unsettled, path: the precarious was, for me, more dependable than the secure. As time went on, an at times reckless commitment to instability and uncertainty migrated into a form of perception, and from perception into an interest in the limits of order, the outer rims of sense. These became the basis for a poetics. I came to want to write poems that did not offer the reader, or listener, calmly composed reflections, neat epiphanies of recognition or identification, but instead poems that ruptured, confused, suspended, the charmed solace of such expectations. As I write this, I realize it sounds both perverse and elitist, the worst kind of deliberate obfuscation. But this is not the case; I want my work to exhilarate, to awaken and stimulate, indeed, to unsettle. I want to invite readers and listeners to the edge or boundary of their assumptions about how language constitutes, or reconstitutes, the self and the world, and how these in turn constitute how we use language. It is this essential reciprocity that guides what I do.

I am by nature restless and impatient, and in order perhaps to accommodate these character flaws and deficits, I have given myself permission to think of my job as a kind of scanner. I net language from its free-floating, ubiquitous circulation, and give to it a matrix in which musical phrase and spatial display are coordinates. My poems are often destabilized narratives, where moments of connectivity are placed against fragments, abbreviated notes, pieces of linguistic thread that are not woven into the substance, but act as floating remnants, leftovers, frayed edges. These loose constructions sign to me and I hope to my listeners and readers a kind of layered indeterminate field, from which incidents erupt and consequences—the great syntactical order—sometimes, but not always, obtain. I want to convey that making sense and finding meaning are what we do when we use language, but that these senses and these meanings are never stable and fixed, but responsive to temporal and spatial conditions, to the specificity and particulars of context. Each person in this room has a different notion, a different picture, to go with the word *tree*.

In choosing to be a poet, I took a path that led toward the unknown, perhaps to the unknowable. My future had only the most furtive of shapes; my aspiration, the most chancy, digressive routes. Language came to me as the most potent, and yet most ephemeral, of commitments. To this day, I am not sure what a poem is. Each time I write one, it becomes the particular, the example, but the next one may not resemble the one before it, or the one to come. Poetry, like so much else in life, can be known only by example. To write a poem is, in the first place, to be curious about what a poem is.

As we witnessed the demise of an active readership, a general public, for all but the most trivial and obvious poems, I and many of my peers have retreated into the protection of the academy, there to teach another generation how to love if not poetry, at least language. I have had moments of doubt. "What are poets for in a destitute time?" the German philosopher Heidegger asked; and the great cultural critic Theodor Adorno, commented that "after Auschwitz, lyric poetry is barbaric." It is often difficult, given the state of the world, to believe that there is any merit, any reason, in making another poem. And yet, poets and books of poems and little magazines devoted to poetry proliferate, readings occur in small towns and large cities across the nation, often to only a handful of persons, all under the radar of general interest, out of the searchlight of celebrity exposure, million-dollar book deals, late night chat shows. A discipline of extraordinary variety and hybridity, moving between fact and fiction, narrativity and fragment, formal orders and chance operations, poetry foregrounds at all times the value of the single word. As the poet Lyn Hejinian has commented, "writing develops subjects that mean the words we have for them."

There is a far-flung but enduring community of poets, who connect with each other not only on the Internet, but in person, where hands and faces, tones of voice and gestures, contribute to the nuance and intricacies of a shared interest in each other and in each other's work. Poetry is a culture of presence and immediacy, of gathering around, listening, exchanging, thinking aloud. It constitutes an oddly familiar community, inflected with small town gossip and mean spirited jealousies, love affairs, marriages and deaths; we write to and for and about each other, often with admiration, pleasure, and joy. We are on the whole lucky to spend our lives in such close proximity to the primary engine of human communication. This intimacy, this primal attachment to language, is convertible to the needs and ambitions of persons who may not be poets, may not want to become poets.

The core of our moral shape begins with our finding out to what we are attached by birth, geography, disposition, intellect, talent. Our initial attachments lead to others, and those to others still, and as we age, we become more clear about those that were given to us, and those that we choose. If we are lucky, they eventually merge, the given and the chosen, into forms of attention that can be communicated to others. These habits of mind, of predilection and practice, are the most valuable tools of a life well spent.

But as long as works of imaginative response and interpretation, by which I mean not just poems, but all creative work, painting and music, dance and sculpture, film and fiction, are viewed by the culture at large, the general public, as either decorative entertainment, or private, elitist distraction, and not, to borrow Emerson's phrase, as "beautiful necessity," then we are in danger of a perfunctory, reductive literalism. We lose our bearings, become mere tokens of political or commercial expedience. Imaginative work is grounded in thinking about, and thinking through, the immediacy of events, both private and public, in order to draw from them objects, materials rendered into forms, that bring us closer to our sense of connection, our personal agency. Art asks to be interpreted, not just consumed; it asks us to suspend our judgment while we engage our senses. If the so-called real world of events is always remote, no matter how close our computer and TV screens, then our sense of engagement and response is in danger of shutting down. Art is a language which anneals individuals to each other through experiences that are uniquely human, that demand connection at the level of making meaning. If we lose our ability to make meaning, that is, to interpret, to find form in the raw materials of life, then we stand in danger of having meaning made for us, a rupture between what is said and what is done, between false intentions and disastrous consequences.

If the word *freedom* begins to sound hollow in our ears, if every person who is not one of us is against us, if restraint is confused with constraint, and liberty with unregulated self-advancement, regardless of consequences, then the Experimental Poem called "America" is at risk. If scholars withdraw into the protective worlds of their scholarly pursuits, if the academy is perceived by the rest of the public as a place of dubious benefit, with too-long holidays and too high salaries, if art is cordoned off as somehow only relevant, if at all, to the consuming rich, then our great experiment is at risk. As I think Emerson understood, the power of faith must be turned toward the world as it is, to its secular institutions, both public and private, its schools and colleges, libraries, museums, parks, hospitals, laboratories, its local communities and their local associations. We, and this "we" now includes you, need to have faith in these, to bring to them our resources, our curiosity and knowledge, our purposes and protections. As Emerson writes at the end of *Experience*, "Never mind the ridicule, never mind the defeat: up again, old heart—it seems to say, there is victory yet for all justice; and the true romance which the world exists to realize, will be the transformation of genius into practical power."

Notes

1. Martin Tamny, the former Dean of Humanities at City College, asked Ann Lauterbach to speak in May 2004 to the initiates to the City College chapter of Phi Beta Kappa.

2. Ibid., 176.

3. *Selections from Ralph Waldo Emerson*, ed. Stephen E. Whicher (Boston: Houghton Mifflin, 1960), 168, 70.

4. Ibid., 168.

5. Ibid., 66.

6. Ibid., 75.

7. Ibid., 78.

8. Ibid., 151–52.

Letter to Lucia

Ralph Waldo Emerson

*M*y dear Lucia:—I am afraid you think me very ungrateful for the good letters which I begged for and which are so long in coming to me, or that I am malicious and mean to make you wait as long for an answer; but, to tell you the truth, I have had so many "composition lessons" set me lately, that I am sure that no scholar of Mr. Moore's has had less spare time. Otherwise I should have written instantly; for I have an immense curiosity for Plymouth news, and have a great regard for my young correspondent. I would gladly know what books Lucia likes to read when nobody advises her, and most of all what her thoughts are when she walks alone or sits alone. For, though I know that Lucia is the happiest of girls in having in her sister so wise and kind a guide, yet even her aid must stop when she has put the book before you: neither sister nor brother nor mother nor father can think for us: in the little private chapel of your own mind none but God and you can see the happy thoughts that follow each other, the beautiful affections that spring there, the little silent hymns that are sung there at morning and at evening. And I hope that every sun that shines, every star that rises, every wind that blows upon you will only bring you better thoughts and sweeter music. Have you found out that Nature is always talking to you, especially when you are alone, though she has not the gift of articulate speech? Have you found out what the great gray old ocean that is always in your sight says? Listen. And what the withered leaves that shiver and chatter in the cold March wing? Only listen. The Wind is the poet of the World, and sometimes he sings very pretty summer ballads, and sometimes very terrible odes and dirges. But if you will not tell me the little solitary thoughts that I am asking for, what Nature says to you, and what you say to Nature, at least you can tell me about your books,—what you like the least and what the best,—the new studies,—the drawing and the music and the dancing,—and fail not to write to your friend, R. Waldo Emerson.

Note

Emerson's letter to Lucia was originally contained in LeBaron Russell Briggs's Address at the Emerson centenary (Monday, 25, 1903). By way of introduction, Briggs described Lucia as "a little girl of thirteen who looked up to [Emerson] then and always." After citing the letter, Briggs observed: "The 'wise and kind' sister of [Emerson's] little correspondent was Miss Jackson's closest friend, and stood up with her at the wedding." Miss Jackson was Lydia Jackson, Emerson's second wife, whom he married on September 14, 1835.

Contributors

Douglas R. Anderson teaches philosophy at Southern Illinois University at Carbondale. His interest is in the history of philosophy with a special interest in American thought. He has authored and edited several books, most recently *Philosophy Americana* (Fordham University Press, 2006). He is also a student of American folk and popular musics.

Michael Brodrick works as a graduate assistant in the Department of Philosophy at Vanderbilt University. His interests are in the history of philosophy, metaphysics, and the philosophy of religion.

Lawrence Buell is Powell M. Cabot Professor of American Literature at Harvard. His books include *Literary Transcendentalism* (1973), *New England Literary Culture* (Cambridge University Press, 1986), both Pulitzer Prize nominees, and *Emerson* (Harvard University Press, 2003), which was awarded the Warren-Brooks Prize and the Christian Gauss Award for literary scholarship.

Deborah Digges is the author of *Late in the Millennium* (Knopf, 1989), *Vesper Sparrows* (Knopf, 1996), which received New York University's Delmore Schwartz Prize, and *Rough Music* (Knopf, 1997), which won the Kingsley Tufts Prize. She is Professor of English at Tufts University.

Dorene Evans has published her poems in *Pequod, The Peninsula Review*, and *Bark*, among other journals. She has recently completed a manuscript of poems, *The Solstice of Sparrows*. She lives on Long Island with her husband and their four Australian shepherds, Basho, Zooey, Vico, and Yahzee.

Len Gougeon is Distinguished University Fellow and Professor of American Literature at the University of Scranton. He is the author of *Virtue's Hero: Emerson, Antislavery, and Reform* (University of Georgia Press) and coeditor (with Joel Myerson) of *Emerson's Antislavery Writings* (Yale University Press). His most recent book is *Emerson and Eros: The Making of a Cultural Hero* (State University of New York Press, 2007).

William Heyen was awarded the Eunice Tietjens Memorial Prize from *Poetry* magazine and the Witter Bynner Prize for Poetry from the American Academy and Institute of Arts and Letters. He is Professor of English and Poet in Residence at State University of New York, Brockport.

Paul Hoover has published eleven volumes of poetry, including *Edge and Fold* (Apogee Press, 2006) and *Poems in Spanish* (Omnidawn, 2005). He is editor of the anthology *Postmodern American Poetry* (Norton, 1994) and, with Maxine Chernoff, the literary magazine *New American Writing*. He is Professor of Creative Writing at San Francisco State University.

David LaRocca trained as a philosopher at State University of New York-Buffalo, UC Berkeley, Vanderbilt, and Harvard. He is the author of *On Emerson* (Wadsworth, 2003) and editor of Stanley Cavell's book *Emerson's Transcendental Etudes* (Stanford University Press, 2003), both under the name Hodge. He photographed *The Gates* on assignment.

Ann Lauterbach is Professor of Language and Literature at Bard College. She is the author of *On a Stair* (Penguin, 1997) and *The Night Sky* (Viking, 2005), among other books. She was a John D. and Catherine T. MacArthur Fellow in 1993.

Arthur S. Lothstein is Professor and former Chair of the Department of Philosophy at the C. W. Post Campus of Long Island University. He has received awards for teaching excellence both from Long Island University and New York University. He is the editor of *All We Are Saying . . . : The Philosophy of the New Left* (G. P. Putnam's Sons, 1971), and is the author of a number of anthologized journal articles on John Dewey, Martin Buber, and American philosophy. He is a past winner of the John Dewey Essay Prize awarded by The Dewey Center at Southern Illinois University, and has recently completed a book on the Emersonian teacher (*Setting Hearts Aflame: An Essay on the Emersonian Teacher*). He is also a recorded song writer.

John Lysaker is Associate Professor and Department Head of Philosophy at the University of Oregon. He works between American and Continental philosophy, addressing issues of aesthetics, ethics / politics, and philosophical psychology. He is the author of *You Must Change Your Life: Poetry, Philosophy and the Birth of Sense* (Penn State, 2002) and *Emerson and Self-Culture* (Indiana University Press, forthcoming).

David Marr is the author of *American Worlds since Emerson* (University of Massachusetts Press, 1988). He teaches at the Evergreen State College.

John J. McDermott is Distinguished Professor of Philosophy and Humanities, and Abell Professor of Liberal Arts at Texas A&M University. He is also Professor in the Department of Humanities and Medicine at the Texas A&M University College of Medicine. He is the author of *The Culture of Experience: Philosophical Essays in the American Grain* (New York University Press, 1976), *Streams of Experience: Reflections on the History and Philosophy of American Culture* (University of Massachusetts Press, 1986), and *The Drama of Possibility* (Fordham University Press, 2007). He is also the editor of *The Writings of William James: A Comprehensive Edition* (University of Chicago Press, 1977), of *The Philosophy of John Dewey* (University of Chicago Press, 1981), and of *The Basic Writings of Josiah Royce* (Fordham University Press, 2005). He is cofounder and advisory editor of the nineteen-volume Harvard edition of *The Works of William James,* and is the general editor of the twelve-volume edition of *The Correspondence of William James* (University of Virginia Press).

Mary Oliver is the author of *Dream Work* (Grove/Atlantic Press, 1994), *Long Life* (Da Capo Press, 2005), *Thirst* (Beacon Press, 2006), and many other volumes. She received the Pulitzer Prize for *American Primitive* (Back Bay Books, 1983). She lives in Provincetown, MA.

The late **Robert C. Pollock** (1901–1978) studied under Alfred North Whitehead and William McDougall at Harvard and under Etienne Gilson at the Medieval Institute, Toronto, Canada. He was Professor of Philosophy at Fordham University from 1936 through 1966 and is the author of a number of seminal essays on classical American philosophy, including "Emerson and America's Future" in *Doctrine and Experience*, edited by Vincent G. Potter (Fordham University Press, 1988). Pollock was a brilliant scholar and gifted teacher whose lectures inspired many generations of students.

Gary Snyder is Emeritus Professor of English at the University of California, Davis. He is the author of *The Practice of the Wild* (Shoemaker and Hoard, 2003), *Back on the Fire: Essays* (Shoemaker and Hoard, 2007), and many other books. He received the John Hay Award for Nature Writing (1997) and the Bollingen Prize for Poetry (1997). He was awarded the Pulitzer Prize for *Turtle Island* (New Directions, 1974).

Mark Strand is Professor of English and Comparative Literature at Columbia University. He is the author of more than ten books of poetry, including *Blizzard of One* (Knopf, 2000), which won the Pulitzer Prize, and *Man and Camel* (Knopf, 2006). He has served as Poet Laureate of the United States. His most recent book is *New Selected Poems* (Knopf, 2007).

Index

Aaron, Daniel, 173, 178n46
Adorno, T. W., 124, 206
Aristotle, 23, 142, 201
Arnold, Matthew, 45
Augustine, Saint, 70, 79, 163

Bachelard, Gaston, 92
Barthes, Roland, 91
Benjamin, Walter, 86, 135
Bierstadt, Albert, 71, 89
Blau, Joseph, 50, 62
Bloom, Harold, 71
Bloomberg, Michael, 109, 120n17
Briggs, LeBaron Russell, 210
Bronte, Emily, 192n7
Brooks, Van Wyck, 60
Brownson, Orestes, 28, 42
Buber, Martin, 51, 62, 70, 82, 87
Buell, Lawrence, 165, 177n12, 178n53,
    192n21, 194n42

Cairnes, James E., 168
Capra, Frijof, 68
Casilear, John Willam, 89
Carlyle, Thomas, 4, 7, 171, 197
Cavell, Stanley, 71, 75, 77, 92, 95,
    121n32, 123, 130, 134, 148
Celan, Paul, 126, 134, 135
Cezanne, Paul, 95
Chang, P.C., 188
Channing, William Ellery, 5, 123, 125
Church, Frederic Edwin, 165
Coetzee, J.M., 200
Cole, Thomas, 71
Coleridge, Samuel, 4, 6, 7, 73, 74, 125,
    197

conditions for experience, 103, 105,
    107, 112
Conway, Moncure, 164
Cudworth, Ralph, 86

Darwin, Charles, 175
De Stael, Madame, 125, 192n13
DeTocqueville, Alexis, 185
Dewey, John, 50, 55, 61, 62–63, 77, 93,
    94–95, 133, 145, 155
Dickinson, Emily, 85
Digges, Deborah, 69
Douglass, Frederick, 167, 171
Dubois, W.E.B., 76
Du Bos, Charles, 44
Durand, Asher, 89, 98n15
Durrell, Lawrence, 95
Dylan, Bob, 196

Eagleton, Terry, 203
Edwards, Jonathan, 42, 61, 79
Emerson, Mary Moody, 39, 67, 197
Emerson, Ralph Waldo
    act of beholding, 144
    aeolian universe, 68
    aesthetic pedagogy, 67
    aesthetics of the ordinary, 18, 24, 45,
        53, 66n54, 79, 93–94,105
    "central doctrine" of "the infinitude
        of the private man", 78–79
    metaphysics of relations, 94
    as a painter, 70–71, 81
    philosophical postures of song and
        dance, 68–70, 97n2
    issue of his "philosophicality", 75
    synoptic vision, 25

Emerson, Ralph Waldo (*continued*),
  and abolition, 6, 18,165, 167, 169,
    186, 189, 193n28
  and Calvinism, 39–40
  and cynicism, xi, 145, 157
  and esthetic sensibility, 10, 35, 38
  and evil, 20–23, 127, 164
  and experience, xi, 11–14, 22, 31, 41,
    52–57, 73, 134, 144–145, 183,
    202, 205
  and idealism, 16, 151–152, 155,
    165
  and individualism, 25, 27, 30, 93,
    136, 173, 188, 190, 194n39
  and individuality, 26–31, 187–188
  and mechanistic philosophy, 13–14,
    18
  and optimism, xi–xii, 20–22, 59–60,
    199
  and Platonism, 19–20, 33–34, 36
  and pragmatism, 85, 96
  and Puritanism, 38–41
  and radical empiricism, 53, 57, 64n13,
    95
  and romanticism, 37–38
  and self-culture, 26–27, 29 122–123,
    125–127, 131, 137
  and self–reliance, 43, 69, 72, 74, 75,
    80, 83, 92, 93, 95, 128, 132, 173,
    183, 190, 194n37, 204
  and skepticism, 103, 148, 204
  and stoicism, 19–20, 33
  and super-string theory, 68, 203
  and Taoism, 69, 70, 75, 93, 95
  and transcendentalism, 6, 42, 51, 71,
    74, 75, 94, 151, 162, 165, 173
  on the American scholar, 3, 52–53,
    58, 68, 77, 79, 84, 86, 92, 94, 96,
    122, 179–181, 183–184, 186, 189
  on "bipolarity", 85
  on higher education, 78, 170
  on slavery, 18, 163–175, 185–189,
    193n28, 193n29
Emerson String Quartet, 76
Empedocles, 73
Euclid, 184

Galileo, 145, 146–147
Garfield, James A., 185, 194n39
Garrison, William Lloyd, 167
Garvey, T. Gregory, 163–164
Gass, William, 87, 128, 135
Gay, Peter, 94
Giamatti, A. Bartlett, 173
Gnosticism, 96
Gougeon, Len, 193n28
Greene, Brian, 68

Hafiz, 68
Hawthorne, Nathaniel, 5, 60
Hedge, Frederick Henry, 51, 151
Hegel, G.W.F., x, 71, 135
Heidegger, Martin, 88, 126, 130, 134,
  206
Hejinian, Lyn, 206
Heraclitus, 93
Herbert, George, 73
Herndon, William, 165–166
Higginson, Thomas Wentworth, 164
historicism, 133–134
Holmes, Oliver Wendell, 64n14, 167
homonymy principle, 141–142
Howe, Julia Ward, 172
Hyter, Nicholas, 68

Ignatieff, Michael, 188
Ives, Charles, 76

Jackson, Lydian, 4, 210
Jaeger, Werner, 91
James, Henry, 45, 46
James, William, xii, 25, 30, 50, 56–58,
  61, 64n11, 65n35, 65n39, 69, 70,
  76, 81, 82, 83, 84–85, 93, 95, 125,
  155, 198, 199
Jamison, Kay Redfield, 85
Jehlen, Myra, 194n39
Jung, C.G., 91

Kabbalistic, 86
Kafka, Franz, 74
Kant, Immanuel, xi, 53, 73, 125
Kensett, John Frederick, 89

King, Martin Luther, 76, 174, 199
Kozol, Jonathan, 68

Leopold, Aldo, 159
Leverenz, David, 91
Lewis, Meriwether (and William Clark),
    89
Lincoln, Abraham, 165–166, 168–169,
    175–176, 187
Locke, John, 73, 91
Longfellow, Henry Wadsworth, xi,
    167,
Longinus, 86
Lothstein, Arthur, 98n13, 98n27
Lowell, James Russell, 64n14, 167,
    168

Machiavelli, Nicolo, 188, 204
MackIntosh, James, 73
Macleish, Archibald, 96
Malik, Charles Habib, 188
Mann, Thomas, 29
Martineau, Harriet, 7
McCarthy, Cormac, 69
McDermott, John J., 70, 72, 73, 77, 79,
    84, 87, 93, 94, 95, 96
Mead, George Herbert, 63n3
Mill, John Stuart, 4, 168, 194, 197
Miller, Dickinson S., 59
Miller, Perry, 197
Milton, John, 123, 184
Montaigne, Michel, 81, 84
Muir, John, 154, 155, 159, 181
Munsterberg, Hugo, 76

Newfield, Christopher, 194n39
Nietzsche, Friedrich, 67, 68, 69, 76,
    82, 85, 96,124,125, 133
Noyes, Alfred, 13

Oliver, Mary, 75
Olmsted, Frederick Law, 102, 103,
    104, 110, 112

Paley, William, 73
Parker, Theodore, 165, 166

Patterson, Anita Hayes, 174
Peirce, Charles Sanders, 42, 51, 55,
    56,145–148, 151, 155
Peter, Paul, and Mary, 196
Phillips, Wendell, 167
Pinchot, Gifford, 155, 156, 159
Pindar, 90, 134
Plotinus, 51, 73
Poe, Edgar Allen, 60
Poirier, Richard, 87
Pollock, Robert C., 50
Pope, Alexander, 73
Porte, Joel, xiii, 95
Pound, Ezra, 203
Proclus, 73

Quine, Willard Van Orman, 141–142

Reed, Sampson, 30
Richardson, Robert D., 165
Rilke, Rainer Maria, 75, 88, 89, 94
Robinson, Crabb, 7
Roosevelt, Eleanor, 188
Rorty, Richard, 151
Royce, Josiah, 50, 51, 53, 55–56, 58,
    61–62

Santayana, George, ix, 20, 32, 50, 51,
    58, 59–61, 66n43
Saturday Club, 167, 168
Schell, Jonathan, 203
Schelling, F.W.J., 51, 64n14, 151–153,
    159
Shakespeare, William 123, 126, 131
Shaw, Robert Gould, 168
Shelley, Percy Bysshe, 91
Spinoza, Baruch, 73
Stein, Gertrude, 201
Stevens, Wallace, 69, 82, 83, 87, 93,
    94, 199–200
Stewart, Dugald, 73
Storey, Moorfield, 173
Strand, Mark, 81
Sturzo, Don Luigi, 37
Sumner, Charles, 166, 168
Swedenborg, Emanuel, 6, 91

Thoreau, Henry David, xi, 5, 73, 75,
    77, 80, 84, 89, 92, 125, 152, 156,
    159, 181, 185, 194n37, 203
Thompson, Francis, 34
Trismegisti, 73
Tucker, Ellen, xi, 4, 197

Very, Jones, 5, 80,

Weir, Peter, 68
White, Richard, 181

Whitman, Walt, xii, 4, 89, 93, 154
Williams, William Carlos, 86, 93
Wills, Gary, 165
Wordsworth, William, 4, 38, 68, 75,
    84, 181, 197

Yeats, William Butler, 77

Zarathustra, 68, 69